Introduction to the History of English

TEXTBOOKS IN ENGLISH LANGUAGE AND LINGUISTICS (TELL)

Edited by Magnus Huber and Joybrato Mukherjee

VOLUME 6

Thomas Kohnen

Introduction to the History of English

Bibliographic Information published by the Deutsche Nationalbibliothek
The Deutsche Nationalbibliothek lists this publication in the Deutsche Nationalbibliografie; detailed bibliographic data is available in the internet at http://dnb.d-nb.de.

Library of Congress Cataloging-in-Publication Data
Kohnen, Thomas, 1956-
 Introduction to the history of English / Thomas Kohnen. -- Peter Lang Edition.
   pages cm. -- (Textbooks in English Language and Linguistics ; Volume 6)
 Includes bibliographical references.
 ISBN 978-3-631-56004-4 -- ISBN 978-3-653-04171-2 (E-book) 1. English language--History. 2. English language--Middle English, 1100-1500. 3. English language--Early modern, 1500-1700. 4. Historical linguistics. I. Title.
 PE1075.K585 2014
 420.9--dc23
                              2013049721

ISSN 1862-510X
ISBN 978-3-631-56004-4 (Print)
E-ISBN 978-3-653-04171-2 (E-Book)
DOI 10.3726/ 978-3-653-04171-2

© Peter Lang GmbH
Internationaler Verlag der Wissenschaften
Frankfurt am Main 2014
All rights reserved.
Peter Lang Edition is an Imprint of Peter Lang GmbH.

Peter Lang – Frankfurt am Main · Bern · Bruxelles · New York ·
Oxford · Warszawa · Wien

All parts of this publication are protected by copyright. Any utilisation outside the strict limits of the copyright law, without the permission of the publisher, is forbidden and liable to prosecution. This applies in particular to reproductions, translations, microfilming, and storage and processing in electronic retrieval systems.

This book is part of the Peter Lang Edition list
and was peer reviewed prior to publication.

www.peterlang.com

Preface

This book aims to provide an accessible but also comprehensive and reasonably detailed introduction to the history of the English language. After a short overview of the basic facts of language change and the Indo-European background of English, it traces the major periods of the language (Old English, Middle English, Early Modern English and Late Modern English), with a brief examination of the perspectives of present-day English. Each period chapter follows the same pattern, providing information about the socio-historical background and the core areas of linguistic structure, but also about discourse, speech acts and genres. The text is richly illustrated with examples and text excerpts, and each chapter concludes with a section containing study questions and exercises.

I would like to thank Tanja Rütten for her feedback on the manuscript. I would also like to thank Stefanie Leu, who designed the maps and figures, and Kirsten Gather, Leonie Mohr and Christina Rath for their help with the manuscript.

Cologne   Thomas Kohnen
November 2013

Table of Contents

1. Language change and language history 1
2. Tracing the origins of English 11
3. English ca. 450 to ca. 1100 (Old English) 21
   3.1. Political and socio-cultural background 21
   3.2. Language structure 29
      3.2.1. Spelling and pronunciation 29
      3.2.2. Morphology and word-formation 34
      3.2.3. Syntax 42
      3.2.4. Lexis and semantics 48
      3.2.5. Regional and social distribution 52
   3.3. Language use 54
      3.3.1. Discourse and speech acts 54
      3.3.2. Genres 57
4. English ca. 1100 to ca. 1500 (Middle English) 71
   4.1. Political and socio-cultural background 71
   4.2. Language structure 76
      4.2.1. Spelling and pronunciation 76
      4.2.2. Morphology and word-formation 83
      4.2.3. Syntax 90
      4.2.4. Lexis and semantics 97
      4.2.5. Regional and social distribution 101
   4.3. Language use 107
      4.3.1. Discourse and speech acts 107
      4.3.2. Genres 110
5. English ca. 1500 to ca. 1700 (Early Modern English) 123
   5.1. Political and socio-cultural background 123
   5.2. Language structure 129
      5.2.1. Spelling and pronunciation 129
      5.2.2. Morphology and word-formation 133
      5.2.3. Syntax 137

    5.2.4. Lexis and semantics.. 144
    5.2.5. Regional and social distribution 149
  5.3. Language use 152
    5.3.1. Discourse and speech acts 152
    5.3.2. Genres.. 157

6. English after 1700 (Late Modern English) 167
  6.1. Political and socio-cultural background 167
  6.2. Language structure 170
    6.2.1. Spelling and pronunciation... 173
    6.2.2. Morphology and word-formation 170
    6.2.3. Syntax.. 175
    6.2.4. Lexis and semantics.. 178
    6.2.5. Regional and social distribution 182
  6.3. Language use 185
    6.3.1. Discourse and speech acts 185
    6.3.2. Genres.. 188

7. Perspectives on present-day English.. 195

List of References 201

1. Language change and language history

Language is continually changing. Some people may not be aware of this fact, since language change is often slow and hardly perceptible. Probably, innovation will become most noticeable in the field of lexis, when new words are coined to designate new ideas, facts or activities. A few decades ago, nobody would have used the verbs *google* or *download* in the sense that is quite common for us in the year 2013. In the same way, hundreds or even thousands of new words have been added to the English language in the past fifty years. But language change also affects spelling, pronunciation, grammar and language use, and here it may be more difficult to actually "observe" change in the period of a lifetime. In fact, many people will be convinced that the English they use every day is basically immutable as regards its grammatical structure and pronunciation. However, this is far from correct. In the course of its history, English has undergone quite dramatic changes, but in order to see and "appreciate" them we must go back five hundred or even one thousand years and look at the texts which have come down to us.

Below are two short extracts which may illustrate some of these changes. The first text excerpt (example 1) stems from the second half of the tenth century, that is, from the Anglo-Saxon period. Anglo-Saxon or Old English is often called a form of English which is mainly incomprehensible to most native speakers of English without special instruction, but it is still English and not a foreign language. Thus, it can illustrate many of the sweeping changes which English has undergone in its history. The text is a preface to a translation of parts of the Bible. The author, Ælfric, was one of the most prolific writers of the Anglo-Saxon period, and he chose for his preface the form of a letter. The letter is addressed to his patron, Æthelwærd, who commissioned the translation. Æthelwærd was an ealdorman, that is, a nobleman exercising authority under the king.

(1) ÆLFRIC MUNUC GRET ÆðELWÆRD EALDORMANN EAÐMOdlicc.
   Ælfric   monk   greets   Æthelwærd   alderman/ ruler   humbly
   Þu bæde me, leof, þæt ic sceolde ðe awendan of Lydene on Englisc þa boc
   you asked   "dear" that I should (for) you translate from Latin into English the book
   Genesis: ða þuhte me hefigtime þe to tiþienne þæs, ...
   then (it) seemed to me arduous (to) you to grant that

1

"Ælfric, the monk, greets alderman Æthelwærd humbly.
You asked me, dear, to translate ("that I should translate") for you the book Genesis from Latin into English. Then it seemed to me an arduous task to grant you this ..."
(Ælfric, *Preface to Genesis*; late 10th century; DOEC)[1]

I am sure this short extract will appear quite foreign to most uninitiated readers. But the glossing, together with the translation, will perhaps help to make the text a little bit more transparent.

Spelling is among the features of the above text which seem to contribute most to its unfamiliar look. We find unusual letters, for example, *æ* and *Æ* (called ash). They represent the Modern English vowel in words like *cat* and *rat*. Other letters no longer in use are *þ* (called thorn) and *ð* (called eth). They both represent Modern English /θ/ and /ð/, that is, the initial consonants in *thin* and *that*. Generally, the relationship between spelling and pronunciation in Old English was quite different from what we are used to in Modern English. For example, *Ælfric* was probably pronounced /ˈælfritʃ/, *bæde* /ˈbæːdə/ and *þuhte* /ˈθuːχtə/ (with χ representing the consonant in German *ach*).

Some of the words in the text can still be found in Modern English, but they are difficult to recognise because of their unfamiliar spelling (which, of course, also reflects a different pronunciation). For example, in *sceolde* we can recognise Modern English *should*, in *boc* Modern English *book* and in *þuhte* we can find *thought*. In addition, the text contains words which are no longer found in Modern English because they died out, for example, *eadmodlice* "humbly", *awendan* "translate" and *hefigtime* "arduous".

In the field of morphology we find many unfamiliar features as well. For example, the personal pronouns and definite articles comprise a wide range of different forms distinguishing between case, number and grammatical gender. The personal pronouns are *ic* (*ic sceolde*) for the first person nominative (the accusative *me* will create no difficulties) and in the second person singular *þu* for the nominative case (*Þu bæde me* "you asked me") and *þe* for the dative case (*ðe awendan* "translate for you"). The article *þa* in *þa boc* is accusative singular feminine and *þæs* (in *to tiþienne þæs* "to grant that") is genitive singular neuter.

Many more "exotic" features could be pointed out, for example, the so-called impersonal construction *þuhte me* (literally "thought me", that is, "it seemed to

---

1   For the examples in the text the following information is given: author, title, (approximate) date and source. For the abbreviations of the electronic sources see the respective section in the List of References.

me") or the *that*-clause after "asked" (*bæde*), which today would be replaced by an infinitive clause. Thus, to sum up, for many people this text will seem fairly incomprehensible, almost like a foreign text, and it forms quite a striking example of how the structure of English has changed during the last millennium.

But the above extract also shows another aspect of language change, the change of language use. It reflects a different use of address terms and different conventions of letter-writing. The letter form employed by Ælfric seems rather formal and over-official, especially with the formulaic third-person construction ("Ælfric, the monk, greets alderman Æthelwærd humbly"). This form is uncommon today. It would sound fairly stilted and too detached in a contemporary setting, even if we consider that Ælfric is addressing a superior. On the other hand, Ælfric uses the forms *þu* and *þe* to address his patron, singular forms of the second-person pronoun that correspond to the (now mostly extinct) forms *thou* and *thee* in Modern English and which are usually seen as familiar, even intimate options in other languages (German *Du*, French *toi*, Italian *tu* etc.). In Old English, the plural forms of the second person pronoun (*ye* for the subject and *eow* for the object) were not yet used as formal and polite options for addressing a single person (compare German *Sie* or the archaic form *Euch* used to address one person), but exclusively to address two or more persons. In line with this more "informal" and almost intimate touch is the address term *leof* ("dear"). Although this form is sometimes rendered as *Sir*, this seems to be a far too formal translation. The central sense of *leof* is "dear, beloved, agreeable", which clearly is also implied in its use as an address term. Thus, apart from the sweeping structural changes pointed out above, the unexpected combination of formal and informal features of language use found in this letter gives evidence of the pragmatic aspects of language change, in this case, changes in the way people address each other and altered genre conventions.

The second text excerpt that will serve as an example of language change (example 2, below) stems from a letter that was written roughly 500 years later, in 1502, by Agnes Plumpton to her husband Robert. The Plumptons were a well-to-do family that belonged to the Yorkshire gentry. A short look at the text immediately shows that 500 years have passed. It is much more accessible and modern than the previous text, although, to a certain extent, the language may strike you as "unfamiliar", too. But an additional translation (beyond the glosses) for a speaker of English does not seem to be necessary.

(2) To the worshipful Sir Robart Plompton, kt. be thes delivered in hast.
                                          knight this   haste
    Sir, in my most hartiest wyse I recommennd me unto You, desiring to
        most sincere way

heare of your prosperitie and welfaire, and of your good spede in
  well-being *happiness*   *success*
your matters; certyfiing you that I, and my sone William, with
    assuring   *son*
all your children, are in good health ... with all your servants.

Sir, ye, and I, and my sone, was content at your departing, ...
 you   *son*
(*Plumpton Correspondence*, Agnes Plumpton; 1502; HC)

Many words still show irregular spellings (for example, *thes*, *hast*, *prosperitie*, *heare*, *sone*), and some have (slightly) different meanings (for example, *welfaire* and *spede*). Some constructions appear odd (for example, the "double superlative" *most hartiest*), but all in all the text "feels" much more like Modern English than the previous example. In particular in the field of morphology, the distinctions made according to case, number and grammatical gender have been largely simplified. For example, nouns like *prosperitie* and *sone* are not marked for gender and case (note that *prosperitie* follows the preposition *of* and *sone* is part of the subject noun phrase); the general plural marker is *–s* (*matters*, *servants*; the exception *children* is also preserved in Modern English). So, the structure of the language and its vocabulary has moved closer to what we know as contemporary English.

On the other hand, in terms of language use, this letter may strike a modern reader as fairly reserved and formulaic, considering that it was written by a wife to her husband. The text starts with the extremely formal superscript and a passive construction (*be thes delivered in hast*). Also, Agnes Plumpton addresses her husband with *Sir* and the formal *ye* (not the intimate *thou*, since this distinction had by then developed and was certainly among the linguistic repertoire). After the address (*Sir*) she inserts a formula that was prescribed by fifteenth-century letter handbooks and reaches back to the *ars dictaminis* ("the art of dictating") of medieval times (*I recommennd me unto you, desiring to heare ..., certyfiing you that ...*). To modern ears, this formula must sound extremely strange, especially when it is employed by a wife addressing her husband. So, this text suggests that letter-writing conventions were more distanced and formal than those followed today, let alone those practised in emails. And we might speculate whether Anglo-Saxon conventions might also be considered less distanced and formal.

The two examples nicely illustrate that the English language has changed significantly during the centuries. The change involved both linguistic structure (spelling, pronunciation, grammar and lexis) and language use (genre conventions, forms of address etc.). Both changes will be considered in this book.

The two excerpts also show that it is quite wrong to assume that the English of today will not be affected by further changes. In fact, what we see today as "contemporary English" is only a snapshot in a continuous flow of modifications of the language that evolve across time. These alterations may not be as sweeping as those found in the developments from Old English to Modern English. This is due to the preserving effects of dictionaries, grammars and education (among other things), which all focus on what is felt to be some fixed form of Standard English. But it is simply naïve to take for granted that today's English will be used unaltered in two hundred years' time.

Historical linguists found out that the major basis for language change is variation. Native speakers of English will pronounce identical words (for example, *cat, dog, plain* etc.) in slightly differing ways, even in identical contexts. Some slightly different variant may catch on and spread. Once the differing variant has become an option, it may be associated with a particular group, may gain prestige, spread further and be established as part of the standard language. In a similar way, variation, that is, different or alternative ways of saying the same thing, is found at other levels of language and may result in language change. For example, for some time in the history of English, two alternative ways of marking the third-person singular of the present tense of verbs existed, *-s* (a new form, whose arrival is probably due to language mix) and *–th* (the older form). We find forms like *likes, writes* and *sits* next to forms like *liketh, writeth* and *sitteth*, sometimes in one and the same text. In the course of time, that is, during the seventeenth century, the *s*-form had prevailed, and by the nineteenth century the *th*-form is very rare and only found in special kinds of texts.

Since variation is a constitutive feature of language, there will be language change as long as language exists. On the other hand, it is important to see that not every instance of variation will automatically result in language change. Some patterns of variation seem to have been fairly stable for long periods of time. For example, in British English forms like *analyse / analyze* and *institutionalisation / institutionalization* have existed side by side without much difference in connotation and not much indication of change towards one or the other variant.

Traditionally, we can distinguish between language-internal and language-external change. Internal changes are those changes which can (mainly) be described within the internal structure of the language. For example, they occur when speakers assimilate the pronunciation of sounds in a word to the preceding or following sounds. One instance of this assimilation can be found in the vowel of words like *was, what* and *wash*, which was pronounced /a/ before 1700 and changed to the modern pronunciation due to the influence of the preceding /w/ (the retracted tongue position resulting in a "darker" vowel). Internal change also happens when word endings or grammatical endings are "levelled" and dropped (for example, because the full stress of words is placed on the first syllable, with the last syllable becoming "blurred"). Thus, Old English infinitives ending in *–an*, were changed to *–en* and finally dropped (*bindan, binden, bind; standan, standen, stand*, and so on). Similar things happened to many Old English inflectional endings.

External changes are those changes which can be linked to political, social or geographical factors. There are quite a few historical events which have affected the development of English. For example, the Battle of Hastings (1066) had the long-term effect that French became the language of the ruling classes and of the administration in England, which resulted, among other things, in the influx of large numbers of French words. The Industrial Revolution in the eighteenth and nineteenth centuries sent masses of people (mostly from the countryside) to the factories of the ever-growing cities, resulting in a large-scale levelling and loss of rural dialects in city-communities. External change often involves also questions of social identity and social prestige. In the nineteenth century, the rise of a spoken standard and *Received Pronunciation* was mainly due to the upwardly mobile middle class, who sought to maintain their position in society by promoting their ideology of "talking proper" and stigmatising "inappropriate" forms (like h-dropping and g-dropping in words like *hat* [æt] and *singing* [sɪŋɪn]).

Internal and external language changes often act in combination. Sometimes an internal change only gains weight with the help of an external element. For example, a certain variant in the pronunciation is seen as the marker of social identity of a group and thus spreads either within this group or, if it is seen as prestigious, even across society. This book will include language-external as well as language-internal developments in the history of the English language and will try to reveal their mutual relationship in the course of the centuries.

Based on the major language-external and language-internal changes in the history of English, it has become traditional to set up so-called periods. These are Old English (450–1100), Middle English (1100–1500), Early Modern English (1500–1700) and Late Modern English (1700–1900 or 1950). Although the roots of this kind of periodisation go back to the eminent nineteenth-century philologist Jacob Grimm, it should be pointed out that such periods are basically not more than a convenient way of reference to a "typical" state of the language and that the exact dates are purely arbitrary. Language change typically proceeds gradually across space and time, it does not affect language in a categorical fashion. Some language histories (for example, Blake 1992) take 1066, the date of the Battle of Hastings, as the beginning of the Middle English period. This cannot, however, be seen as an exact description of linguistic facts. People did not start speaking Middle English after the battle had ended. Rather, the linguistic developments associated with Middle English took at least 50 years after 1066 to fully emerge. Thus, if the dates of periodisation are to be taken literally, one should rather say that Middle English evolved roughly around the year 1100, with some speakers and some regions being more advanced and some less advanced in this process. All the dates of periodisations should be seen in this light.

With the above qualifications, the structure of this book will follow the traditional periods in the history of the English language. The main part of this book (Chapters 3 to 6) will be devoted to Old, Middle, Early Modern and Late Modern English. Each chapter will start with a short account of the political and socio-cultural background, that is, the most important factors of language-external history. The presentation will then proceed according to the traditional levels of linguistic description (spelling and pronunciation, morphology and word-formation, syntax and lexis), with an additional section on regional and social distribution. The last part will be devoted to a description of important pragmatic changes (discourse and speech acts, and genres). The central section of this book is preceded by a very short overview of the linguistic history before the emergence of (Old) English (Chapter 2). It places English within the "family" of the Germanic and Indo-European languages and gives some information about the languages spoken in England before Old English. The last chapter (Chapter 7) rounds off this presentation of the history of English, offering a few perspectives on the future of present-day English.

The rest of this chapter will deal with two further issues involving language change and language history, the question of data and, most importantly, reasons for studying the history of English. One of the basic shortcomings of a history of the English language (as of any history of any language) is the quality and the quantity of the available data which may serve as evidence for the described changes of the language. First of all, until the nineteenth century there is no direct evidence of spoken language. All we know about the older states of the language rests on written evidence. Then, the available written data are often fragmentary and incomplete, because many texts got lost or were destroyed. Thus, the further we get back in the history of English, the more we must put up with a sketchy, even erratic picture. Also, in many cases we do not know the context and setting of texts, their purpose and aims, their addressors and addressees.

Old English, for example, is comparatively well documented, with a quantity of texts of about 3.5 million words. But also here, we know that many texts were destroyed, for example, in the Viking raids (see Chapter 3.1.). Also, the large majority of texts stems from the religious sphere (since it was basically members of the clergy who were able to write). And a large part of the texts (especially those which are not religious) are anonymous and difficult to date. But despite these shortcomings, the reconstructed account of the linguistic history of Old English clearly goes far beyond speculation because, apart from the direct evidence provided by the texts, it rests on an interlocking mesh of hypotheses and bits of indirect evidence, which rely on each other (on this see Chapter 2).

An introductory text book on the history of the English language should, of course, also address the question why we should study the history of a language. Many reasons, which are often related, have been suggested for the diachronic study of a language, in particular, the English language. One of the more obvious motivations for studying the history of English is probably the general interest of human beings in tracing their history and their roots. Since English is one of the major world languages, it seems quite plausible and in fact relevant for the many native speakers (possibly also the second-language speakers) to study its emergence and development across the centuries. This more general interest in history is linked to three more specific motivations for those people who are more closely or even professionally associated with the English language (among them, of course, students of English).

First, an account of the development of the English language through the centuries may allow a more informed assessment of the present position and possible further developments of English. Once we know about the most important external and internal factors which have influenced the course of English through the centuries, we may be in a better position to assess its present status and possible future developments (although, as we shall see, any clear prognostication seems at best hazardous).

Secondly, knowledge of the past will help to explain and understand the present structure of the language. For example, obvious "inconsistencies" and irregular structures can only be understood adequately if we consult history. Consider the forms *food*, *good* and *blood*. We all know that the vowel in these words is spelled the same way but pronounced differently. For uninitiated learners of English this is probably an annoying nuisance, one of the many seemingly unmotivated irregular structures which impede the struggling learner. Those who are professionally involved with English should perhaps know the reasons behind such irregularities.

The identical spelling of the vowel in these words simply reflects their Middle English pronunciation with a long, half-closed /o:/. In the course of the Great Vowel Shift (on this see Chapter 5.2.1.) this vowel changed into /u:/. This pronunciation still applies to *food*. With *good* and *blood* the /u:/ was shortened and in the case of *blood* the short /ʊ/ assumed the manifestation of /ʌ/. However, the spelling of these words was never altered. The insight about this example is that it does not only explain the differing pronunciation of these three words. All (or almost all) words with long /o:/ changed to /u:/ during the Great Vowel Shift; many of them were shortened later (consider, for example, *foot*, *book* and *look*); and short /ʊ/ alternates with /ʌ/ in many environments (see, for example, *put*, *push*, *bull* vs. *luck*, *cut*, *but*). Thus, through reference to the history of English, these and other irregular structures may become transparent. In this sense we can say that knowledge of the past explains the present.

Thirdly, by following the history of English, students of English may learn about the mechanisms of language change in a more general way, which goes beyond this particular language. As was mentioned before, all languages necessarily change and this change may be caused by internal, structural, and external, political, social or cultural factors. Students can learn that language change is not "bad" or may lead to the "decay" of a language, as the "complaint tradition" will have it, but that it has always occurred. For example, those people who complain about "foreign" influence on their native language should have a closer look at the loanwords it already contains (English acquired tens of thousands of French and Latin loanwords in the course of its history).

A last and slightly different motivation for studying the history of the English language is based on an interest in English literature and may well apply to any student of English. The motivation is simply to acquire competence to read literary texts of the past in their original version. Quite clearly, texts like *Beowulf* (an Old English heroic epic) or Chaucer's *Canterbury Tales* (stemming from the end of the fourteenth century) require more or less detailed instruction if a student prefers to read the original version. But also an in-depth reading of Shakespeare has to rely on information from language history. Most of the editions of plays by Shakespeare present the texts in a modernised and regularised version, which is a far cry, for example, from the *First Folio Edition* from 1623. A fairly crucial aspect involves the pronunciation of Shakespeare's English. Almost all contemporary performances use Modern English. But a short look at Early Modern English phonology tells us that the pronunciation of English at the beginning of the seventeenth century was markedly different from today and any performance in the "original Early Modern English" would leave quite a different impression.

Summary

The two text examples presented in this chapter have shown that the English language has undergone sweeping changes in the course of its history, both in terms of linguistic structure and in terms of language use. Thus, the idea of a stable, immutable language is an illusion. Rather, contemporary English is only a snapshot in a continuous flow of changes that evolve across time. Linguistic variation was identified as the basis of linguistic change. The chapter also introduced the concepts of internal and external factors of linguistic change and their different ways of interaction. Lastly, it illustrated problems of periodisation and of the availability of data, and pointed out some motivations for studying the history of (the English) language.

Further reading

Schendl (2001) is an accessible basic introduction to the major questions of language change and historical linguistics. Hock (1991), Lehmann (1992), and Lass (1997) are standard text books.

Questions and exercises

1. Using some basic reference work on English history (for example, Cannon 2002 or Davies 2000), find prominent instances of external language change in the history of English. Think about the possible impact on the language.

2. This chapter has illustrated some changes in genre conventions of letters from Old English until Early Modern English. How did these genre conventions further change in the twenty-first century and what additional changes may be triggered by the introduction of electronic mail?

3. Try to find out more instances of variation in contemporary English, existing side by side (like *analyse* / *analyze*) without any indication of change.

4. In how far is the year 1476 (when William Caxton put up the first printing press in Westminster) an adequate or inadequate date for delimiting the Middle English from the Early Modern English period?

2. Tracing the origins of English

For many students one of the more exciting questions about the history of the English language is: When did English "start", that is, when did it begin to exist? The traditional view is that English "started" when certain Germanic tribes, who had lived in Northern Germany and Southern Scandinavia, arrived in England in about 450 AD and settled there (for a more detailed account of the arrival of the Anglo-Saxons see Chapter 3.1.). Once these tribes were situated in England and basically cut off from their homelands on the Continent, we say that the language of these tribes is English.

Such an answer to the question about the origins of English may be somewhat unsatisfactory to many students. On the one hand, one might ask why those Germanic tribes did not "speak English" while they were still on the Continent. On the other hand, we know that before the arrival of the Germanic tribes there were other languages spoken on the British Isles (for example, Celtic languages and, in connection with the Roman Empire, Latin). Why would these languages, which were clearly spoken in England at an earlier date, not be called English?

To deal with these legitimate objections, we need to draw a more detailed and comprehensive picture of the languages in Europe, their various affiliations and their relationships to what we now know as the English language. The language, or rather, dialects, of the Anglo-Saxon tribes who settled in England in the fifth century AD links back to the several languages (or dialects) spoken by a range of tribes which are called Germanic. The various languages affiliated to these tribes are called Germanic languages. Some of them have developed to modern national languages (for example, Swedish, Danish, English and German, among others). These languages share several common features. Another way to refer to such affiliated languages is to call them a language family. Since the Anglo-Saxon tribes had settled on a separate island and (later) formed an independent kingdom, it seems legitimate to treat their dialects as a separate language within the Germanic language family.

Celtic and Latin (or rather Italic), on the other hand, form two other language families, each comprising several languages or dialects that share features. But on a higher level, Germanic, Celtic and Latin all seem to be part of an even larger, affiliated group of languages, called Indo-European, which covers languages spoken from Ireland and Portugal in the West to Persia and India in the East. And, of course, English is also part of this complicated network of Indo-European languages. In this chapter we will have a short look at the origins of English in the

11

sense that we will look at the Indo-European group of languages, with a special emphasis on Germanic and English.

Many native speakers of German learning English may be aware of the fact that German and English share some features. For example, one can set up series of corresponding words which differ only in a few sounds. German *Hand, Band, Land, Sand* correspond to English *hand, band, land, sand* and German *Stein, Bein, Heim, Eiche* correspond to English *stone, bone, home, oak*. It is obvious that the vowels /a/ and /ai/ on the German side correspond to English /æ/ and /əʊ/ respectively. Since the resemblance, both of form and meaning, of the German and the English words is too striking to be attributed to mere chance, it is plausible to assume that they had a common ancestor. Such ancestor words are also called cognates.

We can expand the range of cognates and languages, if we focus on the everyday, core vocabulary and on languages whose documentation reaches very far back, for example, by including Latin (earliest documentation from the third century BC) and Sanskrit (earliest texts probably from the fifth century BC, but with an oral tradition reaching very much further back, ca. 1200 BC). Table 1 below includes five words of the core vocabulary of English and their cognates in German, Latin and Sanskrit. (Sanskrit is an ancient language from India, which belongs to the Indo-Iranian branch of Indo-European; see Figure 1 below).

English	*thou*	*three*	*foot*	*father*	*fish*
German	*du*	*drei*	*Fuß*	*Vater*	*Fisch*
Latin	*tu*	*tres*	*pedem*	*pater*	*piscis*
Sanskrit	*tvam*	*trayas*	*padam*	*pitar*	–

Table 1: Some cognates in English, German, Latin and Sanskrit

The data in Table 1 only gives some rudimentary and sketchy information which is supposed to serve as a basic illustration of the similarities found in Indo-European-Languages. The resemblance between the cognates is striking and (if we link it to the additional research on Indo-European languages) cannot be the product of sheer coincidence. Apart from the general pattern of resemblance, the data also show systematic differences. Germanic languages (like English and German) have /f/ and /θ/ (German /d/) where Latin and Sanskrit have /p/ and /t/ respectively (*father* vs. *pater; thou* vs. *tu*). This is part of the so-called Grimm's Law or the First Consonant Shift, which describes one of the major sound shifts that separated the Germanic languages from the rest of the Indo-European family.

During the past two hundred years historical linguists have devoted much effort to revealing the systematic similarities and differences between the various

Indo-European languages. These systematic correspondences do not only involve the sound system but also the morphology, syntax and core vocabulary. All this corroborates the assumption that these languages are indeed related. On the other hand, things are often not quite as straightforward as Table 1 might imply. The sounds in individual languages have changed in quite idiosyncratic ways, especially when neighbouring sounds exerted an influence on their pronunciation to a differing extent. For example, returning to the corresponding cognates of German *Heim* / English *home* given above, one can easily find exceptions which distort a straightforward picture. German *Heide* and English *heath* do not seem to fit the pattern (the English word should be *hoath*). This difference is due to the fact that the English word had changed already in pre-Old English times, as a result of a sound change called *i*-umlaut, which affected sounds followed by *i* or *j* (on *i*-umlaut see Chapter 3.2.2.). The pre-Old English form must have been something like *haþi (where * indicates a reconstructed form). The final *i* changed the *a* to *æ* and was lost later. Thus, the Old English form was *hæþ* (not *haþ*), which "regularly" developed into Modern English *heath*. Another source of complications may be early loanwords. They may suggest a common ancestry which is actually not there. For example, Modern English *coast* and German *Küste* do not follow the above *home* / *Heim* pattern, because both go back to French loans (*coast* goes back to Middle English *coste*, which comes from Old French *coste*). But despite all these difficulties in comparison and reconstruction, researchers of Indo-European languages have built up a fairly coherent descriptive outline where the individual pieces all fit, similar to the pieces of a jigsaw.

Figure 1 below gives an overview of the major branches of Indo-European. The Indo-Iranian branch comprises languages which are spoken in the easternmost parts of the area covered by the Indo-European languages, mostly Iran and India, with neighbouring countries. Here we find, among others, Persian, Kurdish, and Sanskrit and some other languages, which are spoken in India (for example, Hindi). The Balto-Slavic branch consists of the Baltic languages (for example, Latvian, Lithuanian and Old Prussian) on the one hand, and the Slavonic languages (among them Russian, Polish, Czech and others), on the other. The Greek branch comprises several old Hellenic dialects. Modern Greek derives from one of them, Attic. There are four minor branches of Indo-European, which can be neglected in the present context, Albanian, Armenian, Tocharian and Anatolian. The remaining branches, Italic, Celtic and Germanic, are more relevant here because they involve the history of the English language more directly.

Italic comprises several dialects spoken in ancient Italy (for example, Umbrian, Oscan and, of course, Latin). Latin (or rather, the variety of Vulgar Latin) branches off

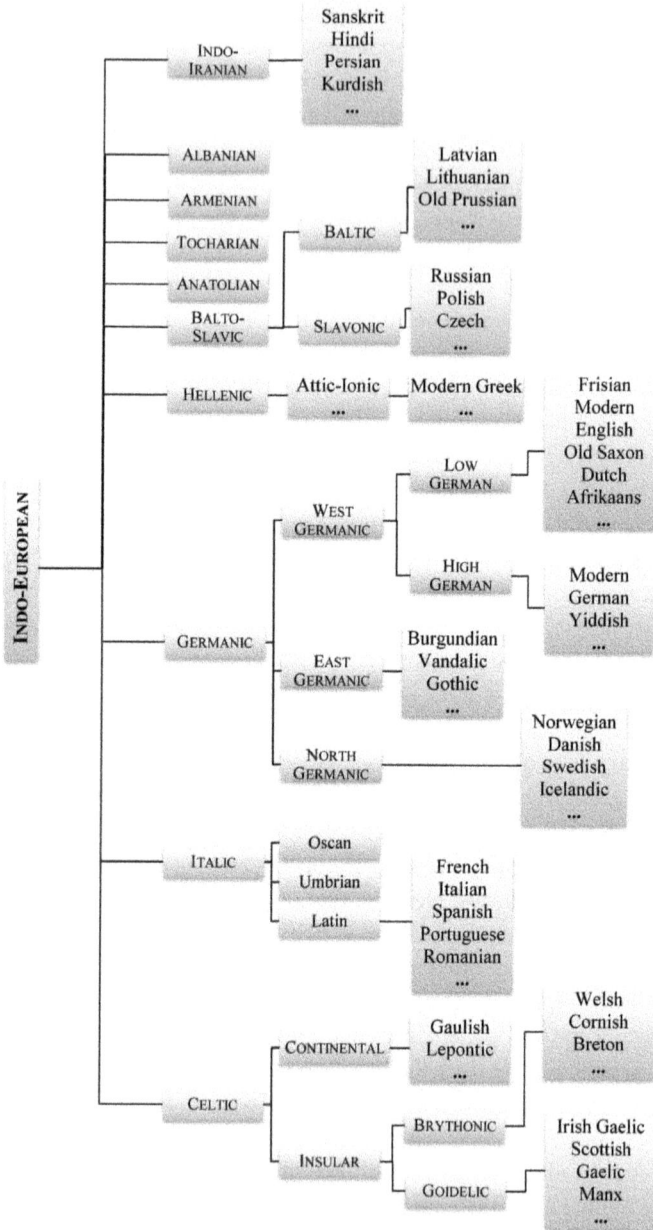

Fig. 1: Major branches of Indo-European

into the various Romance languages of today (among them French, Italian, Spanish, Portuguese and Romanian). As was mentioned above, Latin was spoken in Britain as long as it was part of the Roman Empire. At the beginning of the fifth century AD, however, the Romans left Britain because the Roman Empire was attacked from all sides, and defending Britain does not seem to have been among their top priorities. We know that the superior Roman culture soon vanished in England. An influence of the variety of Latin which might still have been present on the British Isles after the Romans had left, is quite difficult to prove. But Latin influence marks large parts of the history of English and the first attested Latin influence does not stem from the Roman province Britannia but rather from contacts between speakers of Latin and Germanic tribes while these were still on the continent (resulting in such early loans as *wine* and *street*; on this see Chapter 3.2.4.).

The Celtic branch is relevant to the history of English because in the fifth century, when the Anglo-Saxons arrived, Celtic was spoken in all parts of Britain. It is assumed that Celtic peoples had come to Britain from the Continent around the fifth and, later, in the third and second centuries BC. We distinguish the continental and insular group of Celtic languages. The continental group comprises languages which are all extinct (for example, Gaulish and Lepontic). The insular part falls into Brythonic and Goidelic languages. It was the Brythonic languages that were spoken in Britain when the Anglo-Saxons arrived. These are Welsh, Cornish and Breton. (Breton is today spoken in Brittany. It is assumed that the speakers fled from England during the invasion of the Anglo-Saxons). Goidelic falls into Irish Gaelic, Scottish Gaelic and Manx. Originally, Gaelic belonged to Ireland, but in the forth century it spread to the Isle of Man (Manx) and in the fifth century it entered Scotland (Scottish Gaelic).

The common view is that Celtic did not exert much influence on the English language. Some traces can be found in names of places and rivers. Recently this view has been questioned. Some researchers point to parallel forms in Celtic languages and English and maintain that considerable influence on English might have been exerted in spoken language varieties, which have not received any documentation. But this kind of influence is difficult to prove and this approach remains mostly controversial.

English is, as has been mentioned several times by now, a Germanic language, and the Germanic languages are the last section of Indo-European to be covered in this short survey. The Germanic branch of Indo-European is usually divided up into North Germanic, East Germanic and West Germanic. North Germanic comprises the modern Scandinavian languages (Norwegian, Swedish, Danish and Icelandic). Among the East Germanic languages (Burgundian, Vandalic, Gothic) we have only records of Gothic (the language of the Goths). The evidence preserved is mainly the fragmentary remnants of a Bible translation made by Bishop Wulfila in the fourth century, which is preserved in documents from the sixth century. The last descendant of Gothic, Crimean Gothic, died out in the eighteenth century.

West Germanic comprises the dialects of High German (resulting in Modern German), of Low German (with its earliest records in Old Saxon), Dutch, Frisian and, of course, English (Afrikaans and Yiddish are also included in this category). The language that is most closely related to English is Frisian. This language was spoken along the Southern North Sea coast and we may assume that the Anglo-Saxons, before they came to England, lived in close proximity to the Frisians. Historical linguists claim a prehistoric Anglo-Frisian parent language, out of which both Old English and Old Frisian evolved.

The Germanic languages share a number of important linguistic features. For example, they introduced the category of so-called weak verbs, which form the past tense with a dental or alveolar consonant (in Modern English the "regular" verbs with the dental suffix [d, t, ɪd], like *love, loved*; *kick, kicked*; *hunt, hunted*). At the phonological level the Germanic languages share several features as well. As was mentioned above, the Germanic languages were separated phonologically from the rest of Indo-European through the First Consonant Shift (or Grimm's Law). The consequence of this was, among other things, that Indo-European voiceless stops (/p, t, k/) became Germanic voiceless fricatives (/f, θ, χ/; see Table 1 above). The Germanic languages also tended to stabilise the accent on the first syllable of words, which in many cases had the effect of levelling or even losing the unstressed final syllables (in Chapter 1 we mentioned the example of the English infinitive forms *bindan, binden, bind*; *standan, standen, stand*, and so on).

After this short overview of the Indo-European and Germanic languages let us turn to some of the methodological problems Indo-European linguists have to cope with, especially those connected with the reconstruction of older stages of languages and their assumed family relationships. While it is beyond doubt that Indo-European and Germanic languages share common features, we should be careful to take the representation of the links between languages as a family tree too literally. In many cases the family tree can be a convenient way of showing similarities between languages, but it should not automatically be taken as a model of a historic evolution by which one parent language directly spread out into daughter languages.

A case which is often presented as one of the best historically attested examples of parent and daughter languages is the development of Vulgar Latin into the several Romance languages (Italian, Spanish, French, Portuguese etc.). Here we know that the Roman Empire disintegrated and left the local varieties of spoken Latin in relative isolation. The various political and socio-historical developments across the centuries contributed to the evolution of different varieties, sometimes national languages, which are different enough not to be mutually intelligible but which can still be systematically related to their parent language Latin. However, in many cases things are much more complex and fuzzy. In particular, the further we go back historically, the less hard-and-fast evidence can be produced for clear-cut branches in the Indo-European family of languages. Decades of research have made it clear that there does not seem to be a completely satisfactory way of representing the various similarities and differences between the Indo-European languages in terms of branches which divide and further subdivide. For example, Greek and Sanskrit are two languages which are usually placed on different branches but which share a number of features in syntax and lexis.

Nevertheless, the basic idea that the diversity of different languages may have evolved out of a reduced number or even only one parent language, has been fascinating because it also implies that the ancestor language was spoken, possibly several thousand years ago, by one community of speakers in a particular location. In the case of Indo-European, historical linguists have tried to reconstruct the underlying parent language (Proto-Indo-European) and speculated about the provenance of its speakers and the characteristics of their culture and society. Here the traditional view is that the Indo-Europeans were a nomadic or semi-nomadic people living in the Southern steppes of Russia. But there is a variety of views on the home of the Indo-Europeans, as well as on the period when they started to spread (ranging from 7000 BC until 3000 BC). It seems likely that no final and definitive answer to this question will be found.

Another problem involves the interpretation of the available evidence and the reconstruction of stages of a language (or a proto-language) where no evidence is to be had. As was mentioned in the previous chapter, historical linguists have to rely mostly on written evidence. The interpretation of written language in terms of speech can often create difficulties. Just imagine how we were to know the different pronunciation of <oo> in *food, good, blood* in the absence of any contemporary spoken evidence. Beyond the transformation of written signs into spoken sounds, historical linguists also attempt to reconstruct stages of a language (or proto-language) for which there is no evidence available at all. For example, for the pre-Old English predecessor of Modern English *heath* (*hapi) mentioned above we have no documentation. But knowledge about other Germanic languages (for example, Gothic *haiþi*) and knowledge about general phonological processes allow us to reconstruct this form, that is, to assume that in the pre-historic stage of

Old English this word was probably pronounced like this. This method is called comparative reconstruction.

The method of comparative reconstruction is often conveniently illustrated by examining selected words from Romance languages and relating them to their Latin source (see, for example, Lehman 1992: 6–7, 9–10). As can be seen in Table 2 below, the word *dear* is in French *cher*, and in Italian, Spanish and Portuguese *caro*. English *field* is in French *champ*, and in Italian, Spanish and Portuguese *campo*. English *candle* is in French *chandelle*, in Italian and Spanish *candela* and in Portuguese *candeia*.

French	*cher*	*champ*	*chandelle*
Italian	*caro*	*campo*	*candela*
Spanish	*caro*	*campo*	*candela*
Portuguese	*caro*	*campo*	*candeia*
Latin	*carus*	*campus*	*candela*

Table 2: Some cognates in Romance languages and in Latin

Based on this evidence, we can see that the initial consonant in French /ʃ/ corresponds to /k/ in all the other languages and /k/ can be reconstructed as the sound of the parent language Latin, which in fact it is.

This reconstruction is less arbitrary than it might appear at first sight (and in the absence of the Latin source). It is based on two principles, the majority principle and the principle of phonetic plausibility. The majority principle says that the sound which is encountered more frequently is likely to be the sound of the parent language. In other words: It is rather unlikely that the /ʃ/ (or another consonant) changed in three languages and was kept in only one. The principle of phonetic plausibility requires that the sound change should be phonetically plausible and should have been documented in other languages. For example, it would not make sense to assume that the initial sound in the source language had been /æ/ since this sound change is neither plausible nor ever recorded.

However, there always seems to be the potential risk of error. This risk may in fact be not so large, because there are several ways of checking our hypotheses and assumptions, both with regard to the reconstruction and the interpretation of evidence.

Firstly, the accumulated evidence and the various hypotheses all form a coherent network where one item depends on or is linked to the other items. If one item is "wrong", the validity of all the related items is threatened as well. And any new hypothesis must fit this mesh of interlocking evidence. Otherwise it will hardly be worth considering.

A second check relates in part to the principle of phonetic plausibility mentioned above, but here it is expanded to all levels of linguistic description. Any of the structures or changes of structures which are hypothesised should be known from other languages and their histories. Otherwise the hypothesis would hardly be acceptable. Knowledge from other languages may also be helpful in other respects. For example, when Old English was put to writing, monks employed the Latin alphabet in order to construct a viable spelling system. Since we basically know about the sound values of the Latin letters, we have valuable clues for reconstructing Old English pronunciation.

Thirdly, the linguistic descriptions must be supported by the available non-linguistic evidence. They must fit the known facts of the political, socio-cultural and economic history of the language community. For older stages of a language, archaeological discoveries may substantially contribute to a fuller understanding of the society and the context in which the language was embedded. For example, recent findings of pottery, grave furniture etc. improved our picture of Anglo-Saxon England, in particular our views on the early settlement history. There is also more indirect evidence which may help to verify our assumptions. For example, exceptional phonetic spellings in letters may give valid clues about pronunciation. If we find several writers who spell *daughter* as *dafter*, we have reason to believe that this word was actually pronounced with an /f/. Similar evidence can be found in rhymes and puns. We also find explicit metalinguistic discussions and comments, in which writers give descriptions of the pronunciation of words or the "correctness" of certain constructions. Many such comments on spelling and pronunciation can be found starting from the sixteenth and seventeenth centuries. But most of them tend to be fairly subjective and focus on one (fragmentary) aspect of the language.

So, despite the various restrictions and drawbacks historical linguists are faced with, there are several ways of checking the hypotheses against the background of language-internal and language-external data.

Summary

In this chapter we had a short look at the origins of the English language, relating it to the Indo-European language families, in particular to the Germanic languages. The chapter also dealt with important methodological difficulties involved in comparative reconstruction. Despite the many qualifications and restrictions, the hypotheses and assumptions about past stages of the English language form a fairly reliable network of interlocking evidence, where one item depends on the validity of many related items.

Further reading

Lehmann (1992) offers a detailed discussion of comparative reconstruction, using helpful illustrations from Indo-European. Campbell (1998) also includes numerous examples of sound changes from Indo-European. Lass (1994) has a short instructive chapter, guiding the way from Indo-European to West-Germanic. Anttila (1989) used to be a standard textbook on historical and comparative linguistics, while Clackson (2007) is a more recent introduction to Indo-European linguistics.

Questions and exercises

1. Find more series of matching words in English and German (like *hand, band, land* or *stone, bone, home* and their corresponding German forms mentioned in this chapter). What are the underlying sound correlations and are there any exceptions?

2. Look again at Figure 1 in this chapter, with the major branches of Indo-European. Why would Yiddish and Afrikaans be West-Germanic languages?

3. The following extract from a private letter (Jane Pinney, 1686, taken from the *Helsinki Corpus*) includes several idiosyncratic spellings. Which spellings could give hints about the author's pronunciation?

   My dare
      heare yo^u see what yor dafter doe write that shee have ... yor writetinges, that is true but what doe thay sicknifie unles old pimer had given him mony in consederation of it yo^u most com and take bands of her and her housban if yo^u can get thim to give yo^u bands be fore it runes to fare; for shee is wth childe and how can you neglecke such athinge as this what doe yo^u kno ~ how god may deale wth her such alittill cretuare and old to, ..., I will say noe more the lorde dericke yo^u for the best, but I most tell yo^u it is so bad heare, yo^u cannot besensabell unles yo^u ware hare to see and heare, and yo^u may travill as safe heare as thare, till the sogers doe com backe from the campe ...

3. English ca. 450 to ca. 1100 (Old English)

3.1. Political and socio-cultural background

Old English is without doubt the longest period among the traditional periods in the history of the English language. The usual approximate dates given to Old English are ca 450 and ca 1100, resulting in an era which lasted for more than 600 years. It is instructive and important to form an adequate picture of the sheer length of this time-span. Imagine the end of Anglo-Saxon England had happened during the past few years: We would then have to go back at least as far as 1400 AD to reach the beginnings of Old English. This imagined shift is instructive because it brings home the vast time proportions involved and shows the great difficulties associated with any general or definitive statements about the developments of language and communication in a period of that length. It is only natural to assume that during six hundred years Anglo-Saxon England must have seen significant changes in terms of politics, society, religion, cultural life, and communicative behaviour. But it is often extremely difficult to determine when these changes happened and what they involved.

The traditional start of the Old English period is 449. This is the date given by Bede, one of the most prominent scholars of Anglo-Saxon England, in his Latin *Historia ecclesiastica gentis anglorum* ("The ecclesiastical history of the English people", completed in 731). Bede says that in 449 the Germanic tribes of the Angles, Saxons and Jutes, who had left their continental homelands in Denmark and Lower Saxony, arrived in England and settled there. The exact date given by Bede cannot be trusted and we lack enough definite evidence to attempt any exact reconstruction. The settlement of England by Germanic-speaking tribes must have happened in the fifth and part of the sixth century. Archaeological evidence confirms that the three tribes were involved, but the Franks and the Frisians should probably also be included. It is likely that the newcomers first settled in the south and the east of England and gradually spread to the west and the north (see Map 1 below). Bede says that the Jutes settled in Kent and on the Isle of Wight, whereas the Angles spread north of the Thames. It may be that Bede oversimplified the situation here since it seems that the Germanic tribes had already mixed on the Continent before they arrived. So there could have been a mixed Anglian and Saxon culture in those areas described by Bede as Anglian.

The languages or dialects spoken by the tribes which settled in England belonged to the West-Germanic branch of the Germanic language family (see Chapter 2).

They had enough similarities due to their family association but also because the tribes, as was said before, seem to have mixed already on the Continent. The common core of these West-Germanic dialects of the invaders formed the basis for Old English and the English language, while the differing places of settlement marked the initial borderlines of the Old English dialects.

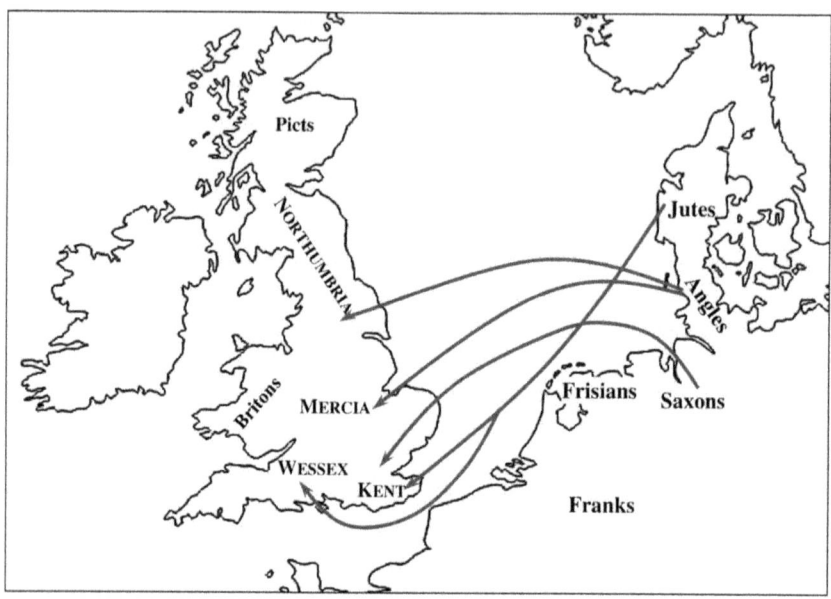

Map 1: Anglo-Saxon migration routes and settlements

When Anglo-Saxon rule was established in England, most of the former inhabitants, the Celtic Britons, were driven to the fringes in the West and North (Wales, Cornwall, Cumbria). Those who stayed seem to have served as slaves. It is instructive to follow the meaning of the Old English word *wealh*, the common designation for the Celtic Britons. Initially it means "foreigner" and "Celt, Briton", but then also "slave, servant", a development of meaning which cannot but be linked to the socio-political background. Linguistically, the Celtic inhabitants only left scarce traces, the most obvious ones being place names and names of rivers (for example, the names of London and Leeds, and the rivers Thames and Avon are Celtic).

The first centuries of Anglo-Saxon rule in England were marked by fragmentation, not by a united kingdom. The few extant sources indicate about twelve different independent kingdoms of varying size by the year 600. Later we find a so-called

Heptarchy, an association of seven kingdoms, with their respective rulers. But the exact number of such "kingdoms" and their exact borderlines is rather vague and has often been questioned. The number of the individual realms was further reduced by wars and conquests, leaving just four kingdoms by ca. 800: Northumbria, East Anglia, Wessex and Mercia. This process of reduction was further accelerated by the Viking invasions, which wrecked all kingdoms except for Wessex (see Map 2 below).

Map 2: The Anglo-Saxon Heptarchy, the Viking invasions and the Danelaw.

In the end, it was the kings of Wessex who united England in one kingdom. Before that, there was a shifting supremacy among the several Anglo-Saxon kingdoms.

During the seventh century the Northumbrian kings seem to have enjoyed an exceptional position, during the following century this eminent rank was covered by the Mercian kings and later by the rulers of Wessex. Some sources imply that the king who held this status had a special function with regard to the whole of England. He is, for example, called Bretwalda ("ruler of Britain"). It seems that this superior position required the other kings to pay tribute, to seek agreement in important matters and to fight under his leadership. But it did not include any sense of unification or a feeling of national unity.

One of the most important developments in the history of Anglo-Saxon England was Christianisation. Christian missionaries entered England from two different directions: St. Augustine and his team, who were sent by Pope Gregory, came from Rome and entered England from the South. Irish monks, invited by King Oswald of Northumbria, started from the Irish-Scottish monastery Iona in the North. Bede says in his *Historia Ecclesiastica* that Augustine arrived at the Isle of Thanet in Kent in 597. He started his missionary activities at the court of the Kentish king Æthelberht and made his way further north. Later he founded the three bishoprics of Canterbury, Rochester and London. The Celtic monks who were called to Christianise Northumbria and Mercia stemmed from the tradition of Irish Christianity. Ireland had already been Christianised in the fifth century by St. Patrick, but the Irish church had later been separated from Rome. As a consequence, Christianity in Ireland followed different regulations, for example, with regard to determining the date of Easter. The conflict over differences between Celtic and Roman Christianity, also over the date of Easter, was solved in 664 at the synod of Whitby. Here the traditional view of Rome prevailed.

The profound and pervasive impact of Christianisation on Anglo-Saxon language and culture cannot be overestimated. First of all, Christianisation and the Christian religion were the agents of literacy in Anglo-Saxon England. The foundation of monasteries and subsequent establishment of monastic schools laid the foundations for the documentation of Anglo-Saxon texts and the passing on of literary knowledge. It is probably safe to say that, had there been no Christianisation, hardly any Anglo-Saxon texts would have come down to us. As a consequence, the primary users of written language were members of the church - despite the fact that in many cases the functions of the texts were determined by secular matters. The large majority of the genres and texts which have survived from Anglo-Saxon times are religious in nature and function. The corpus of Old English is mostly biased towards religious genres. Christianity was also mainly shaped by the use of Latin. The new ideas and concepts which Christianity introduced in Anglo-Saxon England were mostly expressed by words borrowed from Latin or formed according to Latin models (on Latin influence on Old English see Chapter 3.2.4.).

Initially, the level of scholarship attained by Anglo-Saxon monks was exceptional and highly esteemed throughout Europe. Bede, the author of the *Historia Ecclesiastica*, is one of the most prominent scholars of the (early) Middle Ages. Alcuin of York, another Anglo-Saxon scholar of the early period, had such a high reputation that he was summoned to the court of Charlemagne. Later on, this high level seems to have declined, and one of the initiatives to revive and reform monastic life in England had linguistic consequences. This is the so-called Benedictine Reform of the second half of the tenth century, which was led by Bishop Æthelwold of Winchester, together with the Archbishops Dunstan and Oswald. The primary aim of the reform was to reduce secular influence in the monasteries and to enforce the Benedictine Rule as the only and obligatory guiding principle for monastic life in the whole of England. One of the consequences of this reform was a renewed flourishing of scholarship and vernacular translations, above all in Winchester. Æthelwold emphasised the importance of the vernacular for religious instruction and it seems that the Winchester school laid the foundations for a more or less uniform language use which formed the basis for much of the literary language used in the manuscripts dating from the (late) tenth and the eleventh century. This language has often been called the Winchester literary standard.

Another development with an outstanding importance during the Anglo-Saxon period, exerting a similarly profound influence, is the Viking invasion, or rather the Viking invasions (see Map 2 above). The plural is adequate because the Vikings came in several incursions covering basically the time between ca. 787 and 1042 (including the rule of Danish kings). Several reasons have been suggested for the Viking invasions: overpopulation of their native countries with their poor natural resources, internal or political conflicts, and the reduced power of the Frisians, who had blocked the southern access to England. The Vikings had been experts in boat-building and highly skilled sailors and navigators for generations. Britain was not the only aim of their multifarious expeditions, which took them as far as Greenland and Newfoundland.

The Viking incursions started with comparatively small expeditions. From ca. 787 onwards English towns and monasteries were attacked, destroyed and plundered by small bands of Viking warriors, but the assailants seem to have left home immediately afterwards. After ca. 850 larger and well organised forces attacked England. They followed the aim of occupation and settlement. The Vikings invaded the eastern part of England and progressed towards the West, overrunning all kingdoms except Wessex. Also, large parts of north-east England were settled by Scandinavians, with far-reaching consequences for the English language (on the Scandinavian influence on English see Chapter 3.2.4.). The Viking progress to the West was stopped by Alfred the Great (871–899). In the Treaty of Wedmore the Viking leader Guthrum agreed not to extend his rule beyond the so-called Danelaw (the land east of a line linking London and Chester). Alfred's successors were able to re-conquer large portions of the Scandinavian territory. Under King Edgar (959–975) Wessex occupied the complete Danelaw. But towards the end of the tenth century England faced fresh large-scale attacks by the Vikings, attacks which King Æthelræd (978–1016) and his nobility were unable to withstand. This led to the rule of Danish kings, which lasted till 1042, when Edward the Confessor, Æthelræd's son, ascended the throne. Edward's childless death in 1066 marked the beginning of the end of the Anglo-Saxon period.

When we compare England in Anglo-Saxon times with the England we know from today, some general and striking differences will have to be considered. First of all, the coastline was quite different from today. For example, in south-eastern England the Isle of Thanet (where St. Augustine and his companions landed) was in fact still an island, quite separate from the mainland, and Canterbury had access to the sea. The landscape was very much characterised by forests, marshes and fens, which seriously impeded transport and communication. Although there is scarce evidence, England's population must have been fairly small. It formed a basically agricultural society, with cattle-raising and grain-growing as major occupations of the majority of the population.

Anglo-Saxon society, too, was quite different from today's society. The basic elements constituting social networks were the loyalty of a man to his lord and the position of a person within the family. The loyalty of a man to his lord was a characteristic of all Germanic tribes and was already part of their description by the Roman historian Tacitus (first century AD). A retainer should not survive his lord in battle but fight on even in the most desperate situation. In return a retainer was given generous gifts (horses, weapons, even grants of land) by his lord. He was allowed to join the feasting in the lord's hall. This situation is depicted in many accounts given in Anglo-Saxon poetry (for example, in the contemporary poem *The Battle of Maldon* and many others). The question is, of course, whether these were literary ideas or social norms. In any way, the relationship between a man and his lord and the lord's protection still seem to have been important factors in Anglo-Saxon society and were in part reflected in Anglo-Saxon laws. A lord was responsible for his man's acts and had to present him in court. The lord also had to take vengeance or to demand compensation if his man was killed. It seems the lord's protection was an important element of public order because people were not likely to molest a man who enjoyed the protection of a powerful lord. By contrast, lordlessness was a suspicious state in Anglo-Saxon society since it was usually the consequence of disloyalty or cowardice.

In a similar way, the family network provided security in a basically violent society. The certainty of vengeance or compensation functioned as a means of maintaining order. The Anglo-Saxon laws described the classes of society in terms of the amount of money which was due if a person of that class had been killed. This "man-price" (*wergild*) became a mark of rank in Anglo-Saxon society. Despite the clearly specified conditions and details of compensation and the strong opposition of the Church, vendettas and family feuds were a notorious characteristic of the whole of the Anglo-Saxon period.

The king had a unique position in Anglo-Saxon society, which could not be challenged. This is also reflected in Anglo-Saxon laws. For example, an attempt to kill the king or even supporting his enemies cost life and all possessions. Similarly, fighting in the king's house cost all the possessions. As the period advanced, the king's person assumed a kind of sanctity. He was seen as the deputy of Christ, who reigned by the grace of God. Starting from the end of the eighth century, ecclesiastical coronation was introduced and special emphasis was placed on the act of anointing the king. The king was usually elected by the council of "wise men" (*witan*). These were the archbishops, bishops, major abbots, the ealdormen and the most important king's thanes. The choice was usually limited to the royal family and it was on most occasions the eldest son of the last king who was elected. The council of "wise men" also had the function to advise the king on important matters, for example laws, policies, and donations of land.

Anglo-Saxon society comprised three major levels: noblemen, freemen and slaves. Noblemen are mentioned with different designations: An early term is *gesīþas* ("companions"), in Kent we find *eorlas* ("warriors"), and *þegnas* ("thanes") is the later common term. The ordinary freemen are called *ceorlas* ("churls"), the designation for slaves is *þeowas*. Anglo-Saxon laws found a very simple norm for distinguishing the classes, the *wergild* ("man-price", mentioned above), that is, the amount of money which was due if a member of the class had been killed. For example, members of the nobility were called "men of twelve hundred" in Wessex, churls were "men of two hundred", and slaves, needless to say, had no wergild at all. It seems that the position of a thane was linked to extensive possession of land (for example, at least five hides (approximately 600 acres). The extant sources indicate that these large estates were mostly spread out across the whole country. The status of a churl was also linked to possession of land, which ranged between one and two hides. Otherwise a churl enjoyed the full rights of a freeman, that is, he could inherit and pass on land, attend the popular assemblies; he had the freedom of movement, and he had to pay the dues to the church and to fulfil military obligations. Otherwise he had the freedom of movement. There is some indication that the position of the churls gradually declined in the course of the centuries and it seems there was a lower standard of living in the South and West of the country. Since many churls were not able to subsist their families with the output of their land, they had to rent land from a lord and gradually had to give up their personal freedom. As a consequence, we find several subclasses of dependent churls, especially in the South and West. There were, of course, also other kinds of non-agricultural occupations, for example, as merchants and craftsmen. Most of them ranked as churls.

Contrary to what one might expect, the available sources indicate that women had a relatively independent position in Anglo-Saxon society (at least those belonging to the class of noblewomen and freewomen). Women could own land, dispose of it freely and defend their rights in the courts. Women were, in fact, much more independent than in the Middle English period after the Norman Conquest. In Christine Fell's study on women in Anglo-Saxon England (1984) the Anglo-Saxon period is even depicted as "a golden age of power and wealth, culture and education" for women (cited in Mitchell 1995: 211).

The defining characteristic of slaves was that they had no wergild. They could be treated as chattel, as moveable possessions with their respective market value. Their position in the law was fairly precarious. They could be flogged, even mutilated or killed without any consequences for their lord. However, there were basic rights of custom, for example, as regards the amount of food they were given. Some of the slaves seem to have stemmed from the descendants of the Celtic population (*wealh*, see above). But the most common kind of slaves were penal slaves, people who were enslaved for crimes they had committed or because the compensation money which was due could not be paid by their families. The setting free of slaves was advocated as an act of Christian mercy by the Church. And in many of the wills that have come down to us slaves are given back their freedom as part of the last will of the testator.

3.2. Language structure

3.2.1. Spelling and pronunciation

Before Christianisation the English tribes, in England as well as on the Continent, had a runic alphabet which was called "futhorc" after the first six letters. Runes were mostly used for carving short inscriptions on wood, metal or stone. We would find them on daggers, swords, horns, boxes and similar objects. The runic writing was kept up for some time in Anglo-Saxon England, but the literacy introduced by Christianisation would inevitably be based on the Latin alphabet. So, later runic writing would not play any major role.

The monks who introduced literacy in Anglo-Saxon England adapted the Latin alphabet to the Anglo-Saxon language, in order to represent some English sounds which were not found in Latin. They set up some special letters, some of them runic signs. There were first of all the "thorn" <þ> and the "eth" <ð>. Both letters were used to denote the dental fricatives (both voiced and voiceless: [ð], [θ]). Whereas thorn was a runic letter, the provenance of eth could have been Irish. The runic "wynn" <ρ> denotes the bilabial /w/. (In most modern editions of Old English texts the wynn is represented as <w>). The letter "ash" <æ> was used to represent /æ/. The letter "yogh" <ȝ> could denote several sounds: /j/, /g/ and the velar fricative /χ/. The letter <y> was used to represent the rounded front vowel /y/ (the sound in German *Hütte* or *Güte*).

Once you are familiar with the special signs, reading an Old English text is not as difficult as one might assume. The relationship between letter and sound is in most cases fairly straightforward and usually each letter is pronounced, that is, you do not "leave out" letters as in Modern English (compare, for example, the pronunciation of *thought* and *Worcester*). Table 1 below lists the vowel, diphthong and consonant phonemes in Old English; Table 2 illustrates the relationship between spelling and pronunciation in Old English, combining graphemes and phonemes / allophones and giving an example. The presentation in the next sections will follow these two Tables.

There are seven short and seven long vowels in Old English. Since vowel length is phonemic in Old English, they can be arranged in pairs of short and long vowels (see Table 1). In modern editions of Old English texts long vowels are usually marked with a macron (for example, ā, ē, ū etc.; but note that this is not a convention found in Old English manuscripts). There were three front-vowel pairs, three back-vowel pairs and one pair with a front rounded vowel /y/. The front-vowel pairs are /i:/ - /i/, /e:/ - /e/ and /æ:/ - /æ/; the back-vowel pairs are /uː/ - /u/, /oː/ - /o/ and /aː/ - /a/; the pair with the front rounded vowel is /yː/ - /y/. As can be seen from the arrangement of the vowels, their representations by letters and the respective examples in Table 2 below, the relationship between letter and sound is quite straightforward with the seven pairs of vowel phonemes.

There are four diphthongs in Old English, which can be arranged in pairs as well: <ēo> - <eo> and <ēa> - <ea>. (Occasionally we also find the diphthongs <īo> - <io> and <īe> - <ie>). Note that the above representation of employs graphemes since the phonological values of the diphthongs are somewhat controversial in the literature. However, in the context of this book it seems justifiable to treat <ēo> as /eːə/ and <eo> as /eə/, <ēa> as /æːə/ and <ea> as /æə/ (see Table 2 below; note the levelled quality of the letter <o> and <a>, represented as schwa /ə/).

vowels		
front	front + rounded	back
iː / i	yː / y	uː / u
eː / e		oː / o
æː / æ		aː / a
diphthongs		
eːə / eə		
æːə / æə		
consonants						
	stops	fricatives/sibilants	affricates	nasal	liquids	approximants
labial	p – b	f – v		m		w
dental		θ – ð				
alveolar	t – d	s – z		n	l – r	
palatal			tʃ – dʒ			j
velar	k – g²	χ – ɣ				

Table 1: Vowel, diphthong and consonant phonemes in Old English

---

2   On /g/ see the commentary in the text.

Spelling	Pronunciation	Example
⟨i⟩	= /iː/ and /i/	līf ("life"), scip ("ship")
⟨e⟩	= /eː/ and /e/	ēþel ("homeland"), efen ("even")
⟨æ⟩	= /æː/ and /æ/	strǣt ("street"), fæder ("father")
⟨y⟩	= /yː/ and /y/	mȳs ("mice"), synn ("sin")
⟨u⟩	= /uː/ and /u/	fūl ("foul"), sunu ("sun")
⟨o⟩	= /oː/ and /o/	gōd ("good"), God ("God")
⟨a⟩	= /aː/ and /a/	āgān ("to go away"), lang ("long")
⟨ea⟩	= /æːə/ and /æə/	ēadig ("happy"), beald ("bold")
⟨eo⟩	= /eːə/ and /eə/	dēop ("deep"), eorl ("nobleman")
⟨p⟩	= /p/	prēost ("priest")
⟨b⟩	= /b/	biddan ("to ask")
⟨t⟩	= /t/	hātan ("to order")
⟨d⟩	= /d/	dēaþ ("death")
⟨c⟩	/k/	bōc ("book"), cunnan ("can"), cniht ("knight")
	/tʃ/	cirice ("church"), tǣcan ("to teach"), cild ("child")
⟨g⟩	/g/ = [g] or [ɣ]	gān ("to go"), gōd ("good") - dagas ("days"), lagu ("law")
	/j/ = [j]	giefan ("to give"), dæg ("day")
⟨f⟩	= /f/ = [f] or [v]	fūl ("foul") - clīfan ("to cleave")
⟨þ, ð⟩	= /θ/ = [θ] or [ð]	þīn ("your"), wiþ ("with") - ōþer ("other")
⟨h⟩	= /χ/ = [h] or [χ] / [ɣ]	hūs ("house") - lēoht ("light")
⟨s⟩	= /s/ = [s] or [z]	swā ("so"), mūs ("mouse") - wesan ("to be")
⟨sc⟩	= /ʃ/	scip ("ship")
⟨cg⟩	= /dʒ/	ecg ("edge")
⟨m⟩	= /m/	mann ("man")
⟨n⟩	= /n/ = [n] or [ŋ]	niman ("to take") - þanc ("to thank")
⟨l⟩	= /l/	lufu ("to love")
⟨r⟩	= /r/	rīce ("kingdom")
⟨u, uu, p⟩	= /w/	word ("word")

Table 2: Spelling and pronunciation in Old English (the order of presentation follows the text, including graphemes, phonemes, allophones and examples)

Things are slightly more complex in the field of consonants. As can be seen in Table 1 and Table 2, there are three voiceless stops /p, t, k/, which are usually designated by the letters <p, t, c> respectively. But originally there were only two voiced counterparts /b, d/. The voiced stop /g/, represented by <g>, was initially a voiced velar fricative /ɣ/, which, however, developed into the voiced stop /g/ in initial position towards the end of the period (for example, in *gān* "to go"). In medial position the voiced fricative [ɣ] was retained (*dagas* "days", *lagu* "law").[3] For the present purposes it seems justifiable to posit a third voiced stop /g/, although we should bear in mind that this description is not quite correct systematically.

With the fricatives we only find the voiceless phonemes /f, θ, χ/ (the velar phoneme /χ/ designates the final consonant in German *ach*). Their voiced counterparts are allophones in complementary distribution. For example, when /θ/ occurred at the beginning or at the end of a word, it retained its voiceless character (*þīn* /θi:n/ "your" and *dēaþ* /dæ:əθ/ "death"), but in medial position it was voiced (*ōþer* /o:ðər/ "other"). The same applied to the other fricatives (see, for example, *fūl* "foul", with a voiceless [f], and *clīfan* "to cleave", with the voiced [v]).[4] In addition, the allophone of /χ/ in initial position developed from [χ] to [h] (for example, *hūs* "house")

The sibilant /s/ has, similar to the three fricatives, a voiced allophone in medial position, whereas the initial and final position have the voiceless sound (thus *swā* "so" and *mūs* "mouse" with [s] and *wesan* "to be" with [z]). The sibilant /ʃ/ (represented by the letter combination <sc>) only appears as a voiceless sound. There were two affricates: /tʃ/, represented by <c>, mostly before front vowels (for example, *cirice* /tʃiritʃə/ "church" and *tǣcan* /tæ:tʃan/ "to teach"), and /dʒ/, usually represented by <cg> (see Table 2).

There were two nasals, /m/ and /n/. The velar nasal [ŋ], contrary to the situation in present-day English, was an allophone of /n/ since it only occurred before /k/ or /g/ (as in *þanc* "thank" or *singan* "to sing"). There were two liquids, /l/ and /r/. While the former was probably pronounced in a similar way as in present-day English, the /r/ was realised quite differently, probably as an alveolar trill or flap. Finally, there were two approximants, /j/ and /w/. While /w/ was denoted by <u, uu, p>, /j/ had mostly <g> before front vowels (for example *gieldan* "to reward", *gefēra* "comrade", *dæg* "day", see Table 2).

---

3   The voiced fricative /ɣ/ is not found in Standard German, but in certain dialects, for example, in *Lage* as pronounced in the area around Cologne and Bonn.
4   Among the three voiced allophones the velar fricative must – at least theoretically – be distinguished from the velar fricative /ɣ/ mentioned above, which developed into the velar stop /g/.

We should add that Old English had so-called geminates, that is, long or double consonants. These occur mostly in medial position (for example *hoppian* "to leap" as opposed to *hopian* "to hope", both with a short /o/ in the first syllable).

Old English words were stressed, as in all Germanic languages, on the first syllable, independently of the fact how long a word was. Thus, words like *efenceasterwaran* ("fellow-citizen") and *æþelfeorþingwyrt* (the name of a plant) had their main stress on the first syllable. There were only a few prefixes which usually were not stressed, like *ge-* in *gewinn* "labour" or *for-* in *forlēosan* "to lose".

During the Old English period and even before the advent of the Anglo-Saxon tribes in England, we can trace quite a few sound changes which contributed to the further development and diversification of the language and which eventually tended to make the language less transparent. If we know them, we can link words which seem to be quite unrelated from a contemporary perspective to a common source. Here we will deal with two important sound changes, i-umlaut and breaking.

I-umlaut, also called i-mutation, was the result of the influence of an [i] or [j] on the preceding syllable in a word. For example, in proto-Old English the word for *mouse* was *mūs, with the plural *mūsi. In *mūsi, the plural *–i* resulted in a fronting and raising of the back vowel /u:/ in the preceding syllable to /y:/. Later on, the *-i* ending was lost. Thus, in Old English we find the singular *mūs* and the plural *mȳs*. In Middle English the /y:/ was unrounded to /i:/, which in turn was diphthongised during the Great Vowel Shift (see Chapter 5.2.1.), resulting in Modern English *mice*, the "irregular" plural form of *mouse*. In all, i-umlaut affected thirteen vowels in Old English (some of them are given in Table 3 below). A few interesting links between (Modern) English words are revealed if we trace the vowel changes due to i-umlaut. For example, the affix **–iþu* could be used to form nouns out of adjectives, **–iþu* of course containing the *i* which could trigger i-umlaut. So the adjective *hāl* ("whole, healthy") formed the basis of the derived noun *hāliþu or – with i-umlaut changing /a:/ to /æ:/ – *hǣlþ* ("health"). In the same way *fūl* ("foul") and *fȳlþ* ("filth") are related due to i-umlaut.

æ	→	e	
ā	→	ǣ	(*hāl* "whole" (+*iþu*) -> *hǣlþ* "health")
ō	→	ē	
ū	→	ȳ	(*fūl* "foul" (+*iþu*) -> *fȳlþ* "filth")

Table 3: Some vowels affected by i-mutation in Old English

33

Breaking is a process which involves diphthongisation of a front vowel (i, e, æ) when it is followed by a velar consonant or group of consonants (for example, /l/, /r/, /χ/ plus another consonant). Thus *wærp* became *wearp*, *bærn* became *bearn*, *werc* became *weorc*, *fæht* became *feaht*, and so on. Breaking seems to have happened in Old English around the seventh century and affected most of the South of the country. Thus, breaking is particularly common in the West-Saxon dialect (see Chapter 3.2.5.).

3.2.2. Morphology and word-formation

inflectional morphology

One of the major features distinguishing Old English from Modern English is that Old English is a predominantly synthetic language, whereas Modern English is largely analytic. What does this mean? Synthetic languages mark grammatical categories and syntactic functions in a sentence mostly by means of inflectional endings; analytic languages do so mainly by using other means, for example, word-order, prepositions and auxiliary verbs.

Look at a simple illustrative sentence.

(1) Se guma geaf þām wīfe þā hringas.
    "The man gave the rings to the woman."

In the Old English sentence the grammatical categories case, number and gender are expressed by inflectional endings and the respective forms of the definite article: *guma*, in combination with *se*, designates the nominative singular masculine ("the man"), *þām*, in combination with *wīfe*, the dative singular neuter ("to the woman"), and *þā*, in combination with *hringas*, the accusative (or nominative) plural masculine ("the rings"). In the Modern English sentence only the category number is expressed by inflectional means (the –*s*, in *rings*, or the lack of the plural forms in the other nouns). In Old English the cases are closely associated with specific syntactic functions, for example, the nominative case usually designates the subject of a sentence (*se guma*), the direct object is usually expressed by the accusative (*þā hringas*) and the indirect object is associated with the dative case (*þām wīfe*). In the Modern English sentence these syntactic functions are marked by word-order and prepositions. The subject is the constituent immediately preceding the verb, the direct object is the constituent following the verb and the indirect object is marked by the preposition *to*.[5] By contrast, word-order in Old English is relatively free. We could easily change the order of the constituents without any significant change of the meaning:

(2) Þām wīfe geaf se guma þā hringas.

(3) Geaf þām wīfe se guma þā hringas.

In Modern English such a change of the constituent order would result in a major alteration of the meaning or in an ungrammatical construction:

(4) The woman gave the man the rings (or: the rings to the man).

(5) *Gave the woman the man the rings.

Given the basic synthetic structure of Old English, nouns and adjectives are inflected for case, number and gender. For nouns there are several paradigms or types of declension. The most important ones are: strong masculine ā (e.g. *stān* "stone"), strong neuter ā (e.g. *scip* "ship"), strong feminine ō (e.g. *giefu* "gift"), strong masculine u (e.g. *sunu* "son"), strong feminine u (e.g. *duru* "door"), strong masculine i (e.g. *wine* "friend"), strong feminine i (e.g. *dǣd* "deed"), weak masculine –n (e.g. *guma* "man"), and weak feminine –n (e.g. *tunge* "tongue"). Traditionally, strong declensions contain vowel stems, whereas weak declensions contain consonantal stems. Some of them are illustrated in Table 4 below.

Even with this restricted selection of noun endings, you may note that many case forms are identical in one paradigm (for example, *-an* covering accusative singular and plural, genitive and dative singular, and nominative plural with *guma*) and some case forms even across paradigms (for example, *-um* marking the dative plural in all the above declensions). It is true that there was a trend towards the levelling or loss of distinctions in case endings at the end of the Old English period. But it seems that during the largest part of the era the inflectional system worked pretty well. This was due to the fact that the declension of nouns was very much supported by the inflectional system of the demonstrative pronouns, in particular the definite article *se*, which showed a full range of case endings (except for gender in the plural; see Table 5 below).

---

5   Alternatively, the indirect object could be placed immediately in front of the direct object, following the verb.

	stān (str, m) ("stone")	*scip* (str, n) ("ship")	*giefu* (str, f) ("gift")
Singular			
Nom	*stān*	*scip*	*giefu*
Gen	*stānes*	*scipes*	*giefe*
Dat	*stāne*	*scipe*	*giefe*
Acc	*stān*	*scip*	*giefe*
Plural			
Nom	*stānas*	*scipu*	*giefa, -e*
Gen	*stāna*	*scipa*	*giefa, -ena*
Dat	*stānum*	*scipum*	*giefum*
Acc	*stānas*	*scipu*	*giefa, -e*
	guma (w, m) ("man")	*tunge* (w, f) ("tongue")	
Singular			
Nom	*guma*	*tunge*	
Gen	*guman*	*tungan*	
Dat	*guman*	*tungan*	
Acc	*guman*	*tungan*	
Plural			
Nom	*guman*	*tungan*	
Gen	*gumena*	*tungena*	
Dat	*gumum*	*tungum*	
Acc	*guman*	*tungan*	

Table 4: Some Old English strong and weak paradigms

	Masculine	Neuter	Feminine	Plural
Nom	se	þæt	sēo	þā
Gen	þæs	þæs	þǣre	þāra
Dat	þām	þām	þǣre	þām
Acc	þone	þæt	þā	þā

Table 5: The demonstratives se, þæt, sēo

Another major field of nominal inflection is the paradigm of pronouns, although it must be noted here that for the third person the forms are not as distinct in terms of case, number and gender as one would expect them to be (see Table 6 below).

		Singular	**Plural**	
First	Nom	*ic*	*wē*	
	Gen	*mīn*	*ūre*	
	Dat/Acc	*mē*	*ūs*	
Second	Nom	*þū*	*gē*	
	Gen	*þīn*	*ēower*	
	Dat/Acc	*þē*	*ēow*	
		Masculine	**Neuter**	**Feminine**	**Plural**
Third	Nom	*hē*	*hit*	*hēo*	*hī*
	Gen	*his*	*his*	*hire*	*hira*
	Dat	*him*	*him*	*hire*	*him*
	Acc	*hine*	*hit*	*hī*	*hī*

Table 6: Old English personal pronouns

A few points should be noted here. In the first- and second-person paradigm there is no distinction between dative and accusative forms (for example, *mē*, *ūs* etc.). Also, there were a few forms which were exclusively used for the reference to two persons (the so-called dual forms, not listed in Table 6; for example *wit, uncer, unc* for the first person), but their use was somewhat restricted. On the other hand, the second-person plural form was used exclusively for plural reference, not for addressing single persons. To address single persons, only the singular forms were used (on the development of plural forms with singular reference see Chapter 5.3.1.). With regard to the third-person paradigm you may note that the feminine form *she* is not yet found (the feminine form is *hēo*), neither the present-day plural forms starting with *th* (*they, them, their*; they are Scandinavian loans; on this see Chapter 4.2.2.). In addition, some case forms are not quite distinct and some forms may in fact be confusing when you find them in actual texts. For example, there is one dative form (*him*) covering the masculine, neuter and plural. One form (*hī*) is found in the feminine accusative and the nominative / accusative plural. To complicate things even more, the texts show a large variety of differing forms for the individual pronouns (for example, *hiene* for *hine*, *heora* for *hira* and so on).

Adjectives, too, are inflected for case, number and gender. They agree in case, number and gender with the noun they modify. Thus in *þæs blindan mannes* ("of the blind man, the blind man's") the form *blindan* agrees with *mannes* since it is genitive singular masculine. However, you will find again that some forms are not very distinct since they cover many slots in the paradigm (compare Table 7 below).

Strong Singular	Masculine	Feminine	Neuter
Nom	blind	blind	blind
Gen	blindes	blindre	blindes
Dat	blindum	blindre	blindum
Acc	blindne	blinde	blind
Plural			
Nom	blinde	blinda	blind
Gen	blindra	blindra	blindra
Dat	blindum	blindum	blindum
Acc	blinde	blinda	blind
Weak Singular	**Masculine**	**Feminine**	**Neuter**	**Plural**
Nom	blinda	blinde	blinde	blindan
Gen	blindan	blindan	blindan	blindra
Dat	blindan	blindan	blindan	blindum
Acc	blindan	blindan	blinde	blindan

Table 7: Strong and weak adjective declension in Old English

With adjective inflection there is an additional complication in Old English. In Old English there are two different sets of inflectional paradigms, the so-called weak and strong inflections. The weak inflection is employed when the construction includes a determiner, that is, when the adjective is preceded by a demonstrative or a possessive (for example, *se blinda mann*). If the construction does not include a determiner, but adjective and noun "stand alone", we find the strong declension, for example, *blind mann*. Both sets are given in Table 7 above. You will find that the weak declension of adjectives has many similarities with the weak noun declension (see Table 4 above), whereas the strong declension tends to follow the strong noun declension.

Adjective declension also includes comparative and superlative forms, for example, *lēof* "dear" has *lēofra* and *lēofost*, *heard* "hard" has *heardra* and *heardost*, and so on. Both comparative and superlative forms are inflected. There are also so-called suppletive forms, similar to the present-day English forms, that is, forms in a paradigm with no resemblance to the base forms, for example, *lȳtel, lǣssa, lǣst* ("little, less, least") or *micel, māra, mǣst* ("much, more, most").

Old English verb inflection follows the categories person (first, second, third), number (singular, plural), tense (present, past) and mood (indicative, subjunctive, imperative). Traditionally, four classes of verbs are distinguished: weak, strong, preterite-present and so-called irregular verbs. The terms "weak" and "strong" are used here quite differently than when describing nouns or adjectives. Weak verbs use the dental suffix *–d–* or *–t–* when forming the past forms (like Modern English regular verbs, for example, *call, called* or *talk, talked*), whereas strong verbs change their stem vowel (similar to present-day English *rise, rose, risen* or *sing, sang, sung*). Preterite-present verbs use formerly past tense forms with a present meaning. Most of them are the predecessors of today's modal auxiliaries (*can, shall, must* etc.). The so-called irregular verbs are extremely variable in their forms and comprise only a few verbs.

Table 8 below contains the major forms of one weak verb (*fremman*, "to do"). Actually, there are three different classes of weak verbs in Old English, but this need not concern us for the present purposes. Also, there are some weak verbs which show changes in their stem vowel (due to i-umlaut in their present-tense forms, which, however, was suspended in their past-tense forms), but which of course retain their dental suffix. They are worth mentioning because they are still preserved in present-day English. Some of them are *sēcan, sōhte, sōht* ("seek, sought, sought"), *sellan, sealde, seald* ("sell, sold, sold"), *þencan, þōhte, þōht* ("think, thought, thought") or *bycgan, bohte, boht* ("buy, bought, bought").

Indicative		
	Present	Past
Sing. 1st	fremme	fremede
2nd	fremest	fremedest
3rd	fremeþ	fremede
Plural	fremmaþ	fremedon

Subjunctive

Sing.	*fremme*	*fremede*
Plural	*fremmen*	*fremeden*

Imperative

Sing.	*freme*	–
Plural	*fremmaþ*	–
Participle	*fremmende*	*gefremed*

Table 8: *Major forms of the weak verb* fremman *"to do"*

As was mentioned above, strong verbs change the stem vowel in the formation of past forms. This change is traditionally called ablaut. Usually seven classes of strong verbs are distinguished. Except for the seventh class, they can be defined by a distinctive combination of vowel and consonant(s), as is shown below. There are four distinct stem forms, the infinitive, the two past tense forms and the second participle.

I	ī + C	scīnan, scān, scinon, scinen ("to shine")
II	ēo + C	crēopan, crēap, crupon, cropen ("to creep")
	ū + C	brūcan, brēac, brucon, brocen ("to enjoy")
III	e/i + CC	findan, fand, fundon, funden ("to find")
IV	e + C^6	beran, bær, bǣron, boren ("to bear")
V	e + C^7	tredan, træd, trǣdon, treden ("to tread")
VI	a + C	faran, fōr, fōron, faren ("to travel")
VII		healdan, hēold, hēoldon, healden ("to hold")
		hātan, hēt, hēton, hāten ("to command")

The major forms of one strong verb (*singan* "to sing") are given in Table 9 below.

Indicative

	Present	Past
Sing. 1st	*singe*	*sang*
2nd	*singest*	*sunge*
3rd	*singeþ*	*sang*
Plural	*singaþ*	*sungon*

---

6 Usually a liquid.
7 Usually a stop or fricative.

Subjunctive

Sing.	singe	sunge
Plural	singen	sungen

Imperative

Sing.	sing	–
Plural	singaþ	–
Participle	singende	gesungen

Table 9: Major forms of the strong verb singan "to sing"

Preterite-present verbs, mostly the predecessors of today's modal auxiliaries, are those verbs which have a strong past tense with a present tense meaning and consequently developed a new weak past. This development of meaning can still be seen in the so-called resultative aspect entailed in the perfect tense of the Latin verb *noscere* ("to get to know"). Once you have come to know somebody, you know him/her. Thus the perfect form *novi* acquired the meaning "I know". Most preterite-present verbs have a modal meaning, that is, a meaning connected with volition and obligation ("be allowed to", "have to", "need to"). In Modern English they have developed into auxiliary verbs, but in Old English they are often used as full verbs, without being tied to another verb (compare **he can English* as opposed to *he can swim*). Some important Old English preterite-present verbs are *cunnan* ("can, to know how to"), with the weak past form *cūþe*, *magan* ("to be able to"), with the weak past form *meahte*, and *witan* ("to know"), with the weak past form *wiste*.

The so-called irregular verbs constitute a small class of four verbs (*bēon* ("to be"), *dōn* ("to do"), *gān* ("to go"), *willan* ("to wish")) with fairly anomalous paradigms. The major forms can be looked up in the common text books or grammars.

word-formation

Morphological structure in terms of word-formation comprises an important part of Old English since in Anglo-Saxon England new words were usually created by "native means", not by borrowing from other languages (on the major exception to this rule, Latin loanwords in connection with Christianisation and the Benedictine Reform, see Chapter 3.2.4). Old English had a remarkable capacity for creating new words by using elements of the existing word stock together with a large inventory of prefixes and suffixes. This resulted in an exceptional resourcefulness of the vocabulary on the one hand, and in a remarkable transparency of the lexicon on the other. The most common processes of word-formation were, as they are today, derivation (prefixation, suffixation) and compounding. The meaning of such word formations may be quite plausible and transparent if the meaning of the constituent parts, that is, the prefixes, suffixes and free morphemes are known. In this way Old English may create new words for concepts using native means. Much of the Old English vocabulary is related by word-formation patterns and a large section of it may be described in terms of morphologically related word-families.

An illustrative example is the word-family constituted by the verb *gān / gangan* "to go" and *gang* "journey" (see Kastovsky 1992: 294–296 for details). Some compounds are *ciricgang* ("churchgoing"), *hingang* ("going hence, death"), *mynstergang* ("entering on a monastic life"), *gangpytt, gangsetl* ("privy"), *gangwīfre* ("spider, a weaver that goes"); prefixes include *begangan* ("to go to, to visit"), *beganga* ("inhabitant"), *foregān* ("to go before, to precede"), *forþgān* ("to go forth"), *ingān* ("to go in"), *ingang* ("entrance"), *niþergān* ("to descend"), *ofergān* ("to pass over"), *þurhgān* ("to go through"), *upgān* ("to go up"), *ūtgān* ("to go out"), *ūtgang* ("exit"), *wiþgān* ("to go against"), *ymbgān* ("to go round"), *ymbgang* ("circuit"), and so on.

In a similar way, Old English has quite straightforward compounds involving changing combinations with one word (*cræft* "skill"), where Modern English (and other modern languages) have completely different forms involving Latin and Greek loans. In Old English the terms "literature", "arithmetic", "grammar" and "astronomy" are compounds based on *cræft*. Literature is "book-skill" (*bōccræft*), arithmetic is "number-skill" (*rīmcræft*), grammar is "letter-skill" (*stæfcræft*), and astronomy is "star-skill" (*tungolcræft*).

In this way Old English achieves a remarkable transparency of its vocabulary. Once you know the most important stems and affixes, you can – in many cases – work out the meaning of the derived or compounded word. Modern English is less transparent here. Due to the borrowing from many foreign languages (above all French and Latin), words with different stems enter a lexical field, making it quite complex and even opaque (see, for example, *heart / cordial, father / paternal, mouth / oral*).

3.2.3. Syntax

Old English syntax is a fairly complex field and this chapter cannot attempt to give even a short comprehensive overview. Rather, it will focus on selected topics which are, without doubt, important elements of Old English syntax and which may illustrate both differences and similarities of Old English with regard to present-day English. We will look at word-order, negation, coordination / subordination, relative clauses and impersonal constructions.

In the last chapter we saw that Old English was a basically synthetic language. Syntactic functions in the clause, like subject or direct object, were marked by inflectional endings, for example, in nouns and adjectives. As a consequence word order, that is the sequence of the constituents in a sentence, was fairly flexible. On the other hand, Old English word order was not completely unrestricted. In fact, we find quite a few recurrent patterns which seem to have been fairly common. Some of them may be quite familiar to speakers of present-day English, but others will appear rather exotic.

First of all, we find the Subject-Verb-Object order, which is prevalent in Modern English.

(6) Se engel $_{[Subj.]}$ gehyrte $_{[Vb.]}$ þā wīf $_{[Obj.]}$.
 "The angel encouraged the women."
 (Ælfric, *Catholic Homilies;* late 10th century; DOEC)

This SVO pattern is found mostly in main clauses and occasionally also in subordinate clauses. But the verb may also appear before the subject, especially when the clause is introduced by an adverbial (for example, þā).

(7) Þā brōhton $_{[Vb.]}$ hī $_{[Subj.]}$ him $_{[indir. Obj.]}$ gebrǣdne fisc $_{[dir. Obj.]}$.
 "Then they brought him baked fish."
 (Ælfric, *Catholic Homilies*; late 10th century; DOEC)

This inverted pattern is also called "verb-second pattern", since the verb phrase appears as the second constituent in the clause. Please note that one phrase or constituent may contain several words. For example, in the above sentence þā could be replaced by *on þām ylcan dæge* "the same day". This pattern is also used for interrogatives, where *do*-support is not yet found:

(8) Hwǣr eart $_{[Vb.]}$ þū $_{[Subj.]}$ nū gefēra?
 "Where are you now, comrade?"
 (Ælfric, *Lives of Saints (Edmund)*; late 10th century; DOEC)

A third important pattern may be called "verb-final pattern". Here the verb phrase forms the last constituent in the clause.

(9) Þā þā hī [Subj.] þis [Obj.] sprǣcon [Vb.]' ...
"When they said this, ..."
(Ælfric, *Catholic Homilies*; late 10th century; DOEC)

This pattern is typically used in subordinate clauses (see the temporal subordinate clause in example 9). Native speakers of German will find the two last patterns quite familiar because they also appear in Modern German (a German translation of examples 8 and 9 will make this immediately clear).

So far, the presentation may have shown a slightly too regular picture. In fact, we find much variation in the Old English word-order patterns. For example, quite often the complex verb phrase (*habban / wesan* plus participle of a full verb, see *wǣron þurfdrifene* "were pierced" in example 10 below) is split up, with the first element after the subject and the second element at the end of the clause.

(10) ... þe [Subj.] wǣron [Vb.] mid næiglum þurfdrifene [Vb.]'
"... that were pierced with nails."
(Ælfric, *Catholic Homilies*; late 10th century; DOEC)

In such cases it may be difficult to decide whether we are dealing with a verb-second or a verb-final pattern. Occasionally we also find a verb-subject order in a main clause, where the verb forms the first element:

(11) Wǣron [Vb.] his fæder & his mōdor [Subj.] būta hǣðen.
"His father and his mother were both heathens."
(Saint Martin, *Vercelli Homilies*; late 10th century; DOEC)

There are many more cases which may illustrate the intricacies of Old English word-order. It has been suggested that Old English word-order also depends on considerations of discourse structure. For example, the weight or prominence of a constituent or phrase in the sentence may determine its position. Pronouns, which are typically "light", because they are short und do not usually contain much (new) information, are usually placed at the beginning of a sentence. Example (12) contains two pronouns (*he hine*), Subject and Object, which are both placed before the verb.

(12) Hē [Subj.] hine [Obj.] genam [Vb.] ðā on his earmum mid micelre onbryrdnesse.
"Then he picked him up ("took him on his arms") with great emotion."
(Ælfric, *Catholic Homilies*; late 10th century; DOEC)

Another syntactic feature which is quite different from present-day English is negation. Usually, to negate a sentence in Old English, the negative particle *ne* is placed in front of the finite verb:

(13) Ne þurfe $_{[Vb.]}$ wē ūs spillan.
"We need not kill each other."
(*The Battle of Maldon*; late 10th century; DOEC)

We should note here that in negative sentences (as in interrogatives) no auxiliaries are used (*þurfe* has the status of a full verb). The rise of *do*-support and the associated developments belong to the Early Modern English period (see Chapter 5.2.3.).

There is also multiple negation in Old English, a feature that in contemporary English is usually associated with non-standard language use (*He didn't do nothing.*). The negation of the full verb can extend to indefinite pronouns and quantifiers, a phenomenon which is also called negative concord.

(14) ... þurh drihten þe **nāne** synne **ne** worhte **ne nān** fācn **næs** on his mūðe gemēt.
"... through the Lord, who committed no sin, neither was there any deceit found in his mouth."
(Ælfric, *Catholic Homilies*; late 10th century; DOEC)

Example (14) contains in fact five negations (the respective words are in boldface). A literal translation that imitates the word order would go like this: "who no sin not committed, neither no deceit was not found in his mouth" (*næs* is a contracted form of *ne wæs*). This "multiplication" of negation is the result of the fact that the negation of the full verbs (*ne worhte* and *næs*) spreads to the indefinite quantifiers (*nāne* and *nān*).

Another interesting feature of negation in Old English is that the negative particle can be attached (or cliticised) to certain preceding words (like the indefinite pronoun). This "negative contraction" can also affect a number of preceding verbs (for example, *wesan* "to be" (compare *næs* in example 14 above; *wille* "will" or *habban* "to have"). Example (15) contains the forms *nabbað* ("we do not have") and *nellað* ("we do not want"). Note also the double negation through *nāne mēde* ("no reward").

(15) ...wē **nabbað** ðēah nane mēde ðǣre heringe, gif wē be sumum dǣle **nellað** onginnan ðæt wē onhyrigen ðǣm ðēawum ...
"we do not have reward for our praise if we will not to some extent begin to imitate the virtues ..."
(*King Alfred's West-Saxon Version of Gregory's Pastoral Care*; late 9th century; DOEC)

As in present-day English, clauses in Old English could be linked by coordination and subordination. Coordination, in which two independent clauses are connected by means of a coordinating conjunction, was fairly common in Old English. The prototypical coordinating conjunction is *and* (often rendered as "&"). Example (16) below contains an extract from the *Anglo-Saxon Chronicle*, which depicts the details of a Viking raid in the South-West of England in the year 997. The typical structure of the text is the enumeration of individual facts by means of the coordinator *and* / &.

(16) Hēr on þissum gēare fērde se here ābūtan Defnanscīre intō Sæfernmūðon. **&** þǣr gehergodon ǣgðer on Cornwealum ge on Norðwalum. **&** on Defenan. **&** ēodon him þā ūp æt Wecedport. **&** þǣr mycel yfel wrohtan on bærnette. **&** on manslihtum. **&** æfter þām wendon eft ābūtan Penwiht steort on ðā sūðhealfe. **and** wendon þā in tō Tamermūðan. **&** ēodon þā ūp oð þæt hī comon tō Hlidaforda. **&** ǣlc þing bærndon **&** slōgon þæt hī gemētton.
"Here in this year the army went around Devonshire into the mouth of the Severn, **and** plundered Cornwall, North-Wales, and Devon, **and** then (they) went ashore at Watchet **and** did much evil there in burning and manslaughter. **And** afterwards they went next around Land's End on the south side, **and** went then to the mouth of the Tamar **and** went up till they came to Lydford. **And** they burnt **and** struck down everything that they met."
(*Anglo-Saxon Chronicle, Laud MS*; late 9th century; DOEC)

In subordination, a dependent clause is linked to a superordinate clause (also called matrix clause) by means of a subordinating conjunction. Although it is often said that Old English, representing a still fairly oral culture, prefers a paratactic style, with many coordinative constructions (see example 16, above), one should not ignore the fact that subordination is quite common in the Old English texts which have come down to us. Here we often find correlative constructions, where two or more clauses are connected with correlative conjunctions (for example, *þā .. þā*).

(17) **Ðā ðā** crīst bebiriged wæs. **þā** cwǣdon þā Iūdēiscan. tō heora ealdermen pilāte ...
"When Christ was buried, the Jews said to their governor Pilate ..."
(Ælfric, *Catholic Homilies*; late 10th century; DOEC)

In the above example the subordinate clause is introduced by the double conjunction *ðā ðā* (which could be translated literally as "then when"), followed by the matrix clause, which similarly starts with *þā*. In most cases the subordinate clause has verb-final word order (*Ðā ðā crīst bebiriged wæs*), whereas the matrix clause has verb-second order (*þā cwǣdon* ...). Apart from the correlative conjunctions Old English also has a respectable inventory of non-correlative conjunctions, for example, *gif* "if", *þēah* "although", *þā whīle þe* "while", *þæt* "that" and so on.

We will finish the syntax chapter by looking at two constructions where Old English again is quite different from Modern English: relative clauses and impersonal constructions. You will perhaps be surprised to hear that Old English knew neither *who* nor *which* as relative pronouns. In Old English, relative clauses could be introduced by the indeclinable relative particle *þe*, by the demonstrative pronouns *se, sēo, þæt* (or their respective forms, see Table 5 in Chapter 3.2.2. above), which were used as relative pronouns, or by a combination of particle plus pronoun.

In example (18) below the relative particle *þe* refers back to the antecedent *þes iunga man* ("this young man"), while in (19) the demonstrative pronoun *ðæs*, which is used as relative pronoun, does a similar job, referring back to *sum cēpemon crīsten* ("some Christian merchant").

(18) hwæt is þes iunga man **þe** ongēan ðē on swā wurðlīcum setle sit.
"Who is this young man, who is sitting opposite you on such an honoured seat?"
(*Apollonius of Tyre*; 11th century; DOEC)

(19) ... sum cēpemon crīsten mid him, **ðæs** nama wæs Felix.
"... some Christian merchant with them, whose name was Felix."
(*Martyrology*; late 9th century; DOEC)

Since the relative particle was indeclinable, thus possibly creating ambiguity, and since the use of demonstratives as relative pronouns was not always easy to recognise, we often find a combination of both. In example (20) below the combination of *þām* (dative singular of the definite article) and the particle *þe* makes it clear that we are dealing with a relative pronoun and that the relative pronoun has a dative case ("whom") and thus functions as an indirect object in the relative clause.

(20) þȳstre genip, **þām þe** se þēoden self scēop nihte naman.
"the dark cloud, for whom the Lord himself created the name 'night'"
(*Genesis*; c1000; DOEC)

One syntactic construction which may appear particularly "exotic" to speakers of Modern English is the so-called impersonal construction. Old English (like many other languages) could form sentences which lacked a nominative subject. This was particularly common with a class of verbs (mostly verbs of physical or mental perception) which could enter a construction involving a dative, a genitive, an accusative or a combination of them, but not a nominative case. In (21) the verb *ðyncð* ("seems") is linked to a dative (*me*). In (22) *lyste* ("pleased") is linked to an accusative (*hine* "him") and a genitive (*nānes ðinges* "of no thing"). In both cases we lack a nominative subject.

(21) Forðȳ **mē ðyncð** betre ...
 "Therefore it seems better to me ..."
 (King Alfred, *Letter to Wærferth*; late 9th century; DOEC)

(22) ðā ðǣm hearpere ðā ðūhte ðæt **hine þā nānes ðinges** ne **lyste** on ðisse worulde, ...
 "when it seemed to the harper that (of) no thing pleased him in this world, ..."
 (Boethius, *The Consolation of Philosophy*; late 9th century; DOEC)

In present-day English we need the so-called dummy subject *it* in order to express these constructions in a grammatical sentence. The underlying function of an impersonal construction seems to be to express a state of affairs where the participants or persons involved do not play such a prominent part but are merely affected to a different extent (in other words, the person is only "affected" by a thought, but does not actively consider it). Some petrified patterns reflecting this construction survived until the Late Modern period (for example, *methinks*).

3.2.4. Lexis and semantics

In the section on Old English word-formation (Chapter 3.2.2.) we saw that the Old English lexicon was fairly transparent. New words were created using elements of the existing word stock, together with a large inventory of prefixes and suffixes. Due to this native resourcefulness, the estimated proportion of loan words in Old English is fairly low (about 3 per cent, as opposed to about 70 per cent in Modern English). This means that the Old English vocabulary was quite different from today's vocabulary. Old English lacks the many loan words (mostly from Latin and French) which are so characteristic of the modern language.

The Old English vocabulary is purely Germanic, that is, it contains mostly words whose cognates we basically find in other Germanic, in particular West Germanic, languages (for example, Dutch or German). Thus, to a native speaker of German, the Old English lexicon may appear far less mysterious than to a native speaker of English. Native speakers of German may easily trace similarities between Old English words and their German counterparts. For example, Old English *niman* ("take") corresponds to German *nehmen*, Old English *weorpan* ("throw") to German *werfen*, Old English *rǣd* ("advice") to German *Rat*, Old English *earm* ("arm") to German *Arm*, and so on (see also Chapter 2 on some phonological similarities between English and German).

You can see from the above examples that many of the Germanic words disappeared at some stage in the history of the English language (most of them during the Middle English period). Of the estimated 30,000 recorded lexical words found in Old English 85 per cent are no longer in use. However, those Germanic words which survived belong to the core section of the vocabulary. They are words which designate fundamental concepts and which are used with a high frequency (for example, the words *mann* ("man"), *wīf* ("woman"), *cild* ("child"), *hūs* ("house"), *gōd* ("good"), *strong* ("strong") and so on). In addition, they comprise function words like pronouns, prepositions, conjunctions, auxiliary verbs (although, as we shall see, not all function words are native Old English words).

Some Germanic words that survived passed through the centuries without much change of meaning (for example, *cild, hūs, gōd, strong*, which were mentioned above). Others, however, show more or less significant modifications of meaning. For example, Old English *hund* ("dog"; compare German *Hund*) lives on in Modern English as *hound*, a word, which has a more specialised sense since it designates a dog kept or used for the chase. Similarly, Modern English *fowl*, with the specialised meaning "farmyard bird", goes back to Old English *fugol* (compare German *Vogel*), which had then the generic meaning "bird". The primary meaning of Old English *wīf* was not "married woman" but "woman, female". And, as we saw in the section on Old English society, Old English *ceorl* referred to the fairly respected rank of a freeman, which is quite different from a person designated by Modern English *churl*.

Although the Old English vocabulary was mainly shaped by native Germanic elements, there was also some foreign influence. The major influence was exerted by Latin, but we must also assume that, due to the Viking invasions, the Scandinavian languages had a significant impact on Old English, although the actual effect is only documented much later. As we have seen, there was also some (limited) Celtic influence. In addition we witness a few words from other Germanic languages and, towards the end of the period, the first loans from Norman French. The following sections will focus on Latin and Scandinavian influence.

Traditionally, Latin influence on Old English is subdivided into three periods (see, for example, Baugh and Cable 2002): continental borrowing, borrowing during the first centuries of settlement and borrowing due to Christianisation. The first period of borrowing reaches back to the time when the Germanic tribes had contacts with the expanding Roman Empire on the Continent. It seems that the borrowings reflecting these contacts were mainly characterised by war and trade, but the list of items also includes articles of domestic life. Typical examples include *camp* ("battlefield, battle"), *weall* ("wall"), *strǣt* ("road"), *catte* ("cat"), *wīn* ("wine"), *cytel* ("kettle"), *cȳpan* ("to buy"). Many of these loans would not go back to classical Latin, but rather Vulgar Latin, the language of the common people. The number of borrowings from Latin which belong to the continental period is estimated at about 170.

The second period refers to the first centuries of settlement during which the Germanic invaders may have picked up Latin words which could still be found after the withdrawal of the Roman Empire in 410. This Latin influence must have been passed on by the Celtic inhabitants, who were left in England, and, as in other areas, this influence was extremely weak. Very few words can be attributed to this period, for example, *ceaster* ("town") and *port* ("harbour"), both of which can be found in many place names.

The third period, borrowing due to the influence of the Christian religion, is often divided into two parts, the first part referring to the period shortly after the establishment of the Christian faith and the church in Anglo-Saxon England, the second part referring to the impact of the Benedictine reform in the second half of the tenth century. Basically one can say that the influence of the Christian religion resulted in a more extensive borrowing from Latin, yielding several hundred words. The first part contains mostly words which belong to the organisation of the Church and matters of education and learning, for example, *abbod* ("abbot"), *mæsse* ("mass"), *canon* ("canon"), *altare* ("altar") and *scōl* ("school"). But it also contains words which refer to domestic life (for example, *meatte* "mat" and *caul* "cabbage"). The loanwords associated with the Benedictine reform show a much more learned character. They reflect written, formal and educated language and can often be traced back to classical Latin. Many of them are religious in nature (*apostol* "apostle", *cella* "cell", *noctern* "nocturn"), but they also include literary and medical terms and names of plants and animals (*accent* "accent", *cancer* "ulcerous sore", *cucumer* "cucumber", *delfin* "dolphin").

The influence of Latin on the Old English vocabulary can also be noticed in the field of word-formation. Here we can see that, in order to form a new term, the Anglo-Saxons imitated or re-created the Latin word, using Old English elements. This process is called loan formation (see Gneuss 1955 and Weimann 1990: 42–47). A native compound or derivation is formed which is modelled on a foreign, that is, Latin pattern. For example, the Old English term for "gospel", *godspell*, is a literal translation of Latin *euangelium* "good news". Different kinds of loan formations can be distinguished, depending on how literal the rendering of the Latin paradigm is. A loan translation is the most literal way of reproducing a Latin formation. The above example of *godspell* belongs here. In a similar way formations like *ymbsnīdennes* ("circumcision") and *welwillendnes* ("benevolence") copy the Latin models *circumcisio* and *benevolentia* in a "morpheme-by-morpheme" fashion. A loan rendition, on the other hand, contains a partial translation. The rest is a more or less free rendering, which includes vernacular word-formation patterns. Thus Old English *hēahfæder* ("patriarch") gives Latin *patriarchus*, where *patri-* is translated as *fæder* and the rest rendered by *hēah* ("high, exalted"), which functions as the first element in a compound. In Old English *leorningcniht* ("disciple"), the *disci-* element of Latin *discipulus* is translated by *leorning*, the first element of a compound with *cniht* ("boy, servant") as the second part. The least literal rendering of the Latin model, loan creation, is a more or less independent version which reflects the meaning of the Latin model. Thus Old English *cwildeflōd* ("slaughter flood", "deluge") gives Latin *diluvium* and Old English *fulwiht* ("complete consecration", "baptism") gives Latin *baptisma*.

The other major influence on the Old English vocabulary was Scandinavian. There are quite a few Scandinavian loanwords in English. We must assume that, following the settlements of the Vikings in the North, the East Midlands and East Anglia, there was a long-term amalgamation of Scandinavian and English speakers, with many intermarriages and close everyday contacts. Thus it seems likely that many loanwords found their way into Old English. They mainly belong to the semantic fields of seafaring and the law but also include a numer of everyday objects and activities. Most of the loanwords do not appear in extant manuscripts until the early twelfth century. Only some 150 are found in Old English sources. This is due to the scarcity of Old English texts stemming from the area of the Danelaw. Some early examples of Scandinavian loanwords are *hæfene* ("haven"), *lagu* ("law") and *feolagu* ("fellow"). Another major contribution were Scandinavian place names, which can be recognised by their specific endings, for example *-by* ("farm, town") as in *Derby* and *Rugby*, *-thorp(e)* ("village"), as in *Bishopsthorpe* and *Linthorpe*, or *-thwaite* ("an isolated piece of land"), as in

Braithwaite and *Langthwaite*. Not surprisingly, most of the localities bearing such names are found beyond the border separating Wessex from the Danelaw.

Another field where Old English borrowed from Scandinavian is function words. The personal pronouns *they, their, them* replace the Anglo-Saxon *hī, hira, him* (although this takes us well into the Middle English period). The prepositions *till, fro* and *though* are Scandinavian in origin, just as the plural form of the verb *be, are*.

3.2.5. Regional and social distribution

Both regional and social dialects in Old English are problematic since we do not know enough about them. Especially social variation must have existed but the texts which have come down to us do not allow any conclusions about spoken language and the language use of the different ranks of society. Literacy was very much an affair of the monastic and aristocratic elite. In addition, most Old English texts which have survived are religious and composed in a more or less formal style. Thus, social variation is a matter of sheer speculation.

With regional dialects the situation is only slightly better. The basic problem, lack of convincing data as evidence for regional variation, is paramount here as well. Traditionally, four Old English dialects are distinguished: Northumbrian, Mercian, Kentish and West Saxon (see Map 3 below). Except for West Saxon, no area is represented by a reasonable number of texts which would allow us to support a sufficient range of distinctive dialect features. Northumbria extends from the lowlands of present-day Scotland to the Humber. It was a cultural centre during the late seventh century, with eminent abbeys (Wearmouth, Jarrow) and famous scholars (Bede). But contrary to its size and importance, there are only few Northumbrian texts, notably the *The Lindisfarne Gospels*, a Latin text with an interlinear gloss in Old English. Mercian, which is enclosed by the river Humber, Wales and the river Thames, poses similar difficulties. The important available texts (above all the *Vespasian Psalter* and *The Rushworth Gospels*) must be associated with the Lichfield area, a rather restricted quarter, given the size of the dialect region. This is particularly deplorable since the Mercian dialect turned out to be a major contributor (in late Middle English) to the emergent Standard English and continuous evidence of the language spoken in this region might be of great interest. With Kentish we find some interesting texts, in particular charters, stemming from the eight and ninth centuries. But later on, the textual evidence shows a mixture of southern dialect features. West Saxon is the regional dialect which is very well documented, but not before the late ninth century. West Saxon had its centre in Winchester and the surrounding area of the Thames Valley. Starting with the achievements of

King Alfred and his successors, West Saxon influence spread East (to Kent and London) and North. The large majority of all Old English documents which have come down to us have a West Saxon origin. In addition, the Benedictine reform, with its centre in Winchester, created a nearly standardised language, which has been called the West Saxon literary standard (although this should not be mixed up with a modern standard language). Thus, given the majority of Late West Saxon texts, one could be led to believe that Old English is identical to Late West Saxon and a fairly homogenous language. But this is certainly wrong.

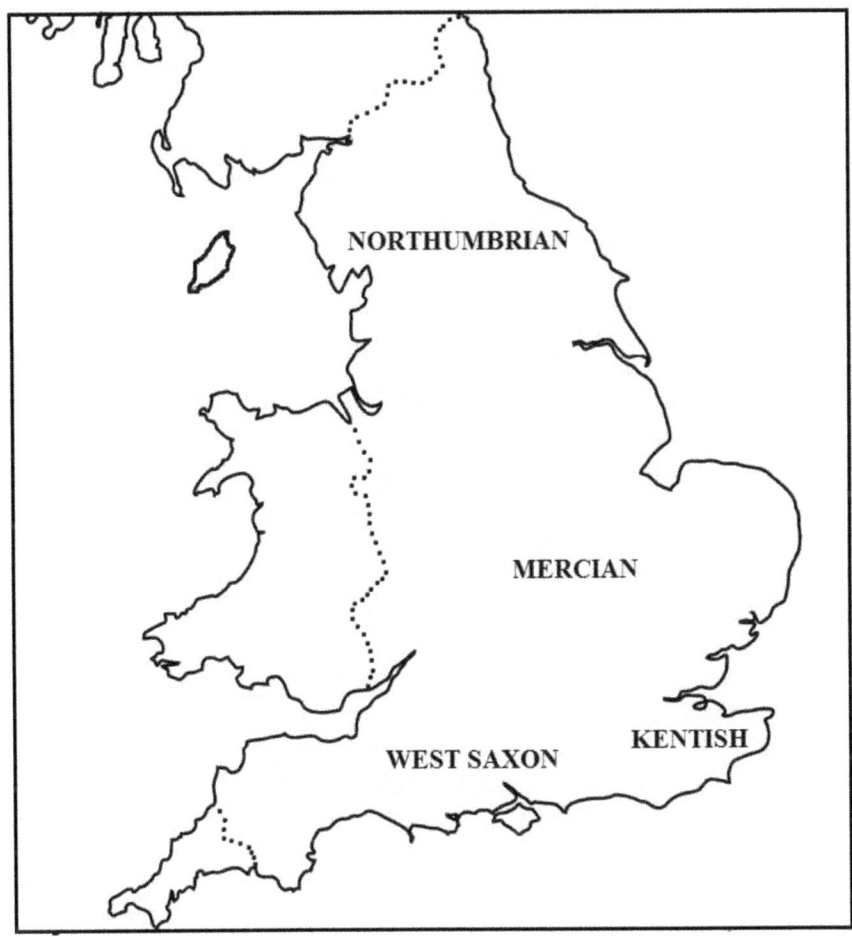

Map 3: The dialects of Old English

As was mentioned above, there are only very few distinct and clearly established regional features in Old English. It seems that breaking of front vowels occurs more often in the West Saxon dialect (on breaking see Chapter 3.2.1.). There is a difference between short *a* before a nasal (*land, hand*), which changes to a short *o* in the North (*lond, hond*). In the Northumbrian dialect we find the new form *aron* (the predecessor of Modern English *are*), which (later) replaces the native West Saxon form *synd*.

3.3. Language use

3.3.1. Discourse and speech acts

One of the distinctive features of the world of Anglo-Saxon discourse is the special blend of Germanic tradition and Christian religion. The Anglo-Saxons were conscious of their Germanic past and proud of the values associated with the Germanic warrior society (courage and fearlessness in battle, loyalty to one's lord, pride of one's ancestry etc.). On the other hand, once Christianised, they knew that this heathen world was in contrast to the values of Christianity. Thus they tried to find a particular "mixture" which included both Germanic and Christian elements. This special blend is most conspicuous in literary discourse. Here we find that traditional Germanic topics and plots were modified in order to meet the requirements of Christianity and the teachings of the Church.

It seems that the particular contrast between the Germanic and the Christian and the different ways of dealing with it are also reflected in Old English speech acts, especially in those speech acts which are called "directives" (that is, orders, commands, requests etc.). Today, directive speech acts are usually seen as face-threatening acts because they are often felt to threaten the addressee's freedom of action and freedom from imposition, that is, the addressee's "negative face". In order to make up for this potential face threat, many languages offer an inventory of so-called indirect directives (for example, *Could you give me a hand? Will you do me a favour?*), which are felt to be more polite, that is, less face-threatening.

Now it seems that this kind of face-work is hardly ever found in Old English, especially in those texts reflecting a Germanic setting. What we do find, though, are directives that reveal what may be called "positive politeness", that is, speech acts which support the addressee's "positive face", for example, that show respect, shared interests and "common ground". However, such directives are mostly found in writings associated with religious instruction, that is, the products of Christianisation. This special distribution will be illustrated in the following sections.

One of the more direct and possibly impolite formulations of a directive is a so-called directive performative. This kind of directive makes the point of the speech act explicit by using a speech-act verb in the first person (for example, *I hereby order you to* ...). A representative study of Old English texts (Kohnen 2000) shows that these constructions were obviously much more common in Old English than they are in Modern (written) English. Two typical examples are given in (23) and (24).

(23) Ac **ic bidde** for Godes lufan and ēac eornostlice **bēode**, þæt man þæs geswīce. Lǣwedum men is ǣlc wīf forboden, būtan his rihtǣwe.
"And I ask for God's love and demand (this) with great concern that people avoid this. Laymen are not allowed to have intercourse with any woman, except their lawful (wife)."
(Wulfstan, *Institutes of Polity*; early 11th century; DOEC)

(24) & ealle Godes þēowas, & hūruþinga sācerdas, **wē biddað & lǣrað**, þæt hȳ Gode hȳran & clǣnnesse lufian & beorhgan him sylfum wið Godes yrre.
"And we ask and instruct all servants of God, and especially (all) priests, to listen to God and love chastity and protect themselves against God's anger."
(Æþelred, *Old English Laws*; late 10th century; DOEC)

In addition to their higher frequency, the Old English performatives did not include any items involving verbs of suggestion or advice (*I suggest that you* ...; *I recommend that you* ...). In fact, none of them could be found in the Old English data. In present-day English *suggest / advise* performatives are typically used as strategies of negative politeness to mitigate the face threats of speech acts.

The results suggest that Anglo-Saxons preferred especially those directive performatives which would be felt as fairly face-threatening today, whereas "face-saving" performatives seem to have been uncommon. This could be explained against the background of the hierarchic structure of the Germanic society: The performatives chiefly occur in an asymmetric communication situation, with the addresser either in a subordinate or in a superior position. Thus there would be no need for politeness or face-work in a "Germanic setting".

Another manifestation of a directive speech act which would seem fairly inappropriate from the perspective of today is the construction involving a second-person pronoun plus *scealt / sculon* ("you must / have to").

(25) ðū **scealt** fēran ond frið lǣdan, sīðe gesēcan, þǣr sylfǣtan eard weardigað,
ēðel healdaþ morðorcræftum
"Thou shalt go and bear thy life, seek out in a journey a place where cannibals inhabit the land, guard the country by murders." (Gordon 1954: 184)
(*Andreas*; late 10th century; DOEC)

In (25) the request is presented in a plain and straightforward way. The obligation is just stated and no further comment seems necessary. The Old English data suggest that this rather direct and straightforward formulation of directives is limited to the secular and / or Germanic settings.

Two other Old English manifestations of directives seem to employ what may be called a common-ground strategy and thus positive politeness. These are constructions with *uton* plus infinitive (usually paraphrased with *let's* plus infinitive), and impersonal constructions with *(neod)þearf* ("it is necessary (for us)").

(26) And **utan** ðūrh ǣghwæt Godes willan wyrcan swā wē geornost magan.
"And let us in every way perform God's commands as carefully as we may be able to."
(Wulfstan, *Homilies*; early 11th century; DOEC)

(27) Ac ūs is mycel **nēodþearf**, þæt wē geþencan, hū drihten ūs mid his þrōwunge alȳsde fram dēofles anwealde.
"But we have great need ("there is great need for us") to consider how the Lord delivered us by his suffering from the devil's power."
(*A Homily for the Sixth Sunday*; 10th century; DOEC)

Both constructions include the addressor (that is, the addressor has to follow the directive in the same way as the addressee). In addition, the constructions stating the necessity of an act relegate the motivation to the sphere of objective duty and can thus be understood as less face threatening.

Here it turns out that constructions involving *utan* are typically found in religious instruction; in a similar way, directives stating some objective necessity are in Old English prose texts mostly found in pieces of religious instruction.

So the results with regard to the directive performatives and the *þu scealt* construction suggest that negative politeness did not play a major role in Anglo-Saxon communication, and the distribution of the data may actually reveal the Germanic side of Anglo-Saxon society. On the other hand, the common-ground strategies involving both addressor and addressee are mostly found in religious discourse. One way of explaining this could be to say that this simply reflects the basic monastic and Christian models of *humilitas* ("humility") and *oboedientia* ("obedience"), major elements of the Benedictine Rule which formed the basis for the life of most monks. Christians should not seek a rank above their fellow Christians, and everybody is bound to follow the requirements of a Christian life. The inclusive *we* found in so many directives of religious instruction may in fact account for this basic monastic or Christian solidarity and obedience. Thus it seems that, with regard to directive speech acts, the Germanic and the Christian element in Anglo-Saxon society are clearly discernible.

3.3.2. Genres

The corpus of surviving Old English texts shows a remarkable richness and variety. There is a large inventory of genres, both in prose and verse. Anglo-Saxon scholars are in fact quite lucky because all extant Old English texts are available (in at least one manuscript edition) in digitised form. This comprehensive database for the study of Old English, with the respectable number of 3.5 million words, is the *Dictionary of Old English Corpus*, which has been compiled at the University of Toronto.

The corpus of Old English is, however, biased in terms of chronology, region and genre. Most of the texts found in the corpus stem from manuscripts which were written in West Saxon monastic centres between the late tenth and the mid twelfth century. They mostly represent the West Saxon dialect of the late period. In addition, most of the texts belong to the religious domain and serve the purpose of religious instruction (they are, for example, homilies, sermons, saints' lives, monastic rules etc.). Thus, although the number of Old English writings which have come down to us may be called quite rich, the corpus of Old English, in so far as it reflects the surviving data, gives undue weight to religious genres.

In the following sections I will first give a short overview of the major Old English poetic texts and then deal with prose texts. The Old English poetic records comprise about 30,000 lines. Most of them are contained in four manuscript collections which are all dated around the end of the tenth and the beginning of the eleventh century. These are the "Beowulf Codex" (containing *Beowulf*, *Judith* and several prose texts), the "Junius Codex" (with several Old Testament pieces), the "Exeter Book" (containing several poems, e.g. the elegies and the riddles) and the "Vercelli Book" (containing, among other pieces, *Andreas, The Fates of the Apostles* and *The Dream of the Rood*).

The Old English poetic records may be divided up into religious and secular texts. The religious poetry comprises poems which retell major stories of the Bible, the majority stemming from the Old Testament (for example, *Genesis, Exodus, Daniel* and *Judith*) but some also from the New Testament (*The Fates of the Apostles* and the dream poem *The Dream of the Rood*). These re-creations typically place the scriptural events in a heroic Germanic setting. Secular poetry shows a preoccupation with the Germanic past and tradition (both real and mythological). It contains a fairly large variety of different genres. There are heroic poems which reach back to the Germanic past (*Beowulf, Deor, Widsith*) and those which narrate contemporary events of Anglo-Saxon history (*The Battle of Maldon*, which took place in August 991, or the *Battle of Brunanburh*, which was fought in 937). Then there are the so-called elegies (for example, *The Wanderer, The Seafarer, The Wife's Lament*), a miscellaneous group of reflective poems which show typical Germanic topics (a wandering exile, a seafarer, a woman involved in a feud and so on) and a dark, sometimes a Christian attitude. We also find metrical charms, magical incantations against several adversities (illness, infertility of the ground etc.). They reflect a basically pagan tradition, although some effort has been made to add Christian elements (for example, prayers). These charms must have been a fairly common genre because they are found in several manuscript collections. Another secular verse genre are the so-called maxims, very short texts which contain aphorisms and sayings about life and society, a genre which is found in most Germanic languages. A last genre to be mentioned here is riddles. Although there is a contemporary Latin tradition of riddles, the ca. 95 Old English riddles which have come down to us are said to represent a fairly independent development. They either contain a personification of an object, which describes itself in a first-person presentation, or the description by the narrator (that is, the riddler). Both end with an explicit request to the addressee to name the subject of the riddle. The vague metaphorical descriptions of the riddles are often deliberately misleading. Riddles cover a fairly heterogeneous range of subjects, sometimes obvious, sometimes opaque. With their humorous character and their implications and double meaning they stand in marked contrast to the dark and rather pessimistic spirit of the other poetic genres.

Old English poetry is characterised by a fairly archaic diction, fixed formulae, verbal patterning, parallelism and repetition. But most importantly, it follows the pattern of Germanic verse. The nature of Germanic verse is mainly determined by the factors stress and alliteration. Each line consists of two half-lines separated by a pause. Each half line comprises two stressed syllables. In example (28) below stressed syllables are indicated by an inverted comma.

(28) 'wēox under 'wolcnum, 'weorðmyndum 'þāh,
(he) grew up   clouds   (his) esteem   increased
"he grew up under the heavens and his honour increased"
(Beowulf, line 8; early 11th century; DOEC)

The two half-lines are linked by alliteration. In (28) the relevant words are *wēox* and *wolcnum* in the first half-line and *weorðmyndum* in the second. The point of alliteration is, of course, that the respective words start with the identical consonant (but vowels do not have to be the same). Usually there is alliteration between one of the two (or both) accented syllables of the first half-line and the first accented syllable of the second half-line. In order to find the alliterating words in a verse, you have to start with the first accented syllable in the second half line (*weorðmyndum*) and look out for accented syllables starting with the same consonant in the first half line (*wēox, wolcnum*). A half-line must have two unaccented syllables but it can have more. Traditionally, the possible combinations of the two accented and the (variable number of) unaccented syllables are described in five patterns, but for the purposes of this book we need not go into detail here (a straightforward overview is found in Mitchell and Robinson 2012).

A question which has often been raised in connection with the assessment Old English poetry is whether it was composed orally. It is true that the poetry which has come down to us in manuscript form still reflects the oral background of its performance (addresses to the audience, repetitions and formulae, use of mnemonic devices and so on). We also know about Germanic wandering minstrels who gave performances in front of warrior bands and their leaders. In fact, some of the surviving poems may have been transmitted orally before they were written down, and even those which were composed in writing still reflect techniques and rhetorical devices which belong to an oral tradition. However, there is no hard and fast evidence that the poems were actually composed orally. The manuscripts in which much of the poetry has survived suggest a rather bookish environment of learning and reading, not the improvised performance of a minstrel.

Now let us turn to Old English prose. Old English prose shows a large inventory of genres, both religious and secular. Many prose texts are translations or adaptations from Latin texts and reflect Latinate patterns to a greater or lesser extent. As was mentioned above, there is a clear predominance of religious texts (for example, homilies, sermons, saints' lives, Bible translations, rules, penitentials and so on). Although most of the prose texts are anonymous (as are all of the poetic records), a number of texts (most of them religious) can be closely associated with three persons: King Alfred, Ælfric, the abbot of Eynesham, and Wulfstan, the archbishop of York.

The term Alfredian prose comprises the Old English translations of Latin texts which are linked with King Alfred's educational program. They were either translated by Alfred himself or commissioned by him. These texts comprise what is usually called early West Saxon and can be dated at the late ninth century. The texts comprise, among others, Boethius's *Consolation of Philosophy*, Augustine's *Pastoral Care* and *Soliloquies* and the famous *Ecclesiastical History of the English People* by Bede.

Ælfric, the abbot of Eynesham, was one of the most prolific writers in Anglo-Saxon England (see also example (1) in Chapter 1). He wrote about 120 homilies, more than 30 saints' lives, translations of parts of the Old Testament and several other works. His texts can be dated at the late tenth / early eleventh century and he is representative of Late West Saxon, his language being influenced by the late West Saxon literary standard of Winchester (see above). Ælfric has been very much praised for the high quality and the achievement of his prose style. It has also been observed that he included alliteration and metrical patterns in his prose to enhance its effect on the reader (or listener).

Wulfstan, the archbishop of York, wrote more than twenty homilies and several long treatises, and he compiled law codes. He is particularly famous for his *Sermo Lupi ad Anglos* ("Sermon of Wolf to the English"), in which he appeals to his countrymen to turn to repentance and reform under the dramatic circumstances of renewed Viking incursions at the beginning of the eleventh century. His prose style, like Ælfric's, has very much been praised because of the impressive use of alliteration, rhyme and rhetorical figures.

In the field of religious prose, there are various anonymous collections of homilies and several other religious texts (translations of the gospels, rules, liturgical texts, prayers etc.) which belong to Late West Saxon.

In the secular sphere we find many, though slightly scattered, examples of several prose genres: a prose romance (*Apollonius of Tyre*), fabulous travelogues (*Letter to Aristotle*), wisdom literature (in the form of a formulaic question and answer pattern), works of science, large collections of medicinal recipes, administrative documents, charters, wills and substantial compilations of laws. While most of these texts are based on a foreign (chiefly Latin) original, another secular genre, chronicles, is represented in an essentially vernacular form. The *Anglo-Saxon Chronicle* is a set of annals which describe British history from the Roman invasion to the second half of the twelfth century (in the continuation of the *Peterborough Chronicle*). The *Anglo-Saxon Chronicle* was probably initially compiled up to the year 892 and subsequently continued at different places to different extents. Seven manuscripts have survived. The *Anglo-Saxon Chronicle* is clearly a monastic production, which was created and carried on in different monastic centres, possibly following a proposal by King Alfred.

Most of the entries of the *Anglo-Saxon Chronicle*, especially the early ones, are typically annalistic in style. They compile the most important events of one year under one heading in a fairly haphazard and fragmentary way. Only later on do they include longer coherent passages, with a more advanced rhetorical style. The *Anglo-Saxon Chronicle* merits special mention because it is one of the most popular and widespread (prose) works in Old English, which was read widely both before and after the Norman Conquest, and it was among the first Old English works to be published in the seventeenth century.

Summary

Old English is the longest period in the history of the English language, spreading out more than 600 years. Although the basic socio-cultural pattern of Anglo-Saxon society was very much shaped by the Germanic tribes who had settled in England during the fifth century (with the central position of the loyalty of a man to his lord), the period was later very much influenced by Christianisation (which laid the foundations for literacy) and the Viking invasions (which had an important impact on the language).

The structure of the language was basically synthetic, with a wide inventory of inflectional endings marking grammatical relations and syntactic functions. There was a fairly close correlation between spelling and pronunciation. Old English lexis is largely characterised by its Germanic word stock. There are few Latin and (later) some Scandinavian loanwords. Evidence of social and regional variation is rather scarce since most surviving texts are more or less formal and influenced by the West-Saxon dialect.

The available evidence in the field of discourse and speech acts suggests that negative politeness does not seem to have been very common in Anglo-Saxon society, especially in a Germanic setting. The Christian values of humility and obedience seem to have resulted in some common-ground strategies. The surviving Old English texts show a remarkable richness and variety, with a wide inventory of religious and secular genres, both in poetry and prose. However, the large majority of texts belongs to the religious sphere.

Further reading

Mitchell and Robinson's *A Guide to Old English* is still the best available introduction to Old English (meanwhile in the eighth edition, 2012). A very good reader is Marsden (2004). Clark Hall (1960) serves as a concise and reliable dictionary when working with non-glossed texts.

Hogg (2002), Lass (1994) and Hogg (1992) are linguistic surveys (with increasing complexity and detail of presentation).

Mitchell (1995) gives a well-illustrated introduction to Anglo-Saxon society and culture, Blair and Keynes (2003) is a standard textbook. Greenfield and Calder (1986), Godden and Lapidge (1991) and Pulsiano and Treharne (2001) give reliable overviews of the literature.

The website of the Dictionary of Old English Corpus is www.doe.utoronto.ca.

Questions and exercises

1. Reviewing Chapter 3.1., work out the most striking socio-cultural contrasts between Anglo-Saxon society and contemporary Western societies, especially with regard to language use.

2. Using the information given in Tables 1 and 2 in Chapter 3.2.1., try to read the text section below.

Ða ðā crīst bebiriged wæs. þā cwædon þā Iūdēiscan. tō heora ealdermen pilāte.
When Christ buried was then said the Jews to their governor Pilate
Lā lēof se swīca þe hēr ofslegen is cwæð gelōmlīce þā ðā hē on līfe wæs. þæt hē
Look Lord the deceiver who here executed is said frequently when he alive was that he
wolde ārīsan of dēaðe on ðām þriddan dæge. Bebēod nū for ðī besittan his
would arise from death on the third day Command now therefore surround his
birigene oð ðone þriddan dæig: þē læs þe his leorningcnihtas cumon & forstēlan
tomb until the third day in case that his disciples come and steal away
his līc. & secgan þām folce þæt hē of dēaðe ārīse: þonne bið þæt gedwyld wyrse
his body and say to the people that he from death arise Then will be that heresy worse
þonne þæt ōðer wære. Þā andwyrde se ealdorman pilātus. Gē habbað weardas.
than that other was Then answered the governor Pilate You have guards
farað tō & healdað. Hī ðā fērdon tō: & mearcodon ðā þrūh mid insegle. &
Go thereto and guard They then went there and marked the sepulchre with seal and

besǣton þā birgine. Þā behēold māria þæs hǣlendes mōder. & þā wimmen þe
surrounded the tomb   Then beheld Mary   the   saviour's mother and the women that
hyre mid wǣron: hwǣr hē bebiriged wæs. & ēodon ðā ongēan tō ðǣre birig &
with her   were where   he   buried   was and went then   back to the city and
sēo magdalēnisce māria & māria iācōbes mōder bohton dēorwyrðe sealfe þe bið
the   Mary of Magdala and Mary James' mother bought precious ointment which is
geworht tō smyrigenne dēadra manna līc mid þæt hī scolon late rotian. & ēodon
prepared to   anoint   dead   men's bodies with that they shall slowly decay. and went
ðā ðā wimmen on þisum dæge on ǣrnemerien. & woldon his līc behwyrfan. swā
then the women on   this   day in early morning and wanted his body prepare   as
hit þǣr gewunlic wæs on ðǣre þēode. Þā cwǣdon þā wīf betwux him. Hwā sceal
it there customary was among the people Then said the women between them Who shall
ūs āwilian þone stān of ðǣre þȳrih. Se stān is ormǣtlīce micel. Þā   ðā hī þis
us roll away the stone from the tomb The stone is extremely   big   When they this
sprǣcon þā wearð fǣrlīce micel eorðstyrung & godes engel flēah of heofenum
spoke then was suddenly big   earthquake and God's angel flew from heaven
tō ðǣre birgene. & āwylte þone stān āweig. & gesæt him uppon þām stāne. Þā
to the sepulchre and rolled the   stone away And sat himself upon the   stone Then
wæs þæs engles wlite swilce līget: & his rēaf swā hwīt swā snāw. Þā wurdon þā
was the angel's countenance like lightning and his clothing as white as snow Then became the
weardmen āfyrhte.   & fēollon adūne   swilce   hī dēade wǣron.
guards frightened And   fell   down as though they dead   were
(Ælfric, *Catholic Homilies*, A Homily for Easter Sunday; early 11th century; DOEC)

Translation

When Christ had been buried, then the Jews said to their governor Pilate: "Look, Lord, the deceiver who has been executed here said frequently, when he was alive, that he would arise from death on the third day. Command now, therefore, to guard his tomb until the third day, in case that his disciples come and steal his body and say to the people that he has arisen from death. Then that heresy will be worse than the other may have been." Then the governor Pilate answered: "You have guards. Go there and guard it."
Then they went there and marked the sepulchre with a seal and surrounded the tomb. Then Mary, the Saviour's mother, and the women that were with her beheld where he was buried. And then they went back to their city, and Mary of

Magdalena and Mary, James' mother, bought a precious ointment, which is prepared to anoint dead men's bodies with, so that they will decay slowly. And the women went there on this day in the early morning, and wanted to prepare his body as it was customary there among their people. Then the women said between them: "Who will roll away the stone from the tomb for us? The stone is extremely big."
When they said this, there was suddenly a big earthquake, and God's angel flew from heaven to the tomb and rolled away the stone, and sat upon the stone. Then the angel's countenance was like lightning and his clothing as white as snow. Then the guards were frightened and fell down as though they were dead.

3. Try to determine the inflectional forms of the nouns and verbs found in the text by Ælfric in exercise 2. Apart from the information given in Chapter 3.2.2., you may use a dictionary (for example, Clark Hall 1960).

4. The excerpt below from the Old English version of Bede's *Ecclesiastical History of the English People* gives an account of the arrival of St. Augustine and his companions in Kent. Look at the main clauses and dependent clauses in the text and the variability of the word order in these clauses (especially the position of subject and verb). What are the differences to Modern English? Can you detect any similarity to other West Germanic languages (for example, German)?

Ðā wæs on þā tīd Æðelbyrht cyning hāten on Centrīce, & mihtig: hē hæfde
Then was at the time Æthelbert king called in Kent and mighty he had
rīce   oð gemæro Humbre strēames, sē tōscēadeð sūðfolc Angelþēode &
kingdom up to edge Humber river which divides "south folk" English people and
norðfolc. Þonne is on ēastewardre Cent mycel ēaland Tenet, þæt is syx hund
"north folk" Then is on eastern half Kent large island Thanet which is six hundred
hīda micel æfter Angelcynnes æhte.   Þæt ēalond tōscēadeð Wantsumo strēam
"hides" large according English people's measure That island divides Wantsum river
fram þām tōgeþēoddan lande. Sē is þrēora furlunga brād: & on twām stōwum is
from the adjoining land It is three furlongs broad and in two places is
oferfērnes, & ǣghwæþer ende līð on sǣ. On þyssum ēalande cōm upp sē Godes
fordable place and both end[s] are on sea On this island landed the God's
þēow Augustinus & his geferan; wæs hē fēowertiga sum. Noman hī ēac
servant Augustine and his companions was he [of] forty one Brought they also
swylce him wealhstodas of Franclande mid, swā him Sanctus Gregorius bebēad.
likewise themselves translators from Franconia with as them Saint Gregory instructed

& þā sende tō Æþelbyrhte ǣrenddracan & onbēad, þæt hē of Rōme cōme & þæt
and then send to Ethelbert   messenger and announced that he from Rome came and the
betste ǣrende lǣdde; & sē þe him hyrsum bēon wolde, būton twēon hē gehēt
best   message carried and he that it obedient   be   wished without doubt he promised
ēcne gefēan on heofonum & tōweard rīce būtan ende mid þone sōþan Gode &
eternal joy   in   heaven   and   future kingdom without end with the   true   God and
þone lifigendan. Ðā hē þā sē cyning þās word gehȳrde, þā hēt   hē hī bīdan on
the   living   When he the king these words heard then ordered he them stay on
þǣm ēalonde, þe hī upp cōmon: & him þider hiora þearfe forgēafon, oð þæt hē
the island, which they upon landed and them there their necessities gave, until that he
gesāwe hwæt hē him dōn wolde.
saw   what he them do wanted

(Bede, Old English Translation of the *Historia Ecclesiastica Gentis Anglorum*; late 10th century; DOEC)

Translation

Æthelbert, then, was at that time king of Kent, and [he was] mighty: He had a kingdom reaching to the edge of the river Humber, which divides the southern part and the northern part of the English people. Then on the eastern half of Kent there is the large Isle of Thanet, which is six hundred hides[8] large after the English people's measurement. The river Wantsum divides that island from the adjoining land. It is three furlongs broad, and in two places it is fordable, and both ends are situated at the sea. On this island God's servant Augustine and his companions landed; he was one (of a group) of forty people. Also, they brought translators from Franconia with them, as Saint Gregory had instructed [them]. And then he sent a messenger to Æthelbert and announced that he had come from Rome, conveying the best message; and he promised them who were willing to follow it, without doubt, eternal joy in heaven and a future kingdom without end with the true and living God. When the king had heard those words, he ordered them to stay on the island where they had landed, and [that] what they needed should be given to them, until he saw what he wished to do with them.

---

8   A "hide" of land was approximately twenty acres.

5. This text excerpt comprises the first eleven lines of *Beowulf*. Read the lines and determine the stressed alliterative syllables.

Hwæt, wē   Gār-Dena in geārdagum,
Listen we [of the] Spear-Danes in former days
þēodcyninga   þrym gefrūnon,
[of the] kings [of the people] glory [have] heard
hū ðā æþelingas ellen fremedon.
how the noblemen bravery performed
Oft Scyld Scēfing sceaþena þrēatum,
often Scyld Scefing [of] enemies bands
monegum mǣgþum meodosetla oftēah,
many tribes mead-benches deprived
egsode eorlas, syððan ǣrest wearð
terrified warriors after first was
fēasceaft funden; hē þæs   frōfre   gebād,
destitute found he [for] that consolation experienced
wēox under wolcnum, weorðmyndum þāh,
grew up under clouds [in] honours prospered
oðþæt him ǣghwylc þǣr ymbsittendra
until him each one there neighbours
ofer hronrāde hȳran scolde,
over whale-road obey had to
gomban gyldan. Þæt wæs gōd cyning!
tribute pay That was good king
(Beowulf, early 11th century; DOEC)

Translation

Listen, we have heard of the glory of the Spear-Danes' kings in former days, how those noblemen performed bravery. Often Scyld Scefing deprived bands of enemies, many tribes of [their] mead-benches, terrified warriors, after he first was found destitute; he found consolation for that, grew up under clouds, prospered in honours, until each of his neighbours by the whale-road had to obey him and pay tribute. That was a good king!

6. The text below is a typical riddle. Again, look at the alliterative structure of the lines. What would you suggest as the solution to the riddle?
Also, give an analysis of the word-formations in the following words: *beadoweorca, gūðgewinnes, forwurde, heardecg, heoroscearp, hondweorc,*

folcstede, dēaðslege. Which of these word-formations are no longer possible in contemporary English?

Ic eom ānhaga,   īserne   wund,
I am a solitary one [by] iron wounded
bille gebennad, beadoweorca sæd,
[by] sword hurt   [with] war-deeds filled
ecgum wērig.   Oft ic wīg sēo,
by [sword-]edges exhausted Often I battle see
frēcne feohtan.   Frōfre ne wēne,
bold ones fight   consolation not hope
þæt   mē   gēoc cyme gūðgewinnes
that [to] me relief come [of] battle-strife
ǣr   ic mid ældum eal forwurðe,
before I among men   all   perish
ac mec hnossiað   homera lāfe,
but me   strikes   the legacy of hammers
heardecg heoroscearp hondweorc smiþa
hard-edged deadly sharp handiwork of smiths
bītað   in burgum;   ic ābīdan sceal
bite [me] in strongholds I wait for must
lāþran   gemōtes.   Nǣfre lǣcecynn
more hostile encounter never   physician
on folcstede findan meahte,
   in   town   find   [I] could
þāra þe   mid wyrtum wunde   gehǣlde,
of those who with   herbs   wounds [might] heal
ac   mē ecga   dolg   ēacen weorðað
but [on] me swords' wounds multiplied become
þurh dēaðslege dagum ond nihtum.
   by death-stroke   days   and   nights
(Riddle 5, late 10th century; DOEC)

Translation

I am a solitary one, wounded by iron,
hurt by [the] sword, filled with war-deeds,
exhausted by [sword-]edges. Often I see battle,
bold ones fighting. I do not hope for consolation

that relief of battle-strife will come to me
before I perish completely among men,
but the legacy of hammers strikes me,
hard-edged, deadly sharp handiwork of smiths
bites me in strongholds; I must wait for
more hostile encounter[s]. Never could I find
a physician in town, of the kind who might heal wounds with herbs,
but swords' wounds become multiplied on me
by death-stroke day and night.

7. The two extracts below stem from a collection of Saints' Lives (the story is about the so-called Seven Sleepers). The text is very much shaped by the values of Christianity and the world of Late Antiquity. While reading the text, look at the specific ways in which requests are formulated here (for example, *Ic wolde georne æt ðe gewitan þissere byrig rihtnaman, gif þu me woldest gewissigan.* "I would like to know from you the correct name of this town, if you would like to instruct me" and *ic wolde, leof, axian, gif ge me secgan woldon* "I would like to ask you, dear sirs, if you would tell me"). Try to assess the politeness of these utterances against the background of what was said about Old English directives in Chapter 3.3.1.

Ðā ofseah he ǣnne geongne man and ēode him tō þǣm ylcan, and ongan hine
Then saw   he   a   young   man and went   to   the   same and began him
āxian, and cwæð, Lā, wel gedō ðē, gōde man.   Ic wolde georne æt ðē gewitan
[to] ask, and said, Look, well "you will do" good man I   would like to of you   know
þissere byrig rihtnaman, gif þū me woldest gewissigan. Ðā cwæð sē geonga tō
[of] this town correct name if you me would   instruct Then said the young [man] to
him, Ic þē wille full hraðe secgan. Ephese hātte þēos burh, and hēo wel gefyrn
him, I you want to very quickly tell   Ephesus is called this town and   it very long ago
swā gehaten wæs. […]
so   called   was
Ðā Malchus þas word gehȳrde þe se portgerēfa him   swā hetelice   wæs tō
When Malchus these words heard that the   mayor   (to) him in such a hostile way was to
spræcende, hē ofdrǣd slōh adūn þǣrrihte   and hine sylfne astrǣhte ætforan
speaking,   he terrified threw down immediately and him   self prostrated before
eallum þām folce, and þā cwæð tō heom eallum mid wēpendre stefne, Lā lēof, ic
all   the people and then said to   them   all   with weeping voice dear [sirs] I
bidde ēow þæt ælmyssan þæt ic mōte ānes þinges āxian, and ic ēow sōna eall
ask   you this   favour   that I may one   thing   ask   and I you soon all

68

wille cȳðan hwæt ic þence on mīnum geþance: þæs ic wolde, lēof, āxian, gif gē
want to tell what I think in my thoughts this I wanted dear ask if you
mē secgan woldon, hwǣr Decius se cāsere sȳ, se þe hēr wæs on þissere byrig?
me say would where Decius the emperor is he who here was in this town
Ðā andwyrde se bisceop him Marinus and cwæð tō Malche, Mīn lēofe cild, nis
Then answered the bishop him Marinus and said to Malchus my dear child not is
nū tōdæg sē cāsere on eorþan lifigende þe Decius sȳ genemned.
now today the emperor on earth living who Decius is named
(Seven Sleepers, *Lives of Saints*; late 10th century; DOEC)

Translation

Then he saw a young man and went to the same, and began to ask and said: "Look, I hope you are well, good man. I would like to know from you the correct name of this town, if you would instruct me." Then the young man said to him: "I will tell you very quickly. This town is called Ephesus, and it was called so very long ago." [...]

When Malchus heard the words that the mayor said to him in such a hostile way, he immediately fell down terrified and prostrated himself before all the people, and then said to them all with a voice full of grief: "Dear sirs, I ask you this favour that I may ask one thing, and I will tell you all soon what I think in my thoughts. This I would like to ask, dear sirs, if you would tell me where Decius the emperor is, who was here in this town."

Then the bishop Marinus answered him and said to Malchus "My dear child, there is no emperor alive on earth today who is named Decius."

4. English ca. 1100 to ca. 1500 (Middle English)

4.1. Political and socio-cultural background

Quite often the Battle of Hastings in 1066 is seen as the beginning of the Middle English period and the start of a separate era, opening up new social, cultural and linguistic dimensions in Britain. This may be true to a certain extent with regard to political and administrative developments, but 1066 is certainly not the boundary line dividing Old English from Middle English. English people just did not wake up one morning in 1066 to find out that they were speaking no longer Old English but some kind of Middle English. Language change is a gradual and extremely complicated process and cannot be captured in precise dates. We know that after 1066 Old English (or some further development of it) was still spoken in large parts of the country, especially in the South West, which had not been exposed to Viking influence. We know about the maintenance of Old English text traditions, and the copying of Anglo-Saxon manuscripts right until the twelfth century. Thus, it is appropriate to say that the Middle English period did not start in 1066 but rather around the first decades of the twelfth century.

While the Battle of Hastings was certainly not the beginning of Middle English, it clearly marked the end of Anglo-Saxon rule and the Anglo-Saxon monarchy. It is interesting to see that the Anglo-Saxon kingdom did not collapse due to bad government or inefficient administration but because of dynastic instability. After the death of Edward the Confessor in January 1066 there were two rivals striving for the succession: Harold, who had already been elected king shortly after Edward's death, and William, Duke of Normandy, who was the second cousin of Edward and thus the closest living relative. The duchy of Normandy went back to fairly recent Scandinavian settlements in Normandy during the ninth and tenth centuries. Relations to the Anglo-Saxon kingdom were complicated because there had been close connections between Normandy and England already before the Conquest: The Anglo-Saxon king Æthelræd (the Unready) had married a Norman wife and his son Edward (the Confessor) had been brought up in Normandy.

As is well known, William defeated Harold and invaded England. On Christmas Day 1066 William was crowned in Westminster. The complete conquest of England took some four more years. One of the immediate consequences of the Conquest was the introduction of a new nobility in England. All large estates and important positions were given to Normans or other foreigners, and this situation persisted for several generations after the Conquest. This meant that French-speaking nobles, together with their retinue, came to England. They maintained strong links with Normandy, where they also kept estates. A similar situation was found in the English church. Here most bishops and abbots were replaced and all important positions were given to Normans. The Abbot of St Stephen's at Caen became Archbishop of Canterbury in 1070, and the other archbishopric (York) was filled with a Norman as well. Within 20 years almost all religious houses found themselves under French-speaking superiors. And there were new foundations established which were entirely peopled by Norman monks. In addition there must have been a significant number of French-speaking merchants and craftsmen who came to England and settled there. And there were, of course, many foreign soldiers who were stationed in the new castles William had built in order to consolidate his rule.

It is quite difficult to estimate with any accuracy the number of Norman or French people who settled in England during the first century or so after 1066, but their number must have been rather moderate. Here the Norman Conquest differed radically from the arrival of the Germanic tribes in England in the fifth century or the Viking invasions of the latter period in Anglo-Saxon England. On these occasions large numbers of people had occupied the country and settled there, either driving out the former population (the Celts) or mingling with it to a considerable extent (as the Vikings had done with the Anglo-Saxons). But the Norman Conquest only resulted, roughly speaking, in the substitution of the Anglo-Saxon members of the ruling class in state and church by Normans. This does not mean that the Conquest had no consequences. The effects were just different, as will be pointed out below.

The establishment of the new Norman nobility created strong links between England and Normandy, because most members of the nobility had possessions both in England and France. Starting from the coronation of William I until 1204, the kings of England were also dukes of Normandy. With the expansion of the estates in France (especially under the long reign of Henry II, 1154–1189), attention was often focused on the affairs on the Continent. As a consequence, the English kings and their nobility spent much of their time in their possessions outside England. William, for example, spent about half of the time of his reign in France, Henry I (1100–1135) 17 out 35 years, Henry II nearly two thirds of his reign. This attitude accounts very much for the "French spirit" which prevailed at court and among the Anglo-Norman nobility. The attitude of the ruling classes towards the English language may not be characterised as hostility but rather as sheer indifference.

This indifference had consequences for the linguistic situation in England. The Normans who settled in England spoke their own language, Norman French, a Northern dialect of France. In the course of time, the French used by Normans in England was called Anglo-Norman. Anglo-Norman was the prestigious language used at court and by the nobility. It seems to have remained the first language of the royal family and the aristocracy throughout the twelfth and probably the thirteenth century, a trend which clearly weakened during the fourteenth century. The first English king after the Norman Conquest whose maternal language is said to have been English was Henry IV, who was born in 1366.

Another domain where Anglo-Norman was used was administration. English-speaking people serving a Norman lord (for example, as stewards and bailiffs on manors or as clerks in town) had to learn French. Whoever wanted to get on in society had to be able to speak French. Thus we may assume that the use of French was not necessarily an ethnic (Norman) but a social feature. The prestigious position of French is also reflected by its use as the language of literature. In early Middle English we find a rich body of Anglo-Norman literature, which was mainly written during the twelfth century in England.

On the other hand, it is quite evident that English was and remained to a considerable extent the language of the common people. So it seems there was no large-scale bilingualism in post-Conquest England, especially not from the perspective of the spoken language of native speakers of English. Bilingualism was certainly found in the written language, especially in the fields of administration, management, in manorial records and Parliament proceedings.

The thirteenth century witnessed a considerable change in the relationship between French and English and this change was first of all triggered by a political event. In 1204 King John lost Normandy to the French king, due to his high-handed proud conduct and bad luck in his military activities. The loss of Normandy had manifest political and cultural consequences. The immediate upshot was that the nobility who owned lands both in England and in Normandy were forced to decide which possessions they would keep, that is, they had to give up one or the other. The long-term effects were that England now tended to be seen as a separate kingdom with its own interests politically and culturally, and even nationally. During the thirteenth century members of the (formerly) Norman nobility would gradually consider themselves more English. In addition, the advent of large numbers of French people, who were given important positions and favourable marriages, during the following decades (especially during the reign of Henry III, 1216–1272), triggered a negative attitude towards the French, which actually reached hostility and a kind of national feeling. Afterwards, the so-called Hundred

Years' War (1337–1453) against France would hardly diminish the antagonism felt against France and the French language.

These changing attitudes certainly had their effect on the role of Anglo-Norman in England and the knowledge of French in the upper classes. From the thirteenth century onwards we witness a decreasing knowledge of French, from about the middle of the century phrase books and teaching manuals for learning French appear, and in the course of time it seems that the practice of speaking French becomes increasingly artificial.

This artificial or stilted character of Anglo-Norman certainly had to do with another development during the thirteenth century. Then a different and more prestigious variety of French had become important in England as almost everywhere in Europe: the variety of French which was spoken in the *Ile de France*, also called Central French or Parisian French. This international prestige variety of French was associated with polite discourse throughout Europe; it was used in administration, law and literature. As a consequence, Anglo-Norman was degraded to a low-prestige provincial dialect. In fact, Anglo-Norman, due to its separation from the homeland and its permanent contact with English, must have sounded fairly peculiar. Thus, we may assume that the practice of French in England was either in decline or oriented towards the new prestigious variety. The upper classes continued to speak French during the thirteenth century, at least for the most part, but they probably did so because it was considered a prestigious language and because it had been the language of administration and business during the past century. This kind of French, needless to say, must have been either quite dated or imperfect. At least from the beginning of the fourteenth century we know that French was taught in the artificial setting of a classroom or private tuition. In this period we also witness the publication of more phrase books and teaching manuals. Since knowledge of French was linked to training and schooling, it was seen as an achievement of educated (and elegant) people, which was mainly associated with culture and fashion, administration and the law. In the fifteenth century to speak French fluently, was still considered a special accomplishment.

The decline of French in England and the need for formal teaching of French finds a complementary development in what is often called the re-establishment of English. Starting from about the middle of the thirteenth century, English becomes again the main language of the country and emerges as the dominant medium of communication in important domains of language use. This is, however, a gradual development, which reaches well into the fifteenth century. In the course of the thirteenth century English slowly spreads to the upper classes. From this time we also find many more texts which are written down in English (sermons, prayers, romances, songs and so on). The popularity of English and its increasing use as an ordinary means of communication is also reflected in regulations proscribing the use of English at educational institutions. At monastic schools, grammar schools and universities conversations were supposed to be held in Latin (or French). The ban on English had been mainly imposed in order to insure the easy command of Latin. But it also shows the extent to which English was actually used and how artificial the use of French must have been. We also know that English was progressively more employed as a medium of instruction at school.

There are also explicit statements and regulations which recommend or prescribe the use of English in certain institutions. In 1362 the Statute of Pleading commanded that English should be the language of the law courts, which meant that all legal cases had to be conducted in English (however, English was not used consistently in recording the proceedings of courts of law until the eighteenth century). In 1363 Parliament was opened for the first time with a speech in English. In the 1380s the London guilds begin to use English for their records and in 1384 a proclamation by the City of London is published in English. Towards the end of the fourteenth century a general attitude prevails which sees English as the main language of the country and even as a national language.

The re-establishment of English was accompanied and supported by major socio-economic developments which also changed parts of English society towards the end of the Middle Ages. The first important development was triggered by the so-called Black Death or Great Plague. This is the bubonic and pneumonic plague, a highly contagious and deadly disease, which spread in England from about the middle of the fourteenth century. Mortality seems to have been disastrous, ranging, according to some estimates, between a third and a half of the population. The immediate effect of these disasters was a shortage of people and consequently a shortage of labour. It seems that the population of England did not really recover during the fifteenth century. As a consequence, the wages of both farm workers and urban craftsmen kept rising right through the whole period. Thus the Black Death strengthened the position of the labouring classes and, by implication, the importance of English, because these people mainly used the vernacular. On the other hand, the Black Death undermined and basically destroyed the old feudal system. England was still very much an agricultural country, with the large majority of the people living and working in the country. Now land owners came into difficulties because they could not pay the high wages and many of the bonded labourers (villains, serfs) simply left their manors and travelled around the country.

In the towns this development was accompanied by the so-called rise of the "middle classes", especially in the larger towns like London, Bristol, York,

Norwich and Oxford. These towns enjoyed a greater or lesser independence of the king and the local nobility and, with their growing population, assumed increasing importance. Here, again, is a section of the population which mainly used English, not French, and contributed to the re-establishment of English. Especially London had the privilege of self-government and controlled large parts of the local trade (which included a major proportion of the shipping of England). London was rich enough to lend money to the king, and the wealthiest citizens of London were sometimes nearly as powerful as members of the local nobility. The most influential institutions in towns were the craft guilds and merchant guilds, strictly hierarchical organisations of craftsmen and merchants which regulated many aspects of life and exerted great influence on the local government. Most mayors of fifteenth-century London came from the mercers, grocers, drapers, fishmongers and the goldsmiths.

A last important socio-economic factor was the increased migration and movement among the population. With the growth of the towns and increasing urbanisation there was a continual movement of immigration to larger towns, especially to London. On the other hand, there was a movement from town to country when large parts of the woollen and cloth industry moved to the countryside. Socially, there was a mixture between the wealthy merchants and the local gentry, especially in the country. All this mixture and exchange contributed to the strengthening of English as the major medium of communication. But it also might lead to a mixture of dialects since people from different parts of the country, speaking vastly differing regional varieties, met and might live in close proximity, especially in London during the fifteenth century. In the course of time, certain dialect features could be levelled and an incipient local standard could form (on standardisation see Chapter 4.2.5.).

In the second half of the fifteenth century, towards the end of the Middle English period, English thus emerged as the dominant medium of communication in all important domains of language use, both spoken and written.

4.2. Language structure

4.2.1. Spelling and pronunciation

One of the most noticeable, if not notorious, features of Middle English is its extraordinary diversity of orthography. Basically, there is hardly any word which is spelt in an identical way in the period, and the variant spellings of one item sometimes go beyond twenty. For example, the glossary of the collection of early Middle English texts edited by Bennett and Smithers (1968) lists no less than 22 different variants for "noʒt", with the senses "nothing" and "not at all, not". These are:

(1) noʒt, nouʒt, nouʒth, noht, noght, nohht, nocht, nogt, noth, nout, nouth, nouct, nohut, novt, nawt, nowt, nowth, naht, nacht, nauʒth, nowiʒt, noouiʒt
(Bennett and Smithers 1968: 540)

This almost chaotic heterogeneity of Middle English spelling can be explained by three major factors. Firstly, we find that, especially in the century following the Norman Conquest, scribes still kept copying Anglo-Saxon texts and thus followed the Old English writing traditions, although at least some of the sounds were changing. Secondly, as a long-term consequence of the Norman Conquest, we witness new, Norman-French conventions which are introduced in manuscripts produced in England. Thirdly, and quite importantly, Middle English is the period of dialectal diversification of the written language. Since there existed no approximate written standard (comparable, for example, to the late West Saxon literary language in Anglo-Saxon England), people mainly had to follow their own intuitions about spelling, forming their own, often idiosyncratic, habits and reproducing in some way their local pronunciation in writing. Thus, apart from discrepancies in morphology, syntax and lexis, Middle English texts from different dialect regions may show extraordinary differences simply in terms of spelling. There are some Middle English manuscripts which show a certain degree of consistency in their orthography (for example, the texts associated with the so-called Katherine Group or the Ellesmere Manuscript of Chaucer's *Canterbury Tales*), but these are fairly exceptional. Only towards the fifteenth century do we find tendencies towards standardisation of spelling.

The spelling traditions stemming from Old English mainly comprise the special Old English letters which do not form part of the Latin alphabet (see Chapter 3.2.1.). These are the "ash" <æ>, the "thorn" <þ>, the "eth" <ð>, the "yogh" <ʒ> and the "wynn" <ƿ>. They are found in early Middle English texts, but <æ>, <ð> and <ƿ> disappeared gradually, while <þ> and <ʒ> are preserved throughout the Middle English period. <þ> is used for both the voiced and voiceless version of the dental fricative [θ] and [ð], whereas <ʒ> represents mostly /j/ in initial position (ʒer "year", ʒong "young") and /χ/ in other positions (riʒt "right", þurʒ "through"). Sometimes a thorn appears in the guise of the letter <y> (perhaps due to the basic similarity of the two letters, especially in rapid handwriting). Thus *ye* can be read

77

as *þe*, which represents the definite article *the* (*ye* can, of course, also be the subject case of the plural form of the second-person pronoun, "you"; see Chapter 4.2.2.).

The Norman-French conventions include innovations and changes in the Anglo-Saxon system that are mostly preserved in Modern English. In the consonants they often concern combinations of letters. The combination <qu> denotes [kw] (*queen*), <gh> designates the allophones of the phoneme /χ/, [ç] and [χ] (as in *right* "right" and *doughter* "daughter", respectively). The combinations <ch> and <cch> are used for the affricate /tʃ/ (*chirche* "church"), <cg> and <gg> for the affricate /dʒ/ (*brigge* "bridge"), <sh> and <sch> for the sibilant /ʃ/ (*ship*). The letter <c>, when placed in front of <e> or <i>, denotes the fricative /s/ (as in *citee* "city").

For vowels, some typical Norman conventions include: <ou, ow> for /u:/ (*hous*), both <y> and <i> for /i/ (*synne, sinne* "sin"), <ie> for /e:/ in words with French origin (for example, *þief* "thief").

Another important convention was due to the use of minims, that is, the single short down strokes of the pen by which the letters <m, n, u> and others were represented in manuscripts (for example, *сitтеtt* for *cumen* "come"). In order to enhance the readability of words which include many minims, for example, combinations of <m, n, u>, where many down strokes would add up and the individual letters could not easily be distinguished from each other (see the example of *сitтеtt* mentioned above), minims which represent <u> were written as an <o>, whenever two or three other minims follow. Thus, we find <o> denoting /u/ in Middle English *comen* and *love* (the Old English spelling had been *cuman* and *lufu*).

Given the diversity and the rapid change which is so characteristic of the Middle English period, it is hardly possible or appropriate to design a systematic description of the vowel and consonant phonemes and their most common orthographic realisations that would be valid for the whole period and all regions. Rather, I will sketch a short overview which is typical of the language of Chaucer and make some remarks about the most important differences and developments in terms of chronology and region.

The Middle English system of vowel phonemes is slightly different from the Old English system because long and short vowels do not pattern as nicely as in Old English. There are three pairs of front vowels (/i:/ - /i/, /e:/ - /e/, /a:/ - /a/) and two pairs of back vowels (/u:/ - /u/, /ɔ:/ - /ɔ/), but also two (single) long vowels, the front vowel /ɛ:/ and the back vowel /o:/ (see Table 1 below). In addition, it is by no means clear whether the pairs only differ in quantity but also in quality (height), as Modern English long /i:/ and short /ɪ/. This detail is neglected here. Old English /y:/ and /y/ is not represented either since these vowels were soon unrounded and only preserved to some extent in the South West.

iː / i	uː / u
eː / e	oː
ɛː	ɔː / ɔ
aː / a	

Table 1: Middle English vowel phonemes

There are six diphthongs in Middle English, /ai/, /ɔi/, /iu/, /ɛu/, /au/ and /ɔu/. None of them is directly taken over from Old English. They derive from a vocalisation of Old English /χ/, /j/ or /w/ (for example, *ploga* becoming *plow*, *dæg* becoming *day*) or they are adopted from French (for example, /ɔi/) or Old Norse.

As you can see in Table 2 below, there is not much difference between the inventory of Old English and Middle English consonant phonemes. Some of the voiced and voiceless allophones in the fricatives have become phonemes since in Middle English minimal pairs can be found: /f/ – /v/ (*leaf* vs. *leave*), /θ/ – /ð/ (*thee* (from *theen* "to prosper") vs. *thee* (dative / accusative of the second-person singular pronoun *thou* "you")), /s/ – /z/ (*asse* "donkey" vs. *as*). The velar fricative /χ/ still has the two allophones [χ] and [ç], similar to German *ach* and *ich*. The same applies to the two allophones of /n/, [n] and [ŋ].

	stops	fricatives/sibilants	affricates	nasal	liquids	approximants
labial	p – b	f – v		m		w
dental		θ – ð				
alveolar	t – d	s – z		n	l – r	
palatal		ʃ	tʃ – dʒ			j
velar	k – g	χ				

Table 2: Middle English consonant phonemes

Due to the great dialectal variability of the Middle English texts, it is impossible to give a straightforward account of the relationship between spelling and pronunciation that would cover all Middle English texts. The short overview presented below will focus on the language of Chaucer, that is, the late Middle English variety of the second half of the fourteenth century, characteristic of the London area. Even here, not all the letters but only the more "difficult" and important facts will be included. In many cases, in order to reconstruct the Middle English pronunciation of a letter, it is important to know the Modern English equivalent and the developments which led to it. This includes, above all, knowledge about the major sound changes covering the Early Modern English period (1500 – 1700), in particular the Great Vowel Shift. In the section below I will only refer to the more detailed descriptions in later chapters (on the Great Vowel Shift see Chapter 5.2.1.).

Among the single consonant letters there are few problems. Only <c> and <g> may create complications. If <c> appears in front of <e> or <i>, it denotes the fricative /s/ (*certain* "certain", *citee* "city"), otherwise /k/ (*compaignye* "company"). The letter <g> is used for the affricate /ʤ/ or for the plosive /g/. Basically, the situation in Modern English can function as a guideline here: *corage* "courage" and *gyaunt* "giant" have the affricate, *get* "get" and *grene* "green" the plosive. The letter yogh <ʒ> (found in some early Chaucer manuscripts) represents /j/ in initial position (*ʒer* "year", *ʒong* "young"), and the allophones of the fricative /χ/, the palatal [ç] in combination with front vowels (*kniʒt* "knight") and the velar [χ] in combination with back vowels (*thouʒ* "though").

The situation with combinations of letters is not very complicated either. <gh>, which in the course of time replaces <ʒ>, refers to the allophones of the phoneme /χ/, [ç] and [χ], with the same distribution as with <ʒ> (pointed out above). <ch> and also <cch> are used for the affricate /ʧ/ (*chirche* "church"), <cg> and <gg> for the affricate /ʤ/ (*brigge* "bridge"). <sh> and <sch> denote the sibilant /ʃ/ (*ship*).

Spelling	Pronunciation
<c>	/s/ (before front vowels)
	/k/
<g>	/g/
	/ʤ/ (as in Modern English)
<ʒ>	/j/ (in initial position)
	/χ/ [ç], [χ]
<gh>	/χ/ [ç], [χ]
<ch>	/ʧ/
<cch>	
<sh>	/ʃ/

Table 3: Some Middle English consonant graphemes and their sound correspondence

Vowels may present some more problems because more detailed knowledge about the developments up to Modern English is required. The letter <a> can represent both short /a/ and long /a:/. In most cases the length can be determined against the background of Modern English: If the present-day English vowel has an /æ/, it is short (*sak* "sack", *bak* "back"), if the present-day English equivalent is a diphthong /ei/, the vowel is long (*name* "name", *shapen* "shape"). This reflects the development of Middle English /aː/ in the Great Vowel Shift.

The letter <e> could denote a short /e/, a long closed /eː/ or a long open /ɛː/ (both long versions have also <ee>). The short /e/ can usually be assumed if Modern English has preserved the sound (*set* "set", *helpen* "help"). The sound value /eː/ can often be assumed if the Modern English vowel is /iː/ in combination with the spelling <ee> (*fet* "feet", *deed* "deed"); the long open /ɛː/ can often be assumed if the Modern English has /iː/ in combination with the spelling <ea> (*heeth* "heath", *mete* "meat"). This again reflects developments of the Great Vowel Shift.

The letter <i> refers to short /i/ or long /iː/. The short version can be assumed if Modern English has short /i/ as well (*bidde* "bid", *pit* "pit"). The long vowel applies if the Modern English equivalent has the diphthong /ai/ (*lif* "life", *milde* "mild"). The same distribution is found with the letter <y>, which was used indiscriminately for the vowels pointed out for <i> (*pyt, lyf*). But in addition, <y>, in initial position before vowel, could refer to the approximant /j/ (*youth*).

The letter <o> can denote the short vowel /ɔ/, the long closed /oː/, the long open /ɔː/ (the long versions also have <oo>) and in addition, as pointed out above, the short /u/. The short /ɔ/ usually applies if the corresponding Modern English word has a short /ɒ/ (*pot, long*); /oː/ can often be assumed if Modern English has /uː/ in combination with the spelling <oo> (*fool* "fool", *good* "good"); /ɔː/ is most likely if Modern English has the diphthong /əʊ/ in combination with the spelling <oa> or <o> (*boot* "boat", *stoon* "stone"). Short /u/ can be assumed in the neighbourhood of <m, n, v, w>, according to the minim rule pointed out above. A good indication is here the vowel /ʌ/ in the Modern English word (*comen* "come", *monk* "monk"). The letter <u> denoted short /u/ (*ful* "full"), but was probably also used for the diphthong /iu/ in French loanwords (*vertu* "virtue").

Spelling	Pronunciation
<a>	/a/, /aː/
<e>	/e/, /eː/, /ɛː/
<i>	/i/, /iː/
<y>	/i/, iː/, /j/
<o>	/ɔ/, /oː/, /ɔː/, /u/
<u>	/u/, /iu/
<ou>, <ow>	/uː/, /ou/

Table 4: Some Middle English vowel graphemes and their sound correspondence

Finally, a few letter combinations should be mentioned here. The combinations <ou> and <ow> were used for the vowel /u:/, but also for the diphthong /ou/. The long /u:/ can be assumed when the Modern English equivalent sound is the diphthong /aʊ/ (*loud* "loud", *toun* "town", *how* "how"). If Modern English shows a different sound in the respective word, we may assume the diphthong /ou/ /(*soule* "soul", *thought* "thought").

The correspondences shown in Tables 3 and 4 above are helpful as a general guideline (especially when reading texts by Chaucer and his contemporaries). But there are many words (or classes of words) which have developed differently and where the general rules do not apply (for a helpful overview of some of these "irregular" developments see, for example, Sauer 1998: 30–33).

Middle English is a period showing many sound changes. Only the most relevant ones shall be presented here. The first three concern the length of syllables. As we saw in the sections above, the length of vowels can often be found out by connecting the vowel and its development to present-day English. There is, however, another, complementary way of discovering the length of a vowel in a Middle English word, namely by looking at certain sound changes which happened towards the end of Old English and at the beginning of Middle English.

The first sound change is called lengthening of vowels in front of voiced homorganic consonant groups ([mb], [nd], [ld]). These groups are sets of consonants which are produced at the same place of articulation. For example, both [l] and [d] involve the tip of the tongue and the alveolar ridge. Thus, we find long vowels in *child* "child", *feeld* "field", *binden* "bind", *climben* "climb" and so on.

Another sound change, which also seems to have happened towards the end of the Old English period, comprises a complementary process: the shortening of those vowels that occurred in front of consonant groups which were not homorganic, including those that contained three consonants. Thus, we find short vowels in Middle English *kepte* "kept" (as opposed to the long vowel in the infinitive *kepan* "keep") and *mette* "met" (as opposed to the long vowel in the infinitive *metan* "meet"), which is still preserved in the Modern English pattern *keep, kept, kept* and *meet, met, met*. In a similar way, there is a short vowel in *softe* "soft", and a short vowel in the first syllable of *fyftene* "fifteen" (as opposed to a long vowel in *fyf* "five").

A third sound change, which can be attributed to the first half of the thirteenth century, resulted in lengthening. It is the lengthening of stressed short vowels in open syllables, involving first /a, e, ɔ/ and later also /i, u/. Open syllables are those ending in a vowel. Thus we find Middle English *faren* "travel" with a long /a:/, *beren* "bear" with a long /ɛ:/, and *cote* "cottage" with a long /ɔ:/.

Generally, and only with few exceptions, vowels in unstressed syllables, which seem to have been differentiated in Old English, lost their distinctive quality in Middle English and were levelled to schwa [ə] (on this see the section on Middle English morphology in Chapter 4.2.2.).

A last sound change is important because it marks a major dividing line between the Northern and Midland / Southern dialects in Middle English. It involves the rounding of Old English /a:/ south of the Humber into /ɔ:/. Thus, we get *wo* "woe", *stone* "stone", *boon* "bone" in the Midlands and the South, whereas the corresponding northern forms are *wa*, *stan* and *ban*.

The Germanic stress pattern (with the accent on the first syllable of the stem), which was characteristic of Old English, stayed basically in effect. French loan words were gradually adapted, sometimes with a delay. Thus, we find *honóur*, *couráge*, *natúre* still with stress on the second syllable. Only later do we find the stress pattern of Modern English.

4.2.2. Morphology and word-formation

inflectional morphology

In the section on Old English morphology (Chapter 3.2.2.) we saw that one of the major differences between Old English and Modern English is that Old English was a mainly synthetic language whereas Modern English is predominantly analytic. In Old English, syntactic functions in a sentence (like subject, direct object etc.) are typically marked by means of inflectional endings. Most of the important changes which transformed English from a mainly synthetic to a predominantly analytic language can be associated with Middle English, in particular the decline of inflectional endings.

Mossé (1968 [1952]) describes three steps in the decay of the inflectional endings. First, the full quality of the vowels /a, ɔ, u, e/ in unaccented syllables is levelled to the indistinct schwa /ə/ (often written as <e>). Secondly, the final consonants /m/ and /n/ in inflectional endings are lost. Thirdly, the schwa is lost. Thus, an Old English word like *scipum* (dative plural of *scip* "ship") would be reduced to something like *scip* (but note that in the plural the –*s* ending is generalised throughout).

As can be easily imagined, this loss of inflectional endings had serious consequences for the grammatical system of Middle English. In nouns and adjectives it caused a reduction of the number of case forms. For example, the endings of the so-called weak declension (*guma* "man": -*an*, -*ena*, -*um*, see

Chapter 3.2.2.) are lost (on the plural *–s* see above). In addition, grammatical gender was lost. Especially the full vowels in inflectional endings had preserved gender differences (compare, for example, the nominative masculine plural *stā nas* "stones" with the corresponding neuter form *scipu* "ships" and feminine form *giefa* "gifts"). The loss of gender was significantly supported by the simplification of the definite article, which was mostly reduced to the invariable *þe* and thus could not express gender distinctions any longer. Lastly, in the verb, person and mood become indistinct in a similar way in many cases.

The decay of inflectional endings is already visible in the latter part of the Old English period, where vowels in inflectional endings were simply mixed up in the manuscripts. For example, the endings *–on*, *–an* and *–en* in verbs occurred interchangeably, and the dative ending of nouns, *–um*, was realised as *–an* or *–on*.

What may have been the reason for this tremendous loss of inflectional endings? One reason could have been the Germanic stress pattern, which places the accent on the first syllable of a word (or rather stem; see Chapter 3.2.1.). Strong stress on the first syllable of a word can make the special quality of vowels in unstressed syllables less distinctive and can lead to a levelling of the vowel. On the other hand, this process did not occur to such an extent in other Germanic languages, which retained their inflectional system more or less (for example, Modern German). Another factor might have been the contact situation between Old English and Old Norse in the Danelaw (see Chapter 3.1.). Since both languages were similar to a certain extent, with related stems of many words, people, in order to communicate, might just have dropped the endings. This, however, is very much a matter of speculation, but, if it happened, it would surely have accelerated the decay of inflectional endings.

The paradigm of nouns was simplified to such an extent that by late Middle English there is basically only the *–(e)s* ending left, which marks the genitive and the plural. The genitive *–(e)s* derived from the genitive singular of strong masculine nouns (*stānas*, see Chapter 3.2.2.), which became the genitive ending of the great majority of Middle English nouns. The plural *–(e)s* derived from the nominative and accusative plural of strong masculine nouns (*stānas*) and the levelled form came to be the general plural marker for all cases.

For a certain time, especially in the early part of Middle English, the plural marker *–(e)s* had a competitor, *–en* (for example, *shon* "shoes", *sunnen* "sins", *yȝen* "eyes"). This form originated in the Old English plural form of weak nouns (*guman* "men", see Chapter 3.2.2.), which, in the levelled form *–en*, was generalised as plural ending for many nouns in the South. There seems to have been a long rivalry between the two plural endings and it is not until the fourteenth century that the *-(e)s* plural prevailed. In Modern English, the *-en* plural is preserved only in a few words as "irregular" plural (*oxen, children* and *kine*, as archaic plural of *cow*).

Another class of nouns with irregular plural forms in Old English, which are preserved in Middle English, are the so-called umlaut plurals (on i-umlaut see Chapter 3.2.1.). Among the most important Middle English forms are *man – men, fot – fet, gos – ges, toþ – teþ, mous – mys*. You will notice that these forms are also found in Modern English (*men, feet, geese, teeth, mice*).

Middle English adjectives virtually lost all inflections (except for the comparative forms). In early texts, and occasionally in Chaucer and Gower, we find a distinction between strong and weak declension (for example, *god man* as opposed to *þis proude vice* "this arrogant vice"; on strong and weak declension in adjectives see Chapter 3.2.2.). During the fifteenth century this kind of distinction disappears basically in every dialect. The periphrastic forms of the comparative and superlative become quite frequent in late Middle English (for example, *more noble* and *moste noble*). The "irregular" forms (*god, better, best* etc.) are mostly preserved.

As was mentioned above, the Old English determiner *se, þæt, sēo* was radically simplified, the result being an indeclinable *þe* ("the"). The other demonstratives have different forms for singular and plural *that - tho* ("that - those") and *this - thise / these* ("this - these").

The system of personal pronouns undergoes rather drastic changes during the Middle English period. Tables 5–8 below contain the basic paradigms. However, as often in Middle English, there is fairly great variation of forms (for example, the second-person plural dative / accusative *you* in Table 6 below has, among others, the forms *ou, ow*).

The first-person pronouns are fairly straightforward (see Table 5 below). A major point of variation concerns the nominative singular. Here *ich* is the stressed form, which is predominantly found in Southern and Midland dialects, whereas *ik* occurs in the North. This form also appears as an unstressed *I*, which is first used north of the Thames and spreads further to the South. This form is lengthened in the fifteenth century and – after diphthongisation due to the Great Vowel Shift – changes to the Modern English pronoun.

The Middle English paradigm of the second-person pronouns (see Table 6 below) still has the basic singular-plural distinction (*thou – ye*). However, contrary to the usage in Old English, we find in Middle English a polite function of the plural forms addressed to a single person (on this distinction see Chapter 5.3.1.).

	Singular	Plural
Nom	*ich, ik, I*	*we*
Gen	*min*	*ure*
Dat /Acc	*me*	*us*

Table 5: Middle English first-person pronouns

	Singular	Plural
Nom	*thou*	*ye*
Gen	*thin*	*youre*
Dat /Acc	*thee*	*you*

Table 6: Middle English second-person pronouns

	Masculine	Neuter	Feminine
Nom	*he*	*hit, it*	*heo, ʒho, she*
Gen	*his*	*his*	*hire*
Dat	*him*	*him*	*hire*
Acc	*hine*	*hit, it*	*hire*

Table 7: Middle English third-person singular pronouns

The pattern for the third person singular (see Table 7 above) is slightly more complicated. In the neuter we find the forms *hit* and *it* in the nominative. *It* occurs in unstressed positions and is regularly found after the fourteenth century. Note that the dative form for neuter and masculine is *him* and the genitive *his*. In the nominative feminine we find three different patterns: the form which continues the Old English pronoun (*heo*), a pattern containing *ʒho*, and the form *she*, which is the Modern English form. The latter form is found as the most common type from the middle of the thirteenth century onwards. The origin of the *she*-form is very much debated and not quite clear (on a more detailed discussion see Horobin and Smith 2002: 130–131). Many scholars think that it derives from Old English *hēo*, which changed due to contact with Old Norse in the North and East of England.

The Middle English third-person plural pronouns (see Table 8 below) show the most complicated pattern since we find a mixture of native forms (starting with *h-*) and Scandinavian forms (starting with *th-*), which combine in certain dialect patterns. Table 8 shows an approximate dialectal distribution according to three types. The Scandinavian type comprises all the modern plural forms, which stem from Old Norse (ON *þeir, þeira, þeim*; on the background of the language contact see Chapter 3.1.). This type is found in the North and, from the beginning of the thirteenth century, in the East Midlands. The native type includes all the native, Old English forms. It is predominantly found in the South. The mixed type has the Scandinavian form ("they") in the nominative, the other forms ("hem, hire") have native origin. This pattern is basically found in the Midlands and also in the London dialect (including Chaucer).

	North	Midlands	South
Nom	*thai*	*þei*	*hi*
Gen	*thair*	*hire*	*hire*
Dat	*thame*	*hem*	*hem*
Acc	*thame*	*hem*	*hi*

Table 8: Middle English third-person plural pronouns

We now turn to verbs. With verbs, Middle English shows the same categories as Old English: person, number, tense and mood. Also, we find the same general classes of verbs in Middle English as in Old English, weak, strong, preterite-present and irregular verbs (for a definition of these categories see Chapter 3.2.2.).

Indicative		
	Present	Past
Sing. 1st	*here*	*herde*
2nd	*herest*	*herdest*
3rd	*hereth*	*herde*
Plural	*here(n)*	*herde(n)*
Subjunctive		
Sing.	*here*	*herde*
Plural	*here(n)*	*herde(n)*
Imperative		
Sing.	*here*	–
Plural	*hereth*	–
Participle	*heryng(e)*	*(y)herd(e)*

Table 9: Major forms of the Middle English weak verb heren *"hear"*

Middle English weak verbs form their past tense with an -*(e)d* or *–t* ending. As in Old English, the majority of all verbs are weak verbs and they form the most productive class. The number of weak verbs is steadily increasing during the Middle English period. If a new verb is formed or borrowed, it is usually introduced as a weak verb. Table 9 above comprises the major forms of the weak verb *heren* "hear" as they might be found in the fourteenth-century literary language (for example, in Chaucer). But note that there are major dialectal variations, some of which will be discussed below.

As in Old English, a few verbs show a stem-vowel change in the past tense and the second participle (due to i-umlaut; see Chapter 3.2.2.), for example, *tellen, tolde, ytold* "tell, told, told"; *techen, taughte, ytaught* "teach, taught, taught"; *sechen, soghte, ysought* "seek, sought, sought" etc.

There is some major regional dialect variation for many of the endings of the verbs. In the third person singular present tense we find -*es* in the North and North Midlands, but *–eth* in the South and South Midlands. In the plural present tense there is *–eth* in the South and South-West Midlands, -*e(n)* /-*on* in the North-West Midlands and East Midlands (including London) and -*es* in the North. In the present participle a fairly complicated pattern emerges: -*ing* is the general Southern and Midland form; -*and* is found in the North (but occasionally also around London); -*inde* prevails in the South-West Midlands and *–ende* in the East.

The strong verbs, which change their stem vowel for the past tense forms, comprise many of the most common verbs. Their inflectional endings for the present tense are basically the same as those of the weak verbs. This, of course, includes the major variant forms mentioned above. In the past tense they have zero or *–e* in the singular and *–en* in the plural.

The seven classes of strong verbs traditionally distinguished are not as clear-cut and distinct as in Old English, due to several sound changes and analogical changes. The list below gives the stem forms (the infinitive, the two past tense forms and the second participle) of the seven classes as an illustration, leaving out details of stem vowels and pronunciation.

I write, wrot, written, (y)written ("write")
II chese, ches, chosen, (y)chosen ("choose")
III finde, fond (found), founden, (y)founden ("find")
IV stele, stal, stelen, (y)stolen ("steal")
V mete, mat, meten, (y)meten ("measure")
VI faren, for, foren, (y)faren ("travel")
VII fallen, fel, (y)fallen ("fall")

Strong verbs decrease in number during Middle English. Their number dropped firstly because many Old English strong verbs were replaced by loanwords and thus were lost during the Middle English period. Secondly, their number decreased because many of them were treated as weak verbs and quite a few of them eventually became weak verbs. Sometimes we find competing strong and weak forms for one verb (for example, *crope* and *crepte* for *crepen* "creep" and *ros* and *rysed* for *risen* "rise"). There is also a tendency of simplification in strong verbs. The number of differing stem vowels is reduced (for example, in *finde* there are only three or even two stem vowels; see above under class III).

Preterite-present verbs, that is, verbs with a present tense that was originally a past tense (see Chapter 3.2.2.), are found in Middle English as well, although in a slightly different form. Among the most common items are *cunnen* ("to know how to"), *moten* ("to be allowed to, compelled to"), *schulen* ("to have to, shall") and *witen* ("to know"). Although they are still used as full verbs, they develop some of the typical features of the later modal auxiliaries during the Middle English period: they have no non-finite forms (for example, infinitives and participles; in Middle English, however, some of them, like *cunnen* "can" and *durren* "dare" can still have infinitives), they usually have no third person inflection and they can be constructed with the bare infinitive (*we sculen riden* "we must ride").

The so-called irregular verbs are also found in Middle English (*ben* "to be", *don* "to do", *gon* "to go" and *wille* "to desire, to want to"). Due to their anomalous paradigms and the dialectal variety of the transmitted forms in Middle English they show extreme variability in their forms and distribution. The major variants are listed, for example, in Mossé (1968 [1952]: 83–86).

word-formation

Old English very much relied on native patterns of word-formation to augment the vocabulary. Thus, the Old English lexicon was fairly transparent. In Middle English we witness three major developments in word-formation. Due to extensive borrowing during Middle English, the native resources of word-formation were less productive or less exclusively productive than in Old English. As a consequence, many Old English patterns died out. On the other hand, several Old English processes of word-formation continued to be used in Middle English. And thirdly, new prefixes and suffixes came along with the numerous loan words from French.

Among the native elements of word-formation that declined during Middle English were above all many Old English prefixes. For example, the prefix *for-*, which had been used to intensify the meaning of a verb, does not survive the

Middle English period and is today only preserved in formations which basically go back to Old English (for example, *forbid, forget, forgive, forsake* etc.). In a similar way, the prefixes *to-* and *with-* died out, or were no longer productive beyond the Middle English period. Today no words beginning with the prefix *to-* are used and the prefix *with-* is no longer productive. Of course, many of the old formations were replaced by new French-based loan words, for example, *forbærnan* by *consume (by fire)*, *tomearcian* by *distinguish*, *wiþcweþan* by *contradict, oppose*, and so on. Suffixes were affected to a lesser extent (compare the no longer productive forms *–lock* in *wedlock*, and *–red* in *hatred* and *kindred*).

However, many native patterns were preserved, for example, compound patterns with the combinations noun + noun, adjective + noun. Modern prefixes like *un-*, *under-* and *over-* can be traced to Old English (compare Old English *ondōn* "undo", *unbindan* "unbind", *oferflowan* "overflow", *overdōn* "overdo" or *understandan*).

But there were clearly many new prefixes and suffixes which came to be available as a result of the numerous French loan words which entered the English language especially in the thirteenth and fourteenth centuries. Such formations do not turn up until late Middle English. Typical examples are formations with the new French-based affixes *con-, pre-, -ance, -able, -tion* or *–ment* (compare *conjoin* "unite", *prescience* "foreknowledge", *governaunce* "government", *ymaginable* "conceivable", *protestacioun* "declaration" and *jugement* "judgment", which are all found in Chaucer).

4.2.3. Syntax

Similar to the chapter on Old English syntax (Chapter 3.2.3.), this section will not attempt to give a comprehensive overview of the syntactic developments during the Middle English period. Rather, it will focus on the selected topics covered also in the Old English syntax section, word-order, negation, coordination / subordination, relative clauses and impersonal constructions.

Old English word order (that is, the order of the constituents in the sentence or clause) was relatively free. Syntactic functions (subject, direct object etc.) were marked by means of inflectional endings. With the decay of inflectional endings, another way of signalling these functions emerged. Now the major syntactic functions were indicated by the position of the constituents in the clause. The subject is the constituent immediately preceding the verb phrase and the object is the constituent immediately following the verb phrase. This SVO order had already been current in Old English. But the important development in Middle English syntax is the establishment of this fixed pattern in both main and subordinate clauses. Thus, by the end of Middle English SVO is the major word order pattern of English.

Of course, we still find some deviant structures in Middle English, which basically go back to Old English. There is the "verb final" pattern, in which other elements of the clause come between subject and verb. In Old English this pattern was typical of subordinate clauses. In Middle English "verb final" also appears in subordinate clauses, especially when the subject or object is short (see, for instance, the pronouns *they* and *hem* in example 2 below). In (2) we find a temporal subordinate clause introduced by *whan* that shows the verb final pattern (*mysavyse*).

(2) I sey nat this by wyves that been wyse,
But if it be whan they hem mysavyse.
"I am not saying this about sensible wives, unless it should be that they act unadvisedly ("when they for themselves take the wrong counsel")."
(Chaucer, *The Wife of Bath's Prologue*; c1395; HC)

Inverted word order, where the subject follows the verb (VS), was found in Old English especially when the clause started with an adverbial. A similar situation is found in Middle English. Here the VS-pattern is particularly likely in main clauses that are introduced by adverbials, by a negative particle or an indirect object. In example (3) the adverbial *therfore* triggers inversion (*ete I*), in example (4) the VS-pattern follows the negative particle *ne* (note also the direct object *Latin* in initial position).

(3) therfore ete I gladly lyght mete.
"Therefore I gladly eat light meals."
(Caxton, *Reynard the Fox*; 1481; HC)

(4) for Latyn ne canst thou yit but small, my litel sone.
"For you know hardly any Latin yet, my small son."
(Chaucer, *A Treatise on the Astrolabe*; 1391; HC)

The VS-pattern is also found in Middle English interrogatives. In example (5) below the second-person singular of *wille* (*wilt*) is followed by the subject (*thou*).

(5) "A! wilt thou so?"
"Ah, do you want it like this?"
(*Towneley Plays*; a1460; HC)

You will note that *do*-support, which is obligatory in Modern English interrogatives, is not yet found in Middle English (just like in Old English). This is a developed associated with the Early Modern period (see Chapter 5.2.3.).

Do-support is not required either in Middle English negation. Initially, Middle English clauses were usually negated by placing the negative particle *ne* or *na* in front of the finite verb. In example (6) below *ne* precedes the finite verb *haue*.

(6) J ne haue hws, Y ne haue cote.
"I don't have a house; I don't have a hut."
(*Havelok*; c1300; HC)

To reinforce the negation, quite often a post-verbal negative adverb (*nawiht, noght*, or *nat / not*) was used. In example (7) below the verb *cume* ("came") is surrounded by *ne* and *noght*, in example (8) the verb *reyneth* ("rains") by *ne* and *not*.

(7) I ne cume noght for to do my wille, bot my fadirs þat me sent.
"I did not come to carry out my own will, but the will of my father who sent me."
(*Benedictine Rule*; a1425; HC)

(8) it ne reyneth not in þat contree ...
"It does not rain in that country ..."
(*Mandeville's Travels*; c1400; HC)

Later on (basically, from the middle of the fourteenth century onwards), the post-verbal negative, became the common way of negating a clause (see *sey nat* in example (9) and *woot nott* in example (10).

(9) I sey nat this for noght.
"I say this quite seriously ("I don't say this for nothing.")."
(Chaucer, *The Merchant's Tale*; c1395; HC)

(10) I woot nott whethyre I maye trust thys Lady Brandon.
"I do not know, whether I can trust this Lady Brandon."
(*Paston Letters*; 1472; HC)

Since the negative particles *ne* and *noght / not* co-occurred quite often (see examples 7 and 8 above), constructions involving multiple negation (also called negative concord) were quite frequent in Middle English. But fairly often we encounter more than two negations in one clause. Example (11) below contains *ne, nat* and two items of *no*. In Example (12) we find *ne, nævre* and *nan*.

(11) thou ne shalt nat seen in no place no thing of yvil.
"You will nowhere see anything evil."
(Chaucer, *Boethius*; c1380; HC)

(12) ne wæren nævre nan martyrs swa pined.
"No martyrs were ever so tortured."
(*Peterborough Chronicle*; c1150; HC)

It is important to see that the extra negatives serve a purely stylistic function. They increase the effect of the negation. This emphatic multiple negation remained quite common throughout Middle English.

Just as in Old English, we find ample use of coordination in Middle English texts. It seems that coordination was particularly common in earlier texts and in documents associated with oral transmission. The extract in example (13) below is from a sermon cycle designed for itinerant preachers who used to address common people. Note the long series of coordinated sentences linked by *and*.

(13) **And** þus clene loue puttuþ owt alle synne. **And** in þis lore schulden men studye, **and** þis charite schulde moue men to speke stabully herof. **And** among alle men þat synnon aȝenys charite, þes foure sectis ... semon more stefly to synne aȝeyn þe lawe of charite. **And** heere is somwhat to speke aȝenys þe furste of þes foure.

"**And** thus pure love extinguishes all sin. **And** on this conduct people should concentrate, **and** this charity should cause men to speak reasonably about it. **And** among all people that sin against charity, these four orders ... seem to sin more forcefully against the law of charity. **And** here is something to be said against the first of these four."
(*Wycliffite Sermons*; c1400; HC)

In the above example *and* is used in a purely additive way. Any further logical relationships between the sentences must be worked out by the reader (or listener). Most of these links may appear strange and superfluous to a present-day recipient. The style of many Middle English sermons and homilies has been called "rambling" and "conversational", which is, of course, also due to the extensive use of coordinating conjunctions.

On the other hand, we find a significant rise of subordinating constructions in late Middle English. This is due firstly to an increase in the inventory of subordinating conjunctions. For example, Kortmann (1997) lists 40 adverbial subordinators for Old English, but 74 for Middle English. Secondly, Middle English (especially late Middle English) shows a preference for non-finite constructions (that is, above all, infinitive and participle constructions). Look at the participles in examples (14) and (15) below (*thinking* and *knowing* in (14); *compleynyng*, *expleyntyng* and *seying* in (15)).

(14) So this emperoure, Octauyan, was wise and discrete. Thinking and knowing that he was but a man as oþir men be, he durst not take vpon hym þe name of God.
"So this emperor Octavian was wise and prudent. Thinking and knowing that he was just a human being as other humans [are], he did not dare to assume the name of God."
(John Mirk, *Advent and Nativity Sermons*; Powell 1981)

(15) .. þer cam a ȝong man to þis prest, .., compleynyng to þe preste of pouerte & disese whech he was fallyn in be infortunyte, expleyntyng þe cawse of infortunyte, seying also he had takyn holy orderys for to be a preste.
"There came a young man to this priest, complaining to the priest about poverty and illness he had fallen in due to misfortune, explaining the cause of the misfortune, saying also that he had taken holy orders to become a priest."
(*The Book of Margery Kempe*; c1438; HC)

The participle constructions in the two excerpts above very much resemble the constructions in Modern English (as you can see in the parallel translations). They show that by the fifteenth century Middle English already had a certain range of subordinate constructions which may contribute to a more varied and possibly "elegant" style and which may serve a larger range of text functions (in the above case, above all narration and lively description). This increase in subordinating constructions, which we witness towards the latter part of the Middle English period, is continued in the Early Modern period, where it can be seen as one of the major means of elaboration and refinement of text structure.

To a native speaker of present-day English, relative clauses in Middle English may appear more familiar than those in Old English. But they still show considerable differences to those used today. In early Middle English texts, the Old English relative particles *þe* and *þa* are still found, but during the largest part of Middle English the most common relative pronoun was *þat* ("that"). This pronoun was used with both personal and non-personal antecedents. In example (16) *þat* refers back to *an cæste* ("a chest") and in (17) *that* refers back to *God*.

(16) an cæste þat was scort
"a chest that was short"
(*Peterborough Chronicle*; c1150; HC)

(17) ... which may in any manere displese God, that is youre creatour and makere.
"... which my in any way displease God, who is your creator and maker."
(Chaucer, *The Tale of Melibee*; c1390; HC)

We find also uses of *that* as a relative pronoun lacking an antecedent. Such uses can be paraphrased by "he who" or "that which". In example (18) below *þat* can be translated with *him/her who* or *anybody who*.

(18) þe devel have þat reche
"the devil take him /her who bothers"
(Langland, *Piers Plowman;* c1362–1393; CMEPV)

Starting from the fourteenth century, the interrogative pronoun *which* is used as a relative pronoun. Like *that*, *which* can refer to both personal and non-personal antecedents. In example (19) *which* refers to *a thousand men*, in example (20) to *concupiscence*.

(19) ... she may chesen of a thousand men which she wol take to hir housbonde.
"She may choose from a thousand men whom she may take as her husband."
(Chaucer, *The Tale of Melibee*; c1390; HC)

(20) ... thurgh concupiscence, which yet is cleped norrissynge of synne and occasioun of synne.
"... through carnal desire, which is (nevertheless) called nourishing of sin and opportunity for sin."
(Chaucer, *The Parson's Tale*; c1390; HC)

Quite often *which* is accompanied by the determiners *the* or *that*. The combination *the which* or *which that* is fairly frequent (see examples 21 and 22).

(21) So at that tyme there was a knyght, the which was the kynges son of Irelonde ...
"So at that time there was a knight who was the son of the king of Ireland ..."
(Malory, *Morte Darthur*; a1470; HC)

(22) He which that hath no wyf, I holde hym shent.
"A man who has no wife, I think he is ruined."
(Chaucer, *The Merchant's Tale*; c1395; HC)

Sometimes the combination *the which* is attached to the repeated antecedent, which results in a rather stilted construction. Compare *of the which horryble mourdure* ("of which horrible murder") in example (23) below. Here a somewhat idiomatic Modern English translation should start a new sentence.

(23) And thus the said Iohn mourdered horrebely his wijff. of the which horryble mourdure the said Iohn was endyteth ...

"And thus the said John murdered his wife in a horrible way; of this horrible murder the said John was accused ..."
(*Chancery Petitions*; 1433; Fisher et al. 1984: 235)

The genitive form *whos* and the object form *whom* emerge as relative pronouns in Late Middle English. The subject form *who*, however, is almost exclusively used as an interrogative pronoun and hardly ever found as a relative pronoun before the sixteenth century.

A disturbing factor to speakers of present-day English is the fact that in Middle English relative pronouns can be omitted in subject position. In present-day English this is only possible in object position (*The man (whom) I saw is my teacher*). But in Middle English we find the following constructions:

(24) for hym the boght ...
"for him who redeemed you ..."
(*The York Plays*; a1450; CMEPV)

(25) Biforn a cors / was caried / to his graue
"in front of a corpse, which was being carried to its grave"
(Chaucer, *The Pardoner's Tale*; c1392 – 95; CMEPV)

The constructions in (24) and (25) only make sense if we insert *who* / *that* after *hym* and *cors*. To uninitiated readers such relative clauses may be quite confusing.

Now we turn to the impersonal construction. The impersonal construction, an Old English pattern which lacks a nominative subject but can have a dative, genitive or accusative object (see Chapter 3.2.3.), quite interestingly, did not disappear but was expanded in Middle English, with many new verbs entering the pattern. Some typical examples are *me lusteth* "it pleases me" and *me needeth* "it is necessary to me" (see examples 26 and 27).

(26) the leest officer that hym lust meynteigne
"the lowest-ranking officer whom he was pleased ("it pleased him") to support ..."
(*Petitions*; 1388; HC)

(27) hem neded no dwale
"No sleeping potion was necessary to them ("they did not need a sleeping potion")."
(Chaucer, *The Reeve's Tale*; c1388 – 92; CMEPV)

But this construction did not survive very long after the Middle English period and was soon restricted to fixed formulae (for example, *methinks*). Later on it died out and only lives on in certain archaic uses.

4.2.4. Lexis and semantics

Let us recapitulate that the Old English vocabulary was mainly Germanic. It contained some loan words, especially Latin borrowings, most of which were added in the wake of Christianisation. But these loans only formed about three percent of the total word stock. Thus it seems fair to say that the vocabulary of the Anglo-Saxon texts which have come down to us is fairly uniform as regards its origin.

This situation is completely different in Middle English. Middle English is the period when the English vocabulary undergoes a thorough change. The major factors of influence were French, Latin and the Scandinavian languages (whose influence probably reaches back to Anglo-Saxon times). In addition, we witness limited influence from a couple of other languages (for example, Dutch, Spanish, Portuguese, and Irish). The following sections will focus on the impact of French, Latin and the Scandinavian languages.

Since after the Norman Conquest French was the language of the upper classes in England, it seems only natural that French exerted considerable influence on the English vocabulary. As we saw in Chapter 4.1., the position of Anglo-Norman became weaker during the centuries, but Central French remained a highly prestigious language right until the end of the period. Traditionally, two periods of borrowing of French loan words are distinguished, with the middle of the thirteenth century forming a rough dividing line (see Baugh and Cable 2002). In the first period, that is, approximately until 1250, fewer words were borrowed, mostly from Norman French. They reflect the role of French as the language of the upper classes and what native speakers of English would pick up when communicating with them. They include *baroun* "baron", *noble* "noble", *servaunt* "servant", *messager* "messenger", *justice* "law, justice", *obedience* "obedience", *prisoun* "prison", *werre* "war" and others. Most of them still retain specific features of Anglo-Norman phonology in their borrowed form (on this see below). The loan words of the second period, that is, roughly from the middle of the thirteenth century onwards, are much more numerous and derive chiefly from Central French. The loans of the second period obviously reflect the urge of the upper classes to include terms of the international prestige variety in their own language. As a consequence, they are in many cases "elaborate" and "refined" terms. They belong to the domains of administration, law, the church, the army, fashion (including cooking), art and scholarship. Here are a few examples: *religioun* "religion", *omelie* "homily", *governement* "government", *coroune* "crown", *treisoun* "treason", *crime* "crime", *armee* "army", *navie* "navy", *pes* "peace", *robe* "robe", *veil* "veil", *diner* "dinner", *sopere* "supper", *taste* "taste", *peine* "pain", *peinten* "to paint", *palais* "palace", *poete* "poet", *title* "title", *papire* "paper", *studien* "to study".

The loan words of the two periods differ in some specific phonological features. This is because in Central French certain sounds developed differently from the Northern variety of Norman French. For example, Anglo-Norman loans typically contain /ka/, where borrowings from Central French have /tʃa/. Thus, *cattle* contrasts with *chattel*, *catch* with *chase* because both were borrowed from the same French terms, but at different times. In a similar way, Anglo-Norman has /w/ in initial position where Central French has /g/. So we get *warden* vs. *guardian* and *warrant* vs. *guarantee*.

It seems only natural that, with the arrival of hundreds or even thousands of new French words, many native Germanic words were lost. As was mentioned in the chapter on the Old English vocabulary, an estimated 85 per cent of the Old English lexemes are no longer in use. On the other hand, in some cases both native and loan word coexisted, forming slightly different but still more or less synonymous senses (see, for example, *hearty* vs. *cordial*, *house* vs. *mansion*, *doom* vs. *judgment*, *child* vs. *infant* and so on).

As we observed in the chapter on Middle English morphology and word-formation, the vast number of words borrowed from French also resulted in a partial decline of native patterns of word-formation and in the adoption of new French affixes.

The second language which exerted a major influence on the Middle English vocabulary was Latin. Latin had already had a considerable impact on some learned registers of Old English. As the language of international scholarship and the language of the Church liturgy, it maintained this influence also during the Middle English period. However, most loans can be dated at the fourteenth and fifteenth centuries. In contrast to French loans, they reflect language contact in the written medium and language use dominated by men. Major fields of borrowing include law, theology, Bible translation, medicine, science and literature. Here are a few examples: *allegorie* "allegory", *contempt* "contempt", *historie* "history", *infancie* "infancy", *nervous* "nervous", *promoten* "promote", *meditacioun* "meditation", *solar* "solar", *tract* "tract". It is often fairly difficult to tell with certainty whether the word came directly from Latin or whether it entered English via French.

It is frequently said that the various French-based and Latin-based borrowings have enriched the English lexicon. This is, first of all, true with regard to the sheer number of words. English seems to have a fairly large vocabulary (in comparison to other modern Western European languages), and a major step towards this expansion of the word stock happened during the Middle English period (but in this context the influx of loanwords during the Early Modern English period must be considered as well). The size of the growth can also be recognised when looking at the proportion of native words and loan words at the beginning and at the end of the Middle English period. In early Middle English about 90 per cent of the words are estimated to be native; towards the end of the fifteenth century this share has shrunken to 75 per cent. Also, beyond the sheer number of words, English has a large inventory of synonyms. In present-day English several concepts can be expressed in three different ways, using a native, a French-based or a Latin-based term (for example, *ask – question – interrogate, kingly – royal – regal*). On the whole, one can say that French-based and Latin-based synonyms are more learned and literary, whereas the native words reflect "direct" ways of referring to everyday items. But this generalisation certainly needs qualification since there are many French-based loans denoting everyday items in a straightforward manner (for example, *prison, pain, crime, army* etc.).

The third factor which affected the Middle English vocabulary was the influence of the Scandinavian languages. Scandinavian loan words in Middle English reflect the linguistic effects of the Viking invasions which happened in the latter part of the Anglo-Saxon period (see Chapter 3.1.). Due to the overwhelming influence of the West Saxon literary language it is assumed that they did not come to the surface during the Old English period but made themselves felt only in manuscripts starting from the thirteenth century, mostly in the Northern and Eastern regions of the Danelaw, where the major Scandinavian settlements were and Old Norse was spoken. The interchange between the Anglo-Saxons and the Norse peoples must have been intensive, resulting in a fairly profound influence on the language. Scandinavian loans include quite a few common words for everyday objects but also some function words (on these see Chapter 4.2.2.). Some common examples are (*dien* "to die", *knif* "knife", *laue* "law", *skin* "skin", *taken* "to take"; function words include, for example, the third-person plural pronouns starting with *th*). At first, Scandinavian loan words had a specific regional distribution, but they seem to have gradually spread to other parts of the country and soon became part of the common word stock.

Some of the Scandinavian loans developed doublets. Since many words in both languages were comparatively similar in form and meaning (Old English and Old Norse were both Germanic languages), we find Scandinavian forms (e.g. *kyrk* "church", *gyfe* "give", mostly in Northern texts) and native forms (*chirche*, *yive*, mostly in Southern texts). In some cases (for example, in *skirt* vs. *shirt*) the doublets developed different meanings.

One of the most noticeable differences between Old English and Middle English is that especially late Middle English texts strike one as much more modern, that is, so much closer to Modern English than Anglo-Saxon texts. In particular, there are so many words which seem quite familiar to a speaker of present-day English. Such an impression may, however, be quite deceptive because many words, although they are similar in form, have changed their meaning since Middle English times. An instructive example of such a "false friend" is the adjective *nice*, which can be paraphrased with "pleasant, attractive, kind, friendly" in most contexts in present-day English. In Middle English, however, the term was often used with a totally different meaning. In Trevisa's translation of Higden's *Polychronicon*, a copious learned Latin chronicle from the thirteenth century (the translation is from the fourteenth century), we find *nyce* in the sense of "foolish, stupid, senseless":

(28) He made þe lady so mad and so nyce þat she worschipped hym as þe grettest prophete of God Almy3ty.
"He made the lady so crazy and stupid that she worshiped him as the greatest prophet of God Almighty."
(Higden, *Polychronicon*; c1327; CMEPV)

Chaucer uses *nyce* quite often in order to refer to a person as "wanton" or even "lascivious":

(29) Nyce she was, but she mente Noone harme ne slight in hir entente, But oonely lust & jolyte.
"She was lascivious, but she did not intend harm or offence, but only lust and sexual pleasure."
(Chaucer, *The Romaunt of the Rose*; Chaucer 1987: 700)

There are many other words which show similarly profound changes of meaning. Whereas *nice* is used in present-day English in a clearly more positive way than in Middle English (a change of meaning which is called amelioration), the word *silly* shows the opposite development, that is, it has assumed a more negative core meaning in present-day English (this change is also called pejoration). In Middle English it is often used in the sense of "innocent, simple", not in the sense of "stupid". Still another type of change, which is called specialisation, is reflected in Middle English *mete* ("meat"). In Middle English *mete* denotes any kind of food, whereas in Modern English the term was specialised to refer to non-vegetarian food. Some words seem to have lost their neutral core meaning due to the arrival of a synonymous French loan word. Thus, the native terms *smear* and *stench* have adopted more negative connotations since the arrival of the French-based terms *anoint* and *odour*.

Sometimes "false friends" may hide behind absolutely common function words. Middle English *cunne* "can", for example, cannot be equated with Modern English *can* in many contexts. Its core meaning is quite often "to be able to, to know how to". If the present-day meaning is taken for granted, this may result in serious misinterpretations. Look at the following excerpt from Chaucer's *Canterbury Tales*. Here a young knight would like to know what thing women desire most.

(30) "My leeve mooder," quod this knyght,"certain
I nam but deed but if that I kan seyn
What thyng it is that wommen moost desire.
Koude ye me wisse, I wolde wel quite youre hire."
"My dear mother, said this knight. I will certainly be dead ('nam' = *ne am*) unless I am able to tell what thing it is that women desire most. If you could tell me, I would reward your efforts."
(Chaucer, *The Wife of Bath's Tale*; c1395 CMEPV)

Here one might be led to believe that the last line (*Koude ye me wisse, I wolde wel quite youre hire.*) should be paraphrased with *Could you please instruct me? I would certainly reward your efforts*. But in fact the syntactic pattern contains a conditional clause (with inverted VS word order) and a full verb *koude* ("knew how to"), which could be paraphrased as *If you could tell me (knew how to instruct me), I would reward your efforts*. The difficulty of interpretation is here due to the fact that the verb *cunne* was still used as a full verb in this period (in addition to the fact that the inverted clause pattern (*koude ye*) could be used to form a conditional clause).

4.2.5. Regional and social distribution

After the Norman Conquest English lost most of its supralocal, that is, national functions as a means of communication. Its use did no longer include official, administrative or scholarly writing, which was basically the realm of French and Latin. Especially during the first centuries of the period, the number of writings in the vernacular and the range of genres covered by English texts were rather restricted, and it seems that the major function of English was oral communication between the members of the non-upper classes. This lack of a national written standard was in contrast to late Old English, where West Saxon had acquired a more or less regularised use in the written mode, which spread across the country. With the loss of its supralocal functions after 1066, this focussed system dissolved. Now, when English was written down, it was in most cases the local variety and it was most of all more or less idiosyncratic adaptations of the spelling to local pronunciation that appeared in the manuscripts. As a result, linguistic variation is pervasive in Middle English texts, and Middle English has been called the period of dialectal diversification of the written language (for examples of the variability of spelling, see example (1) in Chapter 4.2.1.).

Traditionally, five regional dialects of Middle English are distinguished: Northern, which extends from the river Humber further up North, the East-Midland and the West-Midland dialects, basically covering the Midlands area, Kentish in the South-East and, in the South West, basically on the territory of former West-Saxon, the Southern dialect (see Map 1 below). Of course, such a subdivision into five areas can only give a very broad outline and a very rough sketch. Research has shown that there are no single neat dividing lines between individual regional dialects and that there is a lot of heterogeneity within each dialect. However, despite this great internal variability, it is true that a "typical" text from the North is quite different from a "typical" text from the South and fairly often the difference between these texts can be linked to "typical" dialect features. Thus, there is an inventory of distinctive grammatical endings and spellings which may serve as a broad but instructive first orientation when dealing with Middle English regional dialects.

Such typical indicators of dialectal provenance may, for example, be found in some inflectional endings of Middle English verbs. The third-person singular present tense ending was *–es* in the North and North Midlands, *-eth* in the South and South Midlands. Thus the form *heres* "he hears" would point to the North, whereas *hereth* would be associated with the South. In a similar way, the plural present tense suffix was *–es* in the North, *-e(n)* or *-on* in the North-West Midlands, East Midlands and London, and *-eth* in the South and South-West Midlands. The ending of the first participle (the "*ing*-form" in Modern English) was *–and(e)* in the North, *-inde* in the South-West Midlands, *-ende* in the East, and *–ing* was the general Southern and Midland form. In the section on Middle English pronouns (see Chapter 4.2.2.) we saw that the distribution of the native and Scandinavian plural pronouns was an indicator of region. Those forms which stem from Old Norse (*thai, thair, tham*) are found in the North and later in the East Midlands. The native type (*hi, hire, hem*) is typical of the South. The mixed type, with the Scandinavian form in the subject case and native forms in the other cases, prevailed in the Midlands and in London.

There are also manifestations of individual vowels and consonants (or rather vowel- and consonant-phonemes) which are linked to particular regions. For example, the vowel [a:] in words like *stane* "stone", *hame* "home" and *bane* "bone" is predominantly found north of the river Humber, whereas the version with [o:] (*stone, home, bone*) is found in the South. In a similar way [k], [s] and [f] as Northern forms contrast with the Southern counterparts [tʃ], [ʃ] and [v]. Thus, we find *kirke* vs. *chirche* "church", *sal* vs. *shal* "shall" and *for* vs. *vor* "for".

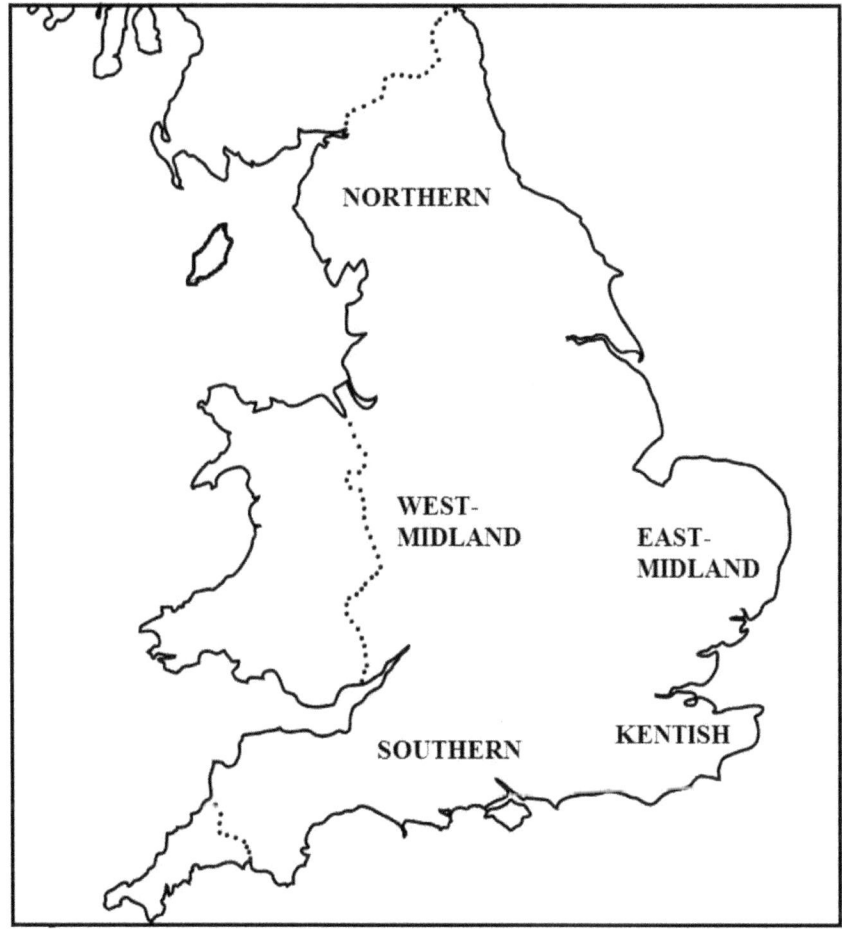

Map 1: The dialects of Middle English

103

It is important to keep in mind that the above features do not necessarily and unambiguously point to a specific origin of a text. As was mentioned before, there are no clear-cut borderlines between the dialect regions and within each dialect there is a lot of internal variation. Although they may very well serve as an initial orientation, it is best to use them in combination when trying to locate a text.

This situation is complicated by the fact that quite a few manuscripts seem to show a mixture of dialects. This may be because the scribe lived in a border area or an area influenced by several major dialects. Many scribes may also have travelled around the country and thus picked up differing features. In addition, manuscripts were often copied, resulting in an idiosyncratic mixture of features. However we may speculate about the background and the reasons, many manuscripts seem to be fairly inconsistent in their use of forms and spelling variants.

A major project at the University of Edinburgh, *A Linguistic Atlas of Late Medieval English* (abbreviated as LALME; McIntosh et al. 1986) has shown the real extent and quality of the complexities associated with the Middle English dialects by including a massive number of (localised) manuscripts and the spelling variants found in them. By plotting the distribution of the spelling variants of individual items (independently of their assumed sound quality) on maps, the atlas is able to give a more accurate picture of the real variability of linguistic forms as represented by (late) Middle English manuscripts. Apart from revealing the complexities of Middle English dialects, the systematic evidence of LALME can also be used to assess the provenance of manuscripts which could not be localised so far.

In the course of late Middle English we can see that the extent of variability slowly declines and certain manuscripts become more consistent in their use of spelling variants. Some texts of the fifteenth century do not show so many characteristic dialect features that may clearly betray their provenance. This process is often called the standardisation of written English. It is closely linked with the re-establishment of English, with English being no longer restricted to local use but emerging as the dominant medium of communication in important domains of language use. It is true that such extended use required a form of language which was more "standardised", that is more consistent. On the other hand, we must accept that late Middle English was far away from a modern standard language, with dictionaries and reference grammars.

Some of these early forms of a more coherent, or focussed, language use have been called "incipient standards" (Samuels 1963). Samuels identified several "types", which stem from the fourteenth and fifteenth centuries and show typical recurring manifestations of variants in several manuscripts. For example, "type

I" stems from the Central Midlands and is associated with the writings of John Wycliffe (and his followers) and some medical treatises. Typical recurring forms are, for example, *sich* "such", *youun* "given" and *si3* "saw". "Type III" is the Ellesmere manuscript of Chaucer's *Canterbury Tales*, with *swiche* "such", *yaf* "gave" and *thise* "these" as typical forms. "Type IV" comprises government documents from the fifteenth century and is called "Chancery English". Examples of typical recurring forms are *such(e)* "such", *gaf* "gave" and *thes(e)* "these". One should note that all of these "incipient standard" varieties (except for Type 1) are London varieties. This, of course, reflects the central importance of London as the major administrative and commercial centre of England.

Given these initial tendencies towards a standardisation of spelling, scholars have asked themselves how and where this written standard originated and by which agency it spread across the country and was more or less consistently accepted. Several contributory factors have been suggested.

Some earlier scholars believed that the initial standard was the achievement of individual authors, especially great writers like Geoffrey Chaucer, but also John Gower and John Lydgate. This tradition is quite old and can be traced back to the first printer William Caxton, who in several of the prefaces to his books says that it was these writers who formed the new modern English language. However, this view is quite questionable and rather unrealistic. Although Chaucer's works were fairly popular, forming a model for many poets of the fifteenth century, his literary language would not have enough social impact to form a written standard that could spread to all sections of society. Literary language has always had rather limited social influence.

A more likely factor which seems to have contributed to the spread of the new standard is the London merchants. As was said above, the new standard was based in London and reflected important dialect features of the capital (although many of them actually belong to the East Midland dialect). The merchants were a powerful group in London and, with their trade routes, maintained an efficient network covering the whole of the country. For example, the wool trade established close links to East Anglia, Yorkshire, Cumbria, Gloucestershire and the South West. So it is quite likely that this network formed a basis for the spread of the forms of the new standard across the country.

A well-documented contribution to standardisation is Chancery English (see Fisher 1996). Chancery English (or King's English) comprises the language of the government documents, which since the beginning of the fifteenth century were more and more frequently written in English. The term "Chancery" refers to the royal administration which, since Edward III, had found a permanent residence at

Westminster. Here the Chancery became a self-perpetuating organisation with a strict hierarchy and a uniform training system. This training system included, among other things, a consistent form of language use, which was passed on to each new generation of clerks. Thus, Chancery English constituted a more or less uniform language usage combined with the high prestige of the king's writ. It is quite likely that Chancery English made a most important contribution to the formation and spread of the new written standard. The more consistent features of Chancery spelling can be noted most clearly in words of Germanic origin because here variability had been greatest. Consistent Chancery usage can also be seen in certain inflectional endings (for example, *-eth*, *-ed*, *-ing/-yng*, *–ly*) and the forms of some pronouns (for example, *I*, *my*, *myn(e)*, *ye*, *you*, *yow*).

Quite interestingly, the focused writing conventions found in the fourteenth and fifteenth centuries (especially Chancery English) formed a blend of dialect forms which did not necessarily bear any direct connection to spoken language. It seems that these patterns were taught to all clerks and scribes, independent of their local background. But it goes without saying that in these documents complete consistency in spelling was not yet achieved. Rather, there emerged a pattern of conformity which differed markedly from previous Middle English writings.

Some scholars claim that the spread and acceptance of Chancery English was due to the influence and support of the Lancastrian monarchy, above all Henry V. In particular, Richardson (1980) has traced Chancery English to the usage of Henry V's Signet Office. Henry V used English for all the letters he sent from France on his second tour (after 1417). Also, the majority of his private correspondence between 1417 and 1422 was written in English. It may also be that Henry used English in order to arouse nationalism and to rally support for his war with France.

So far we have talked about regional variation and incipient standardisation. There is not much clear evidence for social variation in Middle English. It is true that in terms of lexis, the use of French and Latin loanwords was highly prestigious. But this seems to be a matter of different levels of style in literary composition. Whether a certain variety of speech was stigmatised or prestigious is much more difficult to decide. Chaucer, in his *Reeve's Tale*, seems to poke fun at the language of Northerners, and in the *Second Shepherds' Play* a Southern variety is introduced as a somewhat prestigious language form. But in each case it is difficult to work out exactly what communicative intention is linked to the humorous presentation. There is no explicit statement which would clearly designate any of the varieties as either prestigious or stigmatised. Such statements only occur in the Early Modern period or later.

4.3. Language use

4.3.1. Discourse and speech acts

In the section on speech acts in Old English (Chapter 3.3.1.) we saw that the Anglo-Saxons seem to have lacked the kinds of requests we term "indirect" in contemporary English, for example, *Could you give me a hand? Will you do me a favour?* Instead, they seem to have preferred more "direct" manifestations, for example, performatives, that is, directives making the point of the speech act explicit by using a speech-act verb in the first person, or they used the version with "you must / have to". What are typical directive manifestations in Middle English?

In a study on the requests involving speaker volition (Kohnen 2002), that is, first-person constructions with *will* or *would* (for example, *I would like you to do this for me* in contemporary English), it turned out that Middle English, especially in the fourteenth and fifteenth century, showed a high frequency of manifestations with *will* (see *we willen* in example 31 and *we wol* in example 32 below).

(31) we willen and hoaten þæt alle vre treowe heom healden deadliche ifoan.
"We order and demand that all our subjects consider them deadly enemies."
(*Proclamation*, Henry III; 1258; HC)

(32) we wol and charge you. þat ye se and ordeyne þat hasty resticion of þe forsaide goodes be maad ..
"We order and command (you) that you make arrangements that quick restitution of the said goods be made."
(*Letters*, Henry V; 1418; HC)

The above examples stem from proclamations and official letters issued by the king. It is no surprise that the large majority of such items containing *will* are used to perform strict orders and commands, because official documents addressed to subordinates would be a typical occasion for such directives. Quite interestingly, these items form the large majority of the examples found. In fact, most of these Middle English directives involving *will* must be seen as performative uses. The verb *will* is a verb denoting not only speaker volition but also a speech act and can be paraphrased with "order". Typically such formulations with *will* often occur together with other directive speech act verbs (see *hoaten* "demand" and *charge* "command" in the above examples). Thus, it seems that in Middle English the expression of speaker volition could not serve as a means to mitigate the possible threat connected with a directive speech act. Rather, it seems that the statement of speaker volition could serve as a common means of issuing a straight command in an asymmetric communication situation. Today, such unqualified expression of the speaker's will is no longer seen as an appropriate way of making requests.

A similar tendency of Middle English directives to be more "direct" and "straightforward" was revealed in another study of the imperative in religious treatises in Middle English and Modern English (Kohnen 2004). The genre of religious treatise, both in its late medieval and its modern form, has a basic instructional function, which makes it likely for imperatives to be used there. The study showed that imperatives in the period between 1200 and 1375 were fairly frequent (4.5 in 1,000 words), but the frequency went down in late Middle English (1.9). By contrast, the frequency in the Modern English treatises was less than half of that in late Middle English.

One interesting difference between the Middle English imperatives and the Modern English examples was the kind of activity the verb denotes. Whereas the Middle English examples typically referred to concrete actions (*do gode deedis* "do good deeds" in example 33 below and *preie for hem* "pray for them" in example 34), the Modern English items involved mostly cognitive acts involving the reception of the text (for example, *think* in 35). Such requests are, of course, fairly "harmless" as opposed to the concrete instructions contained in the Middle English examples.

(33) þerfore do þou þi-silf alle þe gode deedis wiþ-oute deuocioun, þe whiche þou didist bifore with deuocioun.
"Therefore, do (you) yourself all the good deeds without earnestness which you did with earnestness before."
(*Hilton's Eight Chapters on Perfection*; a1396; HC)

(34) and preie ȝe hertly for hem, that God of his greet mercy ȝeue to hem very knowing of scripturis, and meekenesse, and charite.
"And pray (you) fervently for them, that God of his great mercy may give them true knowledge of the scriptures and meekness and love."
(*Purvey's General Prologue to the Bible*; c1388; HC)

(35) Think of the number of laws that have just as much to do with a man's soul as with his body.
(*LOB-Corpus*, D16, 11–13; 1961)

Another class of speech acts which may reveal interesting differences, but also similarities to Modern English speech-act conventions are insults. In a study on verbal aggression in Chaucer's *Canterbury Tales* (Jucker 2000), the author analyses typical features of late Middle English insults as they are found in the works of Chaucer. Insults serve the basic function of offending and disparaging the addressee (if the addressee is the aim of the insult). Quite interestingly, many of them are religious in nature and often contain pious expressions like *by Jhesu Crist* or *by Seint John*. But we also find name calling and scatology. Look at example (36). In this scene an old man is being insulted by one of three rogues because he did not comply with their request (to tell them whether he had seen Death).

(36) "Nay, olde cherl, by god, thou shalt not so,"
Seyde this oother hasardour anon;
"Thou partest nat so lightly, by Seint John!
Thou spak right now of thilke traytour deeth,
That in this contree alle oure freendes sleeth.
Have heer my trouthe, as thou art his espye,
Telle where he is, or thou shalt it abye,
By god, and by the hooly sacrement!
For soothly thou art oon of his assent
To sleen us yonge folk, thou false theef!"
"'No, you old wretch, by God, you won't,' said another of these gamblers straight away. 'You don't get away so easily, by St. John. Just now you spoke about that traitor Death, who kills all our friends in this district. It's my belief you're his spy. You tell me where he is or you'll pay for it, by God and by the Holy Sacrament! You've clearly ganged up with him to kill us young people, you lying thief.'" (Wilcockson 2008: 537; 539)
(Chaucer, *The Pardoner's Tale*; c1392 – 95; CMEPV)

The insult addressed to the old man contains, first of all, the rather rude terms *olde cherl* ("old wretch") and *false theef* ("lying thief"). But the insult is also accompanied by religious curses, *by God, by Seint John* and *by God, and by the hooly sacrement*. Whereas designations like *olde cherl* and *false theef* may well sound like insults today, the religious curses seem to have lost their force. This is probably because today Christian religion and the teachings of the church are no longer as pervasive in every branch of life as they were in the Middle Ages.

The following excerpt (37) includes a blunt example of scatology, again combined with religious swearing. Here the Host insults the Pardoner (as a reaction to the Pardoner's attempts to sell his relics and make the Host even kiss them).

(37) "Nay, nay! quod he, thanne have I cristes curs!
Lat be," quod he, "it shal nat be, so theech!
Thou woldest make me kisse thyn olde breech,
And swere it were a relyk of a seint,
Though it were with thy fundement depeint!
But, by the croys which that seint eleyne fond,
I wolde I hadde thy coillons in myn hond
In stide of relikes or os seintuarie.
Lat kutte hem of, I wol thee helpe hem carie;
They shul be shryned in an hogges toord!"
"'Oh no,' he said, 'then I would have the condemnation of Christ! Forget it,' he said, 'that's certainly not going to be done! You'd have me kiss your old underpants and swear the relic of a saint, even if they were stained with your bottom. But, by the cross St Helen found, I wish I had your testicles in my hand, instead of relics or a box for them, I'd cut them off and help you cart them around; they could be enshrined in a lump of hog's shit!'" (Wilcockson 2008: 549)
(Chaucer, *The Pardoner's Tale*; c1392 – 95; CMEPV)

The insult begins with the Host comparing the relics to or rather identifying them with the Pardoner's underpants and their stains. He then goes on suggesting that the Pardoner's testicles be cut off and "enshrined in a lump of hog's shit". These scatological references are accompanied by a religious oath (*by the croys which that Seint Eleyne fond* "by the cross St Helen found"). Again, to modern ears the pious oath seems rather lame in comparison to the several scatological references.

These two short examples nicely illustrate that some speech-act conventions may be stable across the centuries, whereas others may change. Oaths referring to the Christian religion do no longer automatically serve as insults whereas references to sex and excrements may still work.

4.3.2. Genres

Generally speaking, the writings from the Middle English period which have come down to us are much more numerous and various than those found in the Anglo-Saxon period. However, this only applies to the late Middle English period, when the vernacular was being re-established as a major means of communication. In the first part of the period, we do not find so many texts written in the vernacular.

In particular, there is a clear religious bias, just as in the Old English period. In this regard, the general picture of Middle English is quite similar to that of Old English. The prevalence of religious discourse cannot be denied (with a similar array of religious genres: sermons, homilies, treatises, saints' lives, rules, liturgical prayer collections etc.). However, during the fifteenth century, the rise of secular genres is clearly visible.

The development of texts of religious instruction in Middle English is closely connected with the decrees of the Fourth Lateran Council (1215). These decrees demanded, among other things, that every Christian layman confess their sins and receive communion once a year. This required an enhanced knowledge about the Christian faith both on the part of the laity and the lower clergy, which resulted in the emergence of a large variety of pieces of religious instruction that focussed on the basic elements of the Christian faith. Other major branches of religious discourse in Middle English comprise the controversial Wycliffite writings (including the Bible translation initiated by Wycliffe) and the so-called mystical tradition associated with Richard Rolle, Julian of Norwich, Walter Hilton and others.

The number of vernacular texts and the variety of genres which developed in the fourteenth and fifteenth centuries is so large that any short survey must necessarily be superficial and leave gaps. There is a substantial body of verse texts, both secular and religious. Among them we find verse chronicles, several religious verse genres (like saints' lives) and verse romances. Most important are, of course, the verse narrative works by Geoffrey Chaucer, William Langland, John Gower and John Lydgate.

We also find a wide range of prose genres in Middle English. Apart from the religious texts mentioned above, prose chronicles (among them the *Peterborough Chronicle*, a continuation of the *Anglo-Saxon Chronicle* and the earliest Middle English record), prose romances, medical and scientific treatises, medical handbooks, administrative and legal writings (petitions, official letters, wills, statutes), and personal letters.

In the following sections I will focus on two genres which may be called "new" genres because they evolved during the Middle English period: personal letters, as a prose genre, and mystery plays, as a verse genre.

Personal letters only emerged as a vernacular genre in late fourteenth-century and fifteenth-century England. The Middle English personal letters which have come down to us mainly belong to three large collections, the *Paston Letters*, the *Stonor Letters* and the *Cely Letters*. Initially, such letters were primarily business letters, whose aim it was to pass on information about trade and commerce and to secure business transactions. They were mostly written by the (lower) gentry and merchants. During the fifteenth century a growing number of letters were also written (or rather dictated) by women who were expected to provide their absent husbands (or parents) with relevant information about their home. Also, more personal matters, like marriage arrangements, love affairs etc. were included. Thus, personal letters do not only provide important information about local and social history, they give vivid depictions of the social and personal life of the middle and upper classes in fifteenth-century England.

From a linguistic point of view, letters are attractive because they tend to include informal, "conversational" language and language use typical of people who may be less educated and literate than renowned authors like Chaucer or learned churchmen. On the other hand, personal letters of the fifteenth century usually follow a fairly formal pattern in their introductory part, which stems from Medieval Latin and was shaped by the tradition of the so-called *ars dictaminis* (see also example 2 in Chapter 1). The *ars dictaminis* is a twelfth-century Medieval Latin term for the art of letter writing (it was also employed for the writing of documents). Its origins lie in Northern Italy, from where it spread to France, Spain and Germany, with vernacular extensions in England in the fourteenth and fifteenth centuries. For personal letters, the *ars dictaminis* prescribed certain fixed sections or steps which the letter writer had to follow when starting a letter and addressing the recipient.

The following example (38) is an extract based on Davis (1965), which gives the basic pattern of an opening section in a fifteenth-century letter "of a formal and respectful kind", but which was also followed in many personal letters we find in the fifteenth-century collections.

(38) Right worshipfull Maister, y hertly comaund me unto you with alle suche servise as y can or may, ... desyring to hire of youre welfare, the which y pray alle mighty Godde to preserve you to youre most pleasure and hertis desire. Please you to have enknowliche of my power welfare: at the making of this my letter y was in gode hele, and y trust in God within short space to be beter.
(Davis 1965: 236–237)

The letter starts with a form of address (usually *right* combined with an adjective of respect and the appropriate title: *Right worshipfull Maister*), which is followed by a formula commending the writer to the recipient (*y hertly comaund me unto you* "I sincerely recommend myself to you") plus an expression of humility (*with alle suche servise as y can or may*). When a child wrote to his or her parents, a request for blessing was added (*besekyng you of your blessing*). In the next step the letter writer was to express his or her desire to hear of the recipient's welfare (*desiryng to hire of youre welfare*), which was followed by a prayer for continuation of welfare (*the which y pray alle mighty Godde to preserve you to youre most pleasure and hertis desire* ("heart's desire")). Then the writer should provide a report about his or her own health, which was introduced by a conditional clause (*Please you to have enknowliche of my power* ("poor") *welfare*) and which usually contained a report of the writer's good health (*at the making of this my letter y was in gode hele, and y trust in God within short space to be beter*) to which thanks to God was added (*thanks bee to God*).

Quite interestingly, this pattern was followed more or less coherently right until the beginning of the sixteenth century. Occasionally, however, if the urgency of the news to be communicated did not leave enough space or time, the pattern could be shortened and some steps be left out.

The so-called mystery plays (together with the morality plays, which will not be dealt with here) mark the beginning of English vernacular drama. The term *mystery play* refers back to the French word *métier* or *mestier* (which in turn goes back to Latin *ministerium*), which means "trade, craft". This designation reflects the fact that the plays were organised and performed by the craft guilds of the major towns in England. They mostly belong to the England of the fourteenth, fifteenth and sixteenth centuries and thus cover a large part of the Middle English period.

The main features of mystery plays again confirm the prevailing influence of the Christian religion during the Middle Ages. Mystery plays were biblical drama, that is, they comprised the history of salvation as traditionally related in the Bible (including also some material which was not part of the official Bible). Thus, they usually started from the Fall of Lucifer and Adam and Eve and stretched out till Judgment Day. The history of salvation was told in selected individual scenes, which related the most prominent "highlights" of the Bible. Since their major point was religious instruction, they included scriptural and homiletic material and aimed at teaching the essential truths of Christianity. Another typical feature was the cyclic character of the mystery plays. The individual scenes of a play were seen as part of the whole organisation of the play and could only be understood in the context of the complete performance.

As was mentioned above, the mystery plays were organised and performed by the craft guilds in towns. The performance happened in so-called pageants. The scenes were given on pageant carts which followed a set route through the town, with fixed stations where the individual scenes were performed. Individual scenes were assigned to individual crafts.

This also meant that the mystery plays were usually amateur productions. From existing town records we know that many cycles must have existed in a variety of places, but only four complete cycles survived (York, Chester, Wakefield (Towneley), and the so-called N-Town play (*Ludus Coventriae*)). We also know from the town records that the authors were mostly anonymous and the plays were in continual revision through the decades. The plays were mostly performed on Corpus Christi (a religious feast first celebrated in 1311), which mostly fell in June. The sheer length of the cycles (in the York cycle 48 scenes are recorded) required the longest period of daylight.

Most plays follow a popular style and provide links to everyday settings. Although mostly written in rhyming stanzas, the language used in the mystery plays includes quite a few informal passages and many elements of humour. This also applies to the extract from the *Second Shepherds' Play*, which is part of the Towneley Cycle and which is included in questions section below.

Summary

Middle English is the period linking Old English and (Early) Modern English. Politically it is marked by the Norman Conquest and the establishment of the Norman nobility in England, leaving Norman French as the language of the court, of government, administration and literature, and English as the language of the common people. However, during the thirteenth century the influence of Anglo-Norman was waning and, until the fifteenth century, English gradually emerged as the dominant medium of communication in most important domains of language use.

Middle English is the period of the dialectal diversification of the written language, with an extraordinary diversity of spelling. In the field of morphology, we witness dramatic changes, which eventually lead to the loss of most inflectional endings, making Middle English a predominantly analytic language, with SVO as the major word-order pattern. The Middle English lexicon undergoes significant changes as well. A large number of French loan words enter the language, together with many Latin borrowings and some Scandinavian influence (which probably goes back to the Old English period). Middle English is the period with a marked regional variation. Only towards the end of the period do we find tendencies towards "incipient standards". In the field of social variation we still lack clear evidence.

Along with the process of the re-establishment of English, the number of vernacular texts and genres which have come down to us is much more numerous than in Old English, especially in late Middle English. Among the new vernacular genres which emerged during the Middle English period are personal letters and plays.

Further reading

Burrow and Turville-Petre (2005) provides an essential introduction to Middle English and includes a variety annotated text excerpts. Horobin and Smith (2002), Mossé (1968 [1952]) and Blake (1992) are linguistic text books on Middle English (with increasing complexity and detail of presentation).
    The standard edition of Chaucer's works is the *Riverside Chaucer* (third edition, 2008). Boitani and Mann (2003) is an excellent survey of Chaucer and his world. Horobin (2013) provides a general linguistic introduction to Chaucer, whereas Sauer (1998) gives instructive information about the pronunciation of Chaucer's language designed for learners with a German background. Edwards (1984) gives a reliable overview of major Middle English prose works.
    The *Middle English Compendium* (http://quod.lib.umich.edu/m/mec/) is an extremely useful website when studying Middle English. It provides, among other things, the *Middle English Dictionary* (*MED*) and a *Corpus of Middle English Prose and Verse*. The *MED* offers a comprehensive analysis of lexicon and usage for the Middle English period, supplemented by a huge number of quotations. The electronic version offers many straightforward and sophisticated search options. The *Corpus of Middle English Prose and Verse* includes sixty-two full texts and several shorter items, again with several search options.

Questions and exercises

1. Based on the information given in Chapter 4.1., reconsider the most important stages by which Middle English developed from a vernacular spoken only by "the common people" to the major medium of communication employed in most domains of society.

2. The text below is from a letter written by Margaret Paston to her husband in April 1448. Reading this text, keep track of the irregular spelling of the words. While the spelling is irregular, is it also inconsistent?

Ryth wyrchypful hwsbond,
Right worshipful husband
I recomawnd me to ȝw, desyryng hertyly to heryn of ȝwr wel-fare, praying
I recommend me to you, desiring heartily to hear of your welfare, praying
ȝw to wete þat I was wyth my Lady Morley on þe Satyrday nexst after þat
you to know that I was with my Lady Morley on the Saturday next after that

ʒe departyd from hens, and told here qhat answere þat ʒe had of Jon Butt;
you departed from here, and told her what answer that you had of John Butt;
and sche toke jt ryth strawngely and seyd þat sche had told ʒw and schewyd
and she took it right strangely and said that she had told you and showed
ʒw j-now qhere-by ʒe myth have knowleche þat þe releve owyth to ben
you enough whereby you might have knowledge that the relief ought to [have] been
payd to here. And sche seyd sche wyst wel þat ʒe delay jt forþe þat sche
paid to her. And she said she knew well that you delay it forth [so] that she
xuld nowth have þat longyth to here ryth. And sche told me hw jt was payd in
should not have that [which] belongs to her right. And she told me how it was paid in
Thomas Chawmberys tym, qhan here dowter Hastyngys was weddyd; and sche
Thomas Chamber's time, when her daughter Hastings was wedded; and she
seyd sythyn þat ʒe wyl make none end wyth here sche wyl sew þer-fore as
said since (that) you will make no end with her she will sue therefore as
law wyl. I conseyvyd be here þat sche had cwnsel to labore aʒens ʒw þer-jn
law will (allows). I conceived by her that she had counsel to labour against you therein
wyth-jn ryth schort tym. …
within right short time...
(Paston Letters; 1448; HC)

3. Using the information given in Tables 1 to 4 in Chapter 4.2.1., try to read the first lines of the *Canterbury Tales* given below (if you need help, you might consider Sauer 1998: 43).

Whan that Aprill with his shoures soote
When (that) April with its showers sweet-smelling
The droghte of March hath perced to the roote,
the drought of March has pierced to the root,
And bathed every veyne in swich licour
And bathed every vein in such liquid
Of which vertu engendred is the flour;
By which power created is the flower;
Whan Zephirus eek with his sweete breeth
When the West Wind also with its sweet breath,
Inspired hath in every holt and heeth
has breathed life into every wood and field
The tendre croppes, and the yonge sonne
the tender new leaves, and the young sun

Hath in the ram his halve cours yronne,
Has   in Aries   its half course   run,
And smale foweles maken melodye,
And small   birds   make melody
That slepen al the nyght with open ye
that   sleep all the   night with open eye
(So Priketh hem Nature in hir corages);
(So incites them Nature in their hearts),
Thanne longen folk to goon on pilgrimages,
Then   long   folk to   go   on pilgrimages,
And palmeres for to seken straunge strondes,
And pilgrims   to   seek   foreign   shores
To ferne halwes, kowthe in sondry londes;
To distant shrines, known in various lands
And specially from every shires ende
And especially from every   shire's end
Of Engelond to Caunterbury they wende,
Of England to   Canterbury they   go,
The hooly blisful martir for to seke,
the   holy blessed martyr   to   seek
That hem hath holpen whan that they were seeke.
Who them has   helped   when   they were sick.
(Chaucer, Canterbury Tales; c1388–92; CMEPV)

4. The text below is an extract from the petition concerning the murder of a certain Isabell by her husband John Carpenter of Sussex in 1433, written in Chancery hand (see Fisher et al. 1984: 235). It spells out in detail the rather shocking and gruesome circumstances of the murder and may thus be a faithful document of life in the first half of the fifteenth century. Analyse the inflectional forms of the verbs contained in the text and determine what classes of verbs they belong to (see Chapter 4.2.2.).

A Roy nostre souerain seigneur
To our royal sovereign master
Besechen humbly youre Comunes of this present parliament. that where one
beseech humbly your Commons of this present Parliament, that where one
Iohn Carpenter of Brydham in the Shire of Sussex husbund-man the   vii daye of
John Carpenter of Brydham in the Shire of Sussex, farmer   the seventh day of
Fevever the yere of youre noble reigne the viiite saying to Isabell his wijff that
February the year of your noble   reign the eighth, saying to Isabell his wife that

117

was of the Age. of xvje. yere and had be maried to him but xv dayes. that they
was of the age of sixteen years and had been married to him but fifteen days that they
wolde go to gedre on Pilgremage and made to arraye hir in hir best arraie and
would go together on [a] pilgrimage and made to array her in her best clothes and
toke hir with hym fro the said Toun of Brydham to the Toun of Stoghton in the
took her with him from the said town of Brydham to the town of Stoghton in the
said Shire. And there in a woode he smote the said Isabell his wijff on the hede
said Shire. And there in a wood he smote the said Isabell his wife on the head
that the brayne wende oute and with his knyff yaf hire many other dedly
that the brain went out and with his knife gave her many other deadly
woundes. And streped hir naked out of hir clothes and toke his knyff and slitte hir
wounds. And stripped her naked out of her clothes and took his knife and slit her
bely fro the breste doun & toke hir bowels oute of hir body and loked if she were
belly from the breast down and took her bowels out of her body and looked if she were
with Childe And thus the said Iohn mourdered horrebely his wijff. of the which
with child. And thus the said John murdered horribly his wife, of which
horryble mourdure the thoursday next after the Fest of Seint Ambrose the Bishop
horrible murder the Thursday next after the feast of St Ambrose the bishop
the yere of your Reigne bi for said the said Iohn was endyteth ...
the year of your reign before said the said John was indicted
(Petition; 1433; Fisher et al. 1984: 235)

5. The text below is an extract from the entry for the year 1137 AD in the *Peterborough Chronicle*. Look at the word order in the main and dependent clauses in this text and work out the proportion of the SV pattern and diverging patterns. Give reasons for the occurrence of the divergent patterns. - Look also at the instances of negation in the text.

Ðis gære for þe king Stephne ofer sæ to Normandi; & ther wes underfangen,
This year went (the) king Stephen over sea to Normandy; and there was welcomed
forði ðat hi uuenden ðat he sculde ben alsuic alse the eom wes, & for he
because they thought that he should be just as the uncle was and because he
hadde get his tresor; ac he todeld it & scatered sotlice. Micel hadde Henri king
had yet his treasure; but he dispersed it and wasted truly. Much had Henry King
gadered gold & syluer, & na god ne dide me for his saule tharof. Þa þe king
gathered gold and silver and no good not did people for his soul of it. When the king
Stephne to Englaland com, þa macod he his gadering æt Oxeneford. & Þar he
Stephen to England came, then made he his council at Oxford. And there he
nam þe biscop Roger of Serebyri & Alexander biscop of Lincol & te canceler
took the bishop Roger of Salisbury and Alexander bishop of Lincoln and the chancellor

118

Roger, hise neues, & dide ælle in prisun til he iafen up here castles. Þa the
Roger, his nephews, and did all in prison until they gave up their castles. When the
suikes undergæton ðat he milde man was & softe & god, & na iustise ne dide,
traitors understood that he mild man was and soft and good and no justice not did,
þa diden hi alle wunder. Hi hadden him manred maked & athes suoren, ac hi
then did they all atrocities. They had him homage done and oaths sworen, but they
nan treuthe ne heolden. Alle he wæron forsworen & here treothes forloren, for
no pledge not held. All they were forsworn and their pledges forlorn, because
æuric rice man his castles makede & ægenes him heolden; & fylden þe land
every rich man his castles made and against him held; and [they] filled the land
ful of castles.
full of castles.
(*Peterborough Chronicle*; c1150; HC)

6. This text is an extract from the *Second Shepherds' Play*, a mystery play that is part of the *Towneley Cycle* (see Chapter 4.3.2.). The scene presented here is remarkable since Mak (one of the shepherds) assumes here the role of a yeoman sent as an envoy from a great Southern lord (*a yoman ... sond from a greatt lording*). In order to render his appearance more plausible, he tries what he considers a Southern accent, which, however, is quickly recognised as a *sothren tothe* ("Southern tooth"), because it does not fit the predominantly Northern features common to their speech. Try to spot typical Southern and Northern features in the text (see also Chapter 4.2.5.).

Mak
what! ich be a yoman / I tell you, of the king;
What! I am a yeoman / I tell you, of the king;
The self and the same / sond from a greatt lordyng,
The self and the same / envoy from a great lord,
And sich.
And such.
ffy on you! goyth hence
Fie on you! Go away
Out of my presence!
out of my presence!
I must haue reuerence;
I must have reverence;
why, who be ich?
why, who am I?

Primus Pastor
Why make ye it so qwaynt? / mak, ye do wrang.
Why make you it so quaint? / Mak, you do wrong.

Secundus Pastor
Bot, mak, lyst ye saynt? / I trow that ye lang.
But, Mak, do you want to be a saint? / I think that you long to.

Tercius Pastor
I trow the shrew can paynt, / the dewyll myght hym hang!
I think the shrew can talk flatteringly, / the devil may him hang!

Mak
Ich shall make complaynt / and make you all to thwang
  I will make [a] complaint / and cause you all to be flogged
At a worde,
at a word,
And tell euyn how ye doth.
and tell even how you do.

Primus Pastor
Bot, Mak, is that sothe?
But, Mak, is that true?
Now take outt that sothren tothe,
Now take out that southern tooth [southern dialect],
And sett in a torde!
and set in a turd!

Secundus Pastor
Mak, the dewill in youre ee / a stroke wold, I leyne you.
Mak, the devil in your eye / a stroke would I give you.

Tercius Pastor
Mak, know ye not me? / by god I couthe teyn you.
Mak, know you not me? / by God I could harm you.

Mak
God looke you all thre! / me thoght I had sene you,
God look (to) you all three! / I thought I had seen you,
ye ar a fare compane. /
you are a fair company. /

Primus Pastor
can ye now mene you?
Can you now remember yourself?

Secundus Pastor
Shrew, Iape!
Shrew, Ape!
Thus late as thou goys,
thus late as you go,
what wyll men suppos?
what will men suppose?
And thou has an yll noys
And you have an ill noise [reputation]
of stelyng of shepe.
of stealing of sheep.

Mak
And I am trew as steyll / all men waytt,
And I am true as steel / all men know,
Bot a sekenes I feyll / that haldys me full haytt,
but a sickness I feel / that holds me full violently,
My belly farys not weyll / it is out of astate.
my belly fares not well / it is out of condition.

Tercius Pastor
Seldom lyys the dewyll / dede by the gate.
Seldom lies the devil / dead by the gate.
(*Towneley Plays*; a1460; HC)

7. Look again at the extract from the letter in exercise 2. Based on the information about the *ars dictaminis* given in Chapter 4.3.2., determine which steps of the opening section of letters are included and which are left out. – Considering addressor and addressee, the topics and the issues raised in this text, why could this extract be called a typical example of a Middle English letter?

121

5. English ca. 1500 to ca. 1700 (Early Modern English)

5.1. Political and socio-cultural background

In the last chapter we saw that the end of the Middle English period was marked by the re-emergence of English as the major means of communication in many important domains of language use. This re-establishment of English and the beginning of standardisation can serve as one criterion for delimiting the opening of the Early Modern English period. In this period, English is used in most areas of life, and in the course of the sixteenth and seventeenth centuries, most of the remaining fields (for example, scientific and academic prose, liturgical religious texts) adopt English as well.

Also, during the last half of the fifteenth century, it becomes increasingly difficult to tell, with the help of dialectal features, where a written text stems from (except for clearly Northern texts). So, at the outset of Early Modern English we encounter an incipient norm of a written (orthographic) standard which is used in the literate sections of society, a standard, however, which will not be codified until the very end of the period.

This incipient standardisation is closely linked to another event, which may be said to introduce the new era, the invention of printing from movable type and the introduction of the printing press in England in 1476 by William Caxton. Printing and the mass production of books very much contributed to standardisation. Other phenomena which are sometimes said to mark the new period are the beginning of the Tudor era (1485) and the Renaissance. These language-external factors, which may serve to delimit the start of Early Modern English, will be dealt with in more detail in the following sections. With regard to language-internal factors for delimitation, the so-called Great Vowel Shift is also mentioned by some scholars (see Chapter 5.2.1. below). But this phonemic change had already started in late Middle English and, with its last repercussions, it clearly extended beyond the year 1700.

The end of the Early Modern English period is less clearly marked. Linguistically, it may be recognised in the extensive regularisation of spelling and in the emergence of a certain homogeneity of the language; politically, in the consolidation reached by the Restoration and the Glorious Revolution towards the end of the seventeenth century.

Seen from the perspective of external history, the Early Modern period can be divided up into several subperiods, depending on the rulers of the country. The first one is the Tudor era (1585–1603), with Henry VIII and Elizabeth I as the most prominent figures. The Tudors manage to give the monarchy new strength and authority; at the same time, the Tudor era is characterised by relatively great social mobility, with many people from the lower classes reaching high positions (for example, Thomas Wolsey, the son of a butcher and inn-keeper, became a cardinal and Lord Chancellor under Henry VIII). The reign of Henry VIII sees the introduction of the Reformation and Renaissance thought in England. The era of Elizabeth I is often thought of as a golden age of prosperity, literature and music. After the death of Elizabeth the monarchy was passed on to James I, who belonged to the House of Stuart. The Stuart era (1603–1649, the second subperiod), especially the reign of Charles I (1625–1649), is characterised by growing social, political and religious contrasts, which eventually lead to the outbreak of the Civil War, the execution of the king, and the establishment of the so-called Commonwealth under the Lord Protector Oliver Cromwell (1649–1660). In 1660, with the Restoration, the monarchy is re-established.

As was said above, one of the major events to start the Early Modern English period, because it was a major factor in the standardisation of English, was the introduction of the printing press in England by William Caxton. Originally, Caxton had been a textile merchant and had lived in Bruges on the Continent for a considerable time. From 1471 until 1472 he stayed in Cologne, where he probably worked in a printing house and learned the art of printing. He returned to Bruges and printed his English translation of a French book, the *Recuyell of the Historyes of Troye* (that is, collection of stories about Troja). This is a significant volume with more than 700 folio pages and the first book printed in English. Caxton later went back to England and in 1476 set up his own printing press in Westminster. In the following years he produced more than one hundred books and shorter texts. Some of these were his own translations, but also works of Chaucer, Gower and Lydgate, chronicles, statutes, grammatical works, religious pieces and others. After Caxton's death, there were mainly two printers who dominated the market, Wynkyn de Worde and Richard Pynson. In the first decades of the sixteenth century these printers produced above all a considerable output of cheap books which aimed at a less educated but larger public. During the sixteenth century book production rose dramatically and the printing press became a most central social and political factor.

How could the printing press enhance standardisation? In the age of handwritten manuscripts, each book had been a more or less unique copy in a hugely variable population of texts and compilations. As we saw in the section on Middle English (see Chapter 4.2.5.), handwritten manuscripts were often highly inconsistent in their spelling. In addition, texts were copied quite often, with scribes adding or leaving out sections of text or making them fit their local vernacular. With the introduction of printing, one identical version of a text could be reproduced hundreds or even thousands of times. At first the individual printing houses followed their own house styles, that is, they decided how words were spelt and texts punctuated, and thus printed texts could be variable, depending on the printer and the edition. Later, with large numbers of copies people developed a sense for the question why texts and, in fact, individual words should not be printed in one identical orthographic form. Thus, the new technology of printing enhanced standardisation.

The dramatic increase in the output of printed books, of course, presupposes a growing number of people who were able to read them. Expanding literacy and education are two major developments characterising the socio-cultural background of the Early Modern English period. Literacy, that is, the extent to which people are able to read and/or write, had been rather limited during the Old English and the larger part of the Middle English period, and had been mostly restricted to the members of the church. In the times of manuscripts, writing was a specialised skill and an arduous task. However, "illiterate" people were not necessarily excluded from participation in written communication. For example, they could do administrative business simply by dictating letters or having documents read out to them, that is, they could do their jobs quite efficiently without being able to read or write. This situation seems to have changed gradually during the fourteenth and fifteenth centuries and the change was accelerated during the Early Modern period. However, although there must have been more people who could read and write, it is quite difficult to assess or measure the extent of literacy which prevailed in a given period. In the literature we find different kinds of evidence, with varying degrees of reliability.

The most straightforward, but least reliable sources are statements made by contemporaries about the level of literacy which prevailed at the time. Such statements are quite rare and also highly subjective, because they mostly reflect the limited perspective and specialised interests of their authors (Bennett 1969 gives a few instructive examples for the Early Modern period). A second source for the assessment of literacy are acts, statutes and petitions referring to reading, writing and printing. Since the distribution of written material was often a socially and politically highly sensible area, there are quite a few legislative documents devoted to this topic. For example, in 1543 an act was passed regulating the reading of the English Bible. It ruled that the reading of the English Bible be restricted according to rank. The nobility and gentry were allowed to read the English Bible to their households; female members of the nobility and gentry were only allowed to read it privately to themselves; the lower ranks were strictly forbidden to read any portions of it. Since you only forbid things which you assume (or fear) people are able to perform, it is quite likely that many members of the lower ranks were in fact able to read. But the evidence based on this kind of legislation can only serve to make rather broad and general assumptions and needs to be supplemented by more concrete and direct data.

Such data may, in a way, be gained if we look at the growth of written or printed material, for example the number of books (or manuscripts) owned by individual people or the number of written items produced during a certain period of time. For example, between the years 1481 and 1490, 136 titles were printed in England, 1,470 titles between 1541 and 1550, 2,987 titles during the last decade of the sixteenth century and 18,530 titles between 1681 and 1690 (see Barnard and McKenzie 2002: 779–84). These sheer numbers suggest a significant increase at least in the ability to read. However, these numbers can only serve as indirect evidence. Even during the Tudor era, listening to texts that were read out was one major way of literary participation, and it is very difficult to asses with any accuracy, based on the number of printed items, the numbers of people of were actually able to read them.

The most reliable way of estimating the literacy in past periods is based on the use of signatures as opposed to simple marks in various documents. For example, in 1642 all men over eighteen had to make the so-called *Protestation Oath*, by which they confirmed their loyalty to the Anglican Church. The lists with the signatures of this oath are at least partly representative of the male population because all social ranks in England were forced to take part in it. What is measured here as an indication of literacy is the fact whether people were able to write their name or not. Since we know that reading was usually taught before writing, the ability to sign one's name can generally be taken as strong indication for the ability to read. The more concrete results of such studies (for example, Cressy 1980) show a fairly high proportion of illiteracy in Tudor and Stuart England. In about 1500 the overall literacy of men in England must have been as low as ten per cent, literacy of women only one per cent. In the middle of the sixteenth century the corresponding proportions are twenty per cent and five per cent, during the time of the Civil War (around 1642) thirty per cent and ten per cent. But there seem to have been large regional and social differences. Literacy was more common in towns and cities (especially London) and less common in the countryside. In terms of social rank, the professions, the nobility and the gentry had very high literacy levels, but the lower ranks, together with women, had fairly low proportions. Although the initial picture of literacy at the end of the fifteenth century seems rather pessimistic, literacy levels seem to have improved considerably during the Early Modern period, and in the course of the seventeenth century illiteracy becomes a distinguishing feature of the poor and lower ranks in society.

The most important traditional institution providing instruction in reading and writing were schools. Here, as well, we can see that Early Modern English is a time of significant growth, above all of grammar schools. During the Early Modern period, as well as in the Middle Ages, primary and secondary education was not a public sector in England. Schools were not financed by the state. Their existence depended mainly on the church, which, during the Middle Ages had provided most if not all of the educational institutions. Starting from the fourteenth century, there were also private secular benefactors who donated means for the establishment of schools. The more important part of the educational system was the grammar school. Grammar schools were comparatively well organised and usually had more funding than schools for elementary education. We already find many grammar schools in the fourteenth century, but their major growth happens during the fifteenth and sixteenth centuries. In his fundamental study on English schools in the late Middle Ages, Nicolas Orme (1973) lists a total number of 105 secular schools for the fourteenth century, but 114 for the fifteenth century and 124 for the years between 1500 and 1530. His later research revealed even more foundations. This sudden growth of grammar schools has been corroborated by further studies. The gifts of land and money which the schools received were mainly based on private initiatives. They came above all from the members of the gentry and the rising middle class.

This process of the strengthening of the educational sector continues during the Reformation, which has traditionally been called the classical period of expansion of educational facilities. For example, more than 300 new grammar schools were founded between 1500 and 1620.

The growing numbers of grammar schools during the Early Modern English period are certainly a clear indicator of the rising levels of literacy. However, they cannot be taken as evidence for increasing attempts at maintaining or enhancing linguistic standards in the use of English. Grammar schools did not teach English, they taught the Latin language and aimed at reading and writing skills in Latin. The teaching of English seems to have happened by indirect means. In many cases English was the language of instruction at school, English was often the implicit background for teaching Latin grammar, and English served as the source or the target language of translations in Latin classes.

The low status of English in the educational system nicely reflects the poor image the vernacular language had at the beginning of the Early Modern English period. With the introduction of Renaissance thought at the beginning of the era, we witness a re-appreciation of the classical languages and a new estimation of the rhetorical skill and refinement associated with classical Latin and Greek. By contrast, the English language was considered "poor", "vulgar" and "barbarous", lacking prestige. Latin, as it had come down to the Renaissance period, appeared as the ideal: elegant, "copious" and never changing. Latin was also the lingua franca of international scholarship, the language of schools, universities and the Church. English, on the other hand, had a limited word stock, appeared unstable and changing, lacking refined syntactical constructions and rhetorical figures. People who published prestigious works in the vernacular had to formulate long forewords where they produced excuses for not writing in Latin and reasons why English was the appropriate means of communication (for example, Roger Ascham and Thomas Elyot). It was only towards the end of the sixteenth century that there was a general shift in this attitude towards English. Now the majority of educated people thought that it seemed to have gained the prestige of an elegant and refined language, with enough words and constructions to express the minute facets and aspects of philosophical, scientific and poetic diction.

One of the major factors which also contributed to the emancipation and renewed appreciation of English was the Reformation. It was also one of the major movements which dominated and polarised religious life and the socio-political scene throughout the Early Modern English period. The first stage of the English Reformation was triggered not by doctrinal but rather political issues over the problem of dynastic succession. Henry VIII wanted the Pope to annul his marriage with Katherine of Aragon, who did not seem to be able to bear him a male heir. The Pope, however, withheld his permission. Thus, Henry broke off relations with Rome and, in the Act of Supremacy (1533), declared himself Supreme Head of the Church of England. Henry confiscated all Church property and, after their dissolution, also the enormous wealth of the monasteries. On the other hand, at least during the reign of Henry, the Reformation was not intended to change religious doctrine. Henry tried to keep the teachings of the Church of England fully Catholic, except for the question of papal sovereignty.

This conservative orientation changed under Edward VI. He introduced the *Book of Common Prayer* (1549), whose articles of faith re-defined the doctrine of the Church of England in Protestant terms. The *Book of Common Prayer* also contained, among other things, the texts for liturgical services and prayers in English, reflecting the basic innovation that Mass was no longer said in Latin. Upon Edward's early death, Mary I attempted a complete return to Catholicism. The years of Henry's, Edward's and Mary's reigns were marked by many disruptions and divisions due to the sudden doctrinal re-orientations. There were martyrs both on the Catholic and the Protestant side. For example, Thomas More (the former Lord Chancellor) and Cardinal John Fisher were executed during Henry's reign because they had refused to sign the Act of Supremacy. Hugh Latimer and Thomas Cranmer (both bishops and prominent supporters of Protestantism) were burnt at the stake under the reign of Queen Mary. During her reign many Protestants of all ranks were forced into exile (the so-called Marian exiles).

Elizabeth I attempted a religious settlement which was to include both traditional as well as more specifically Protestant subjects in the Church of England. The religious settlement was, however, only partly successful, since the Puritans, and other non-conformist Protestants, kept pressing for further and more radical reforms, whereas Catholics were not allowed to be members of the Anglican Church. This contrast between more traditional members of the Anglican Church and increasingly radical dissenters, together with a growing fear of an imminent Catholic "plot", characterised religious life during the seventeenth century and long after the Civil War.

One aspect of Protestant doctrine turned out to be particularly relevant for the English language and for the spread of the vernacular. For Protestants, the "word", that is the text of the Bible was of essential importance for every Christian and his / her salvation. Since the Bible directly reflected God's law and since every Christian was directly responsible to God, the Bible had to be made accessible to everyone, which meant it had to be translated into English. Thus, within the framework of Reformation thought the vernacular in Bible translations represented a pathway to salvation and to heaven. The Early Modern English period is, in fact, an era producing many important Bible translations. And Bible translations, along with the *Book of Common Prayer* and certain martyr stories, became the most popular and well read books during the whole of the period.

5.2. Language structure

5.2.1. Spelling and pronunciation

During the first part of the Early Modern English period we still find some of the special letters that were typical of Middle English. These include thorn <þ>, sometimes used instead of <th> (for example, *þohte* "thought"), and yogh <ȝ>, sometimes used for <g>, <gh> or <y> (for example, *ȝod* "good" and *broȝte* "brought"). People in Early Modern England were also fond of abbreviations. The letter <y> stood for <þ> or <th> (for example, y^e or *ye* "the" and y^t or *yt* "that"), the ampersand <&> often replaced the co-ordinating conjunction *and* and the tilde <~> was a sign for nasals and the Latin-based prefixes *con-*, *per-*, and *pro-* (for example, *who~* "whom", *p~form* "perform" etc.).

While spelling could still be fairly variable during the first decades of the period (especially in more informal genres, like personal letters), we find an increasing tendency towards standardisation during the seventeenth century. As was pointed out in the preceding chapter, this was largely due to the influence of the printing press (see Chapter 5.1.).

The most important change or rather complex of changes affecting the Early Modern English phonological system was the so-called Great Vowel Shift. This is a series of developments which involved all the long vowels of late Middle English and which gradually transformed the sound system of Early Modern English. It started as early as late Middle English and lasted right into the eighteenth century.

Starting from the early fifteenth century, all long vowels were raised (those which were already high, /i:/ and /au:/, were diphthongised). The order and dating of the individual changes is debated and there was probably a large amount of individual and regional variation, but, seen at a more abstract level, the whole complex of changes appears as a chain shift (see Figure 1 below).

The first step in this chain was probably that the late Middle English long vowels /i:/ and /u:/ were diphthongised. These diphthongs had a centralised first element, resulting in /əi/ in *tide* and /əu/ in *house*. It seems that this process was more or less finished by 1500. Towards the end of the seventeenth century these diphthongs resembled very much the respective sounds of present-day English, namely /aɪ/ and /aʊ/. Now the space for the high vowels was vacant and the mid-high vowels /e:/ and /o:/ occupied these positions. Thus words like *see*, *meet* and *keep*, which had had an /e:/ in late Middle English, were pronounced with an /i:/, and words like *food*, *moon* and *boot*, which had had /o:/, shifted to /u:/. It seems that this change was also completed by 1500.

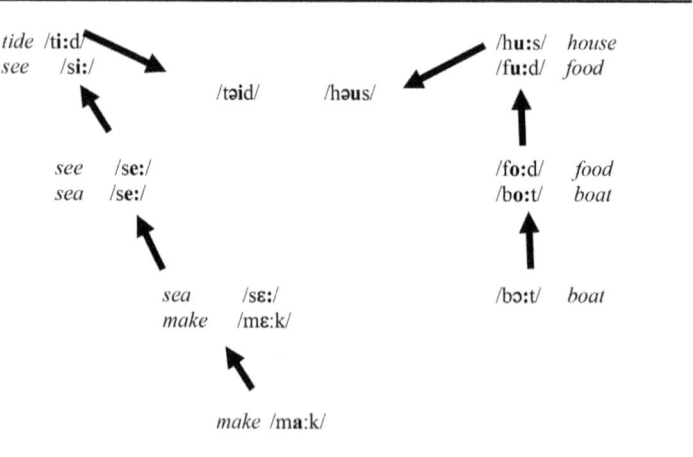

Fig. 1: Major developments of the Great Vowel Shift

Given the simultaneity of the two processes (diphthongisation of /i:/ and /u:/; raising of /e:/ and /o:/), researchers have argued that the chain might be either a pull chain (with the vacant spaces of the high vowels attracting the mid-high vowels) or a push-chain (with /e:/ and /o:/ driving the high vowels out).

The next stage in the shift involved words with Middle English /ɛ:/ (like *sea* and *meat*) and words with Middle English /ɔ:/ (like *boat* and *home*). These vowels were raised to /e:/ and /o:/ respectively, resulting in pronunciations like /se:/ for *sea* and /bo:t/ for *boat*. This process happened during the sixteenth century and was more or less completed by 1600. Later on, towards the end of the seventeenth century, the *sea* and *meat* words moved further up and were pronounced with an /i:/, creating many new homophones (*see/sea, meet/meat* etc.). The *boat* and *home* words continued to be pronounced with an /o:/ throughout the Early Modern period and were diphthongised in the course of the eighteenth century, resulting in the present-day English versions with /əʊ/.

The last step involved the long vowel /a:/ in words like *make* /ma:k/ and *name* /na:m/. This vowel was raised to /ɛ:/ by the end of the sixteenth century, resulting in pronunciations like /mɛ:k/ and /nɛ:m/; later, during the seventeenth century, it became closer and merged with /e:/. During the eighteenth century the vowel in the *make* and *name* words was diphthongised, resulting in the present-day pronunciation /meik/ and /neim/.

Given the variability and fluctuation of the Great Vowel Shift, it seems rather difficult to work out a fixed list for the pronunciation of the long vowels during the Early Modern English period. Some text books have split up the era into several stages, with typical pronunciation patterns (see, for example, the three stages presented in Barber 1997: 108). As a basic orientation and summary of Figure 1, Table 1 below shows the typical manifestations of the long vowels and the diphthongs in about 1600.

tide, side	əi	*house, mouse*	əu
see, meet	i:	*food, moon*	u:
sea, meat	e:	*boat, home*	o:
name, make	ɛ:		

Table 1: Typical manifestations of the long vowels and the diphthongs in about 1600

When considering arrangements like Table 1, we should keep in mind that the Great Vowel Shift was not as regular and uniform a change as the presentation would suggest. For example, many of the changes were not carried out in the northern dialects, and there were quite a few exceptions. If the long vowel was followed by an /r/, many special developments are found (for example, in words like *boar* and *bear* no raising took place; a detailed list is given in Barber 1997: 121).

Another major phonological development involved the Late Middle English diphthongs which were (in most cases) monophthongised and turned into long vowels. Middle English /iu/ (*chew, new, due*) and Middle English /ɛu/ (*dew, few*) both became /ju:/, with the initial element sometimes being lost during the eighteenth century (*chew, brew*). Middle English /aʊ/ became /ɒ:/ in the first half of the seventeenth century (*all, law, taught*), and Middle English /ɔʊ/ (*soul, know*) became /ɔ:/ and later turned into /o:/. This sound thus joined Middle English /ɔ:/ (*boat, home*), which in the course of the Great Vowel Shift had been raised to /o:/. So, in the first half of the seventeenth century words like *rose* and *soap* (Middle English /ɔ:/) as well as *soul* and *know* (Middle English /ɔʊ/) were pronounced with an /o:/. During the eighteenth century they acquired their Modern English format and were diphthongised to /əʊ/. The last Middle English diphthong to be affected by monophthongisation was /ai/ (*day, tail*). In the initial part of Early Modern English the first element of the diphthong was raised, yielding /ɛi/. Around the time of Shakespeare we find the monophthong /ɛ:/, which was raised to /e:/ towards the end of the period. So this sound coalesced with Middle English /a:/ (*make, name*), which during the Great Vowel Shift had been raised to /ɛ:/ and later to /e:/. As a consequence, words like *make* and *name* as well as *day* and *tail* were pronounced with the same vowel in the seventeenth century (either /ɛ:/ or /e:/). In the eighteenth century both were diphthongised and acquired the Modern English form /ei/.

By comparison, the development of the short vowels during the Early Modern period is fairly straightforward. There are only few changes. Middle English short /a/ was raised to /æ/ during the sixteenth century (*hat, bat, cat*). Short Middle English /ʊ/ split up into two separate phonemes in the middle of the seventeenth century (mainly in the South). There was the rounded version /ʊ/ in words like *bull, bush, full, put* and *wolf*. And there emerged an unrounded version /ʌ/, which was used in words like *cut, shut, nun* and *monk*. The unrounded version /ʌ/ acquired the status of a phoneme, since due to the shortening of /u:/ in certain contexts (*book, look* etc.), new minimal pairs emerged (*look* vs. *luck, book* vs. *buck*).

The changes affecting the consonant system during Early Modern English were also fairly limited. Two new consonant phonemes evolved. The sibilant /ʒ/ developed as a result of the merging of /z/ and /j/ in words like *pleasure* and *vision* during the seventeenth century. Thus, *pleasure* turned from /plɛzjər/ to /plɛʒər/. The other new consonant phoneme was /ŋ/. This velar nasal occurred in words like *sing* and *bring*, which were pronounced /siŋg/ and /briŋg/. In these combinations the voiced plosive /g/ tended to be dropped, resulting in pronunciations like /siŋ/ and /briŋ/, and also in new minimal pairs like *sing* /siŋ/ and *sin* /sin/.

Other changes of Early Modern English consonants involved simplification of clusters. For example, initial clusters comprising /wr/, /kn/ and /gn/ were reduced to /r/ and /n/ respectively, yielding the Modern English pronunciations of words like *wry, wrong, knife, knight, gnaw* and *gnat*. The change affecting the /wr/ cluster happened earlier, during the sixteenth century, whereas the simplification of /kn/ and /gn/ was only completed towards the end of the period.

5.2.2. Morphology and word-formation

inflectional morphology

In the field of inflectional morphology, Middle English was the crucial period of change, when English developed from a predominantly synthetic to a basically analytic language. Although later centuries completed this trend towards simplification by levelling and/or dropping of endings, the Early Modern English system is in most respects almost identical to the Modern English one.

With nouns, the *–(e)s* ending had emerged as the marker of both the genitive singular and the plural in the Middle English period. However, the modern distribution of the allomorphs of the plural morpheme [iz, z, s] was not established until the seventeenth century. Also, there were some irregular plural formations, many of which are still found in contemporary English. Plurals ending in *-en* were found with certain words (for example, *oxen* and *children*; formations like *eyen* and *hosen* seem to be restricted to the Early Modern era). Another irregular pattern was the plural formed by the i-umlaut (see Chapter 3.2.1.). Most of these forms are also preserved in contemporary English (for example, *mice, men, geese* etc.). Zero plural forms were also common with certain nouns (for example, *sheep, deer, horse* etc.).

In most cases, there was no orthographic distinction between genitive and plural. The apostrophe placed before the *–s* of the genitive singular was only introduced in the second half of the seventeenth century; the plural genitive was marked only in the eighteenth century. Thus, in most cases, *kings* could be *kings, king's* or *kings'*.

	Subject	Object	Possessive
Singular			
1st person	*I*	*me*	*my / mine*
2nd person	*thou*	*thee*	*thy / thine*
3rd person	*he/she*	*him / her*	*his / her*
	hit / it	*him*	*his*
Plural			
1st person	*we*	*us*	*our*
2nd person	*ye*	*you*	*your*
3rd person	*they*	*them / hem*	*their*

Table 2: *Personal pronouns at the beginning of the Early Modern period*

	Subject	Object	Possessive
Singular			
1st person	*I*	*me*	*my*
2nd person	*you*	*you*	*your*
3rd person	*he/she*	*him / her*	*his / her*
	it	*it*	*its*
Plural			
1st person	*we*	*us*	*our*
2nd person	*you*	*you*	*your*
3rd person	*they*	*them*	*their*

Table 3: *Personal pronouns towards the end of the Early Modern period*

During the Early Modern English period the system of personal pronouns saw a few major changes. Tables 2 and 3 above contrast the inventory of forms at the beginning and at the end of the period.

The possessive forms of the first and second persons singular had originally two alternative forms, one longer form ending in *–n* (*myne*, *thyne*) and a shorter form (*my*, *thy*). The longer forms were used before vowels (*mine arm*), the shorter forms elsewhere (*my leg*). The longer forms were given up in the early seventeenth century (however, the forms ending in *–n* can still be used as independent possessives, for example, *these books of mine*).

At the beginning of Early Modern English, the neuter forms of the third-person subject pronoun still had the aspirated form *hit*, apart from the weak form *it*. The object form was *him*, identical to the masculine case. During the sixteenth century both the aspirated form *hit* and the object form *him* were given up, generalising the weak form *it* for both subject and object case. The possessive form *his* was replaced by *its* not until the beginning of the seventeenth century; *its* became common during the second half of the century. The rise of the new form *its* (which seems to have developed by analogy to the genitive suffix) was probably triggered by the ambiguity of the form *his*, which could indicate masculine and neuter gender.

In the plural, the native forms starting with *h-* had been replaced by the Scandinavian forms with *th-* by the end of the fifteenth century. A few early texts of the sixteenth century may occasionally show forms like *hem*. A major change affected the second-person pronouns. During the sixteenth century, the distinction between the subject plural form *ye* and the object plural form *you* was given up. The form *you* was now generalised to both subject and object positions. Also, *you* was increasingly used instead of *thou* in the course of Early Modern English. Thus, the number distinction was given up for the second-person pronouns. *Thou* (and the related forms *thee*, *thy*, *thine*) can still be found throughout the seventeenth century in many texts, but its use seems to have been quite marked (on the social implications of *thou* and the spread of *you* see Chapter 5.3.1. below).

With adjectives, the analytic forms with *more* and *most*, which were introduced in Late Middle English, compete with comparatives and superlatives formed with the inflectional endings *-er* and *–est* (*more constructive*, *most constructive* vs. *easier*, *easiest*). The distribution of the forms was not yet regulated. For example, we find analytic forms with disyllabic adjectives. Also, Early Modern texts show double comparative and superlative forms, that is, combinations of the analytic and the synthetic forms (*the most highest*). Thus, there may be three comparative forms for *easy*: *easier*, *more easy* and *more easier*.

Early Modern English verb inflection was slightly more complex than the inflection of nouns and adjectives. In the present tense we still find the ending for the second person singular *–(e)st* (for example *thou makest*, *thou hast* etc.), which, however, was given up in the course of the period. It is quite likely that this loss is linked to the demise of the second person singular pronoun *thou*, which usually triggered the respective inflectional ending. The third person singular of the present tense had two alternative forms, *–eth* and *–(e)s*. The *–(e)s* ending, which was the Middle English northern form, had spread south and had replaced the *–eth* ending by the early seventeenth century in many domains, especially in informal texts and spoken language. This form became the new standard form. The *–eth* ending, however, which was the Middle English southern variant, prevailed in formal and conservative writing until the last half of the seventeenth century. This ending also persisted with short common words, for example, *do*, *have* and *say*, sometimes until the eighteenth century. In the present tense plural the Middle English endings (-*(e)s* in the North, -*(e)n* in the Midlands and -*(e)th* in the South) were mostly given up at the beginning of Early Modern English, although some of them may still be found in early sixteenth-century texts. Otherwise, the (Modern English) zero marking is found.

In the past tense the second person singular ending –*(e)st* and the plural ending –*en* are lost during the sixteenth century. The regular allomorphs of the dental suffix for weak verbs –*ed* [d, t, id] are established by ca 1650. In the section on Middle English morphology (see Chapter 4.2.2.) we saw that in the past tense of strong verbs there were competing strong and weak forms for one verb (for example, *crope* and *crepte* for *crepe* "creep" and *ros* and *rysed* for *rise* "rise"). This tendency towards greater variability of forms increases during the Early Modern period. With many verbs we find several, or at least two, different past tense or past participle forms (for example, *holp / helped, chose / chosed, drove / drived, driven / droven* etc.).

Early Modern English saw an increase in the use of the analytic constructions involving the auxiliaries *have* and *be* in combination with the first and the second participle. The present perfect (*have* + -*ed*) was well established, although the construction does not seem to have been as frequent as it is today. Also, with verbs expressing motion (for example, *come, go, run*) and with verbs expressing change of state (for example, *become, grow, change*) the forms of the auxiliary *be* tended to be used, rather than *have* (for example, *he is come, she is changed* etc.). Constructions with *have* spread during the Early Modern period, but the change was not complete until the nineteenth century. In particular, the verbs *go* and *come* resisted the use with *have* fairly long.

The so-called progressive construction (*be* plus –*ing*) was not yet very frequent and the marking of the progressive aspect was still optional (see, for example, the famous question addressed to Hamlet *What do you read, my Lord?*). Also, the paradigm was still incomplete. For example, constructions like *he is being shown* only evolved during the eighteenth and nineteenth centuries.

The subjunctive seems to have played a more prominent role in Early Modern English than it does today. Morphologically, the forms were marked by a lack of the inflectional ending (in the second and third person, for example, *I insist that she leave*). Typically, subjunctive forms are used to express uncertainty, doubt and wishes. The syntactic contexts which required the subjunctive were much more numerous in Early Modern English. For example, it was used in many adverbial and nominal clauses carrying a hypothetical or conjectural meaning. In the course of the Early Modern period the frequency of subjunctive forms declined and it is usually said that modal auxiliary verbs were used instead.

word-formation

Word formation processes are among the major means of creating new words in a language. While Early Modern English is a period of massive gains in the field of lexis, these additions to the vocabulary are often attributed to processes of borrowing (see Chapter 5.2.4.). Still, Early Modern English provided a large number of possibilities of forming new words by means of the standard methods of word formation, above all affixation, compounding and conversion. Not all available options can be covered here. The following short overview will focus on some important examples (for a more detailed treatment see Nevalainen 1999: 376–433; a shorter account is found in Nevalainen 2006: 59–65).

Nevalainen points out that Early Modern English, at the beginning of the seventeenth century, had more than 120 affixes available (the most important ones are listed in Nevalainen 2006: 62–63). Certainly, affixation was the most common method of word-formation. Among the most popular suffixes were *-ness* (*bawdiness, straightness*) and *–er* (*murmerer, examiner*) for nouns, *–ed* (*muscled, rose-lipped*) and *–y* (*bawdy, dirty*) for adjectives. Among the most common prefixes was *un–* (*uncomfortable, unfit*), but also *in–* (*inhospitable*), *counter–* (*counterprove*) and *re–* (*reprint*), to give a few examples (see also Barber 1997: 233–236).

In compounding the most productive type is the combination of two nouns, as it is still in contemporary English (for example, *meadow ground* and *horse mill*). Other productive patterns were, for example, combinations of nouns and adjectives (for example, *lifelong* and *skin-deep*), of nouns and past participles (*hand-made, heaven-sent*) and of particles plus verb (*undersign, overshine, underrate*; Nevalainen 2006: 61).

Another fairly common word-formation process was conversion, and it seems that this process was applied in a wide range of cases. Typically, nouns and adjectives were converted into verbs (for example, the verbs *apprentice, gossip, dirty* and *secure*). But we find also adjectives changed into nouns (for example, *ancient* and *invincible*, both referring to persons) and even function words which are converted to nouns (*the ins and outs*) and verbs (*to up*), or both (*but me no buts*, a phrase formed by Susanna Centlivre in her play *The Busie Body* in 1708).

5.2.3. Syntax

Seen from the perspective of syntactic structures, Early Modern English is a period when major changes happened, which finally made the language quite similar to Modern English. Thus, in the field of syntax and quite in contrast to inflectional morphology, Early Modern English may be seen as a bridge between Middle English and contemporary English. Many of the changes in syntax can be connected with the functional expansion and stylistic differentiation which happened as English became the major means of communication in all domains of language use. The following sections will deal with some of the topics covered in earlier syntax chapters (like word-order, negation, subordination and relative clauses), but will also address new constructions (like *do*-support and non-finite constructions).

During the Early Modern period the subject-verb-object order in declarative sentences, which had already become dominant in Middle English, was further strengthened. However, there were still some deviant word-order patterns. After sentence-initial adverbs (for example, *then, now, here, there, thus, yet*) the order of subject and (finite) verb was often inverted (compare *was this proclamacion made* in example (1), *say thei* in (2), *sayd this holy Kinge* in (3) and *knowe we* in (4) below).

(1) Now was this proclamacion made w^{t}in .ii. houres after y^t he was beheded.
(Thomas More, *History of King Richard III*; 1514–1518; HC)

(2) Thus say thei y^t knew her in her youthe.
(Thomas More, *History of King Richard III*; 1514–1518; HC)

(3) Thus sayd this holy Kinge, when our sauiour as yet had not suffered his passion for him.
(John Fisher, *Sermons*; 1535; HC)

(4) Now knowe we that thou hast the devyll.
(William Tyndale, *The New Testament*; 1534; HC)

It seems that the frequency of this kind of inversion depended somewhat on the author and the genre (for example, Thomas More obviously preferred this kind of construction; it is also found often in religious prose). Fronted direct objects and subject complements could trigger inversion, as well (compare *this* (direct object in example 5 and subject complement in example 6)).

(5) This do wee command you.
(Elizabeth I, *Letters*; 1599; HC)

(6) This was he of whom I spake.
(*King James Bible*, St. John's Gospel; 1611; HC)

Inverted declarative sentences seem to have been relatively frequent during the sixteenth century but became rare in the seventeenth century. Many of the inverted constructions that are found after 1600 are primarily motivated by factors of emphasis in the text or other discourse reasons (see examples 5 and 6, where emphasis seems to be the primary motivation for inversion).

On the other hand, one special kind of inversion, inversion after certain initial negative and restrictive adverbs (for example, *never, neither, hardly, seldom*) became more and more common during the seventeenth century and was obligatory towards the end of the period (see examples 7 and 8).

(7) Never was there anye man that layed anye thynge to my charge.
(*The Autobiography of Thomas Mowntayne*; 1553; HC)

(8) And Iesus saide vnto her, Neither doe I condemne thee: Goe, and sinne no more.
(*King James Bible*, St. John's Gospel; 1611; HC)

Among the more important and conspicuous syntactic developments in Early Modern English was the rise of the so-called *do*-support. *Do*-support comprises the use of the auxiliary *do* in most interrogative and negative sentences and in some other constructions (for example, *do* when used for emphasis or as a prop-word in reduced clauses). Quite interestingly, *do* was used initially fairly often in declarative sentences, mostly for non-emphatic purposes. This development had started with the so-called causative *do*, which was found above all in late Middle English, that is, in the fourteenth and fifteenth centuries. The causative sense is best translated with a construction involving *have* + object + participle or *cause* + object + infinitive. Thus, in example (9) below *I dyde do enprynte a certayn nombre of them* could be rendered as "I had a certain number of them printed", and in example (10) the translation of *whyche he dyde to knowe* could be "which he caused to be known".

(9) And accordyng to the same I dyde do enprynte a certayn nombre of them.
(William Caxton, *Prologue to the Canterbury Tales*; 1477–1484; HC)

(10) whyche he dyde to knowe ouer alle in his lande
(William Caxton, *The History of Reynard the Fox*; 1481; HC)

During the sixteenth century we find quite a few instances of *do* in declarative sentences which do not carry any causative meaning any longer but seem to have no specific function except for indicating tense.

(11) And by this circle wee knowe what starres do continually appeare, and which are continually hidden, also what starres doe rise and goe downe.
(Thomas Blundevile, *A Briefe Description*; 1597; HC)

(12) This church was ruined in the 20th yeare of William the Victor, by a raging fire, which did prostrate the greatest part of the city of London.
(John Hayward, *Annals*; 1627; HC)

(13) After priuat prairs, I did writ a Letter: after, I did breake my fast, then I went about the house.
(*Diary of Margaret Hoby*; 1599; HC)

Several reasons have been suggested why this optional tense marker or "empty *do*" was used (for example, emphasising the topic of the statement, uncertainty about the formation of past tense forms with certain verbs, rhyme and metre). In the above examples, one might speculate that in (11) emphasis might be the motivation for inserting *do*. In (12) we could assume that the verb *prostrate* "throw down" was derived from the Latin participle *prostratus*, which was already marked for past tense. So many language users would be reluctant to add another tense marker. And *write* and *break* in (13) certainly belonged to those verbs in which strong and weak forms alternated and made people unsure about the "correct" form. Whatever may have been the reasons for the rise of empty *do*, during the seventeenth century we witness a serious decline of the frequency of such constructions and by the eighteenth century this construction is extremely rare.

On the other hand, *do* spread in other sentence types. Ellegård (1953) has shown with a representative sample of prose texts that *do* appears first in negative interrogatives. Then it spreads to positive interrogatives, then to negative declaratives and negative imperatives. Towards the end of the period *do*-support is likely to appear in most of the above sentence types, but it is not yet fully grammaticalised. Especially with negative declaratives, there is still a certain proportion of constructions without *do* (see example 14 below). Also, certain verbs resist *do*-support for a considerable time (for example, *know* and *doubt*; see examples 15 and 16).

(14) hee admits him not for his Counsailor
(Shakespeare, *The Merry Wives of Windsor*; First Folio Edition 1623; HC)

(15) ... whether with age or anger, I know not, but she fancy'd the last.
(Aphra Behn, *Oroonoko*; 1688; HC)

(16) I doubt not but at yonder tree I shall catch a *Chub*.
(Izaak Walton, *The Compleat Angler*; 1653 / 1676; HC)

Another important development in the field of syntax involved the spread and the refinement of complex sentences, that is, constructions with a main clause and one or more subordinate clauses. During the Early Modern period we witness an increase in the frequency of both finite and non-finite subordinate clauses (non-finite clauses are infinitive, participle and gerund clauses). The rise of subordinate structures in texts reflects first of all Latin influence that can be felt in the wake of the Renaissance. Authors were trying to imitate the "refined" hypotactic structures of the model texts supplied by Classical Antiquity. A richer inventory of subordinate syntactic constructions was also a precondition for English to become a standard language that can be used in all domains of society. Thus, as was pointed out above, the syntactic development during the Early Modern period reflects the functional expansion and stylistic differentiation connected with standardisation.

A section of subordinate clauses that had already seen a major increase during late Middle English were adverbial clauses. These spread further during the sixteenth and seventeenth centuries. Increased frequency is here accompanied by a finer semantic differentiation of the subordinate conjunctions. Due to the richer inventory of subordinate conjunctions adverbial clauses could be used to express semantic relationships more precisely and more explicitly. At first, most of the conjunctions could be combined with *that* (see *for all that* in example 17 below). Example (18) contains a participle construction introduced with *while*. In example (19) the conjunction *unless* is followed by a subjunctive form of the verb (*be*).

(17) How many of this Citie for all that they are Vsurers, yet would be counted honest men.
(Henry Smith, *Sermons*; 1591; HC)

(18) ... and she vow'd, it was a palace, while adorned with the presence of Oroonoko
(Aphra Behn, *Oroonoko*; 1688; HC)

(19) Nay I add farther, that no man can judiciously embrace the true Religion, unless he be permitted to judge, whether that which he embraces be the true Religion or not.
(John Tillotson, *Sermons*; 1679; HC)

The most frequent type of subordinate clause in Early Modern English seems to have been the relative clause, especially in its non-restrictive form. The Early Modern English inventory of relative pronouns was more or less the same as in Modern English, but some striking differences in use could still be found. The pronoun *which* could still (as in Middle English) refer back to personal antecedents. Such constructions are particularly found in texts of the sixteenth century (see examples 20 and 21 below).

(20) The king would say that he had .iii. concubines, which in three diuers properties diuersly exceled.
(Thomas More, *The History of King Richard III*; 1514–1518; HC)

(21) After me cometh a man, which was before me.
(William Tyndale, *New Testament*; 1534; HC)

During the seventeenth century the distribution of the relative pronouns with personal antecedents slowly approaches the Modern English state. Another differing feature of Early Modern English relative pronouns concerns the zero relative, which can be found in subject position (especially after *there* and *here*; see examples 22 and 23 below; the zero-pronoun is marked with "ø").

(22) There is a willow [ø] growes aslant a Brooke.
(William Shakespeare, *Hamlet*; First Folio Edition 1623)

(23) Sir, here's a woman [ø] would speake with you.
(William Shakespeare, *The Merry Wives of Windsor*; First Folio Edition 1623; HC)

A rather strange construction, which reflects Latin influence, is the so-called continuative relative clause. Here a relative pronoun (instead of a demonstrative pronoun) is used to introduce a new main clause. In example (24) below the relative pronoun *which* (plus the noun *infami*) refer back to the preceding infinitive clause (*to depose the prince & take himself the crown*). However, we do not find a "regular" relative clause; the phrase *With which infamy* starts a new sentence.

(24) ... it shold paraduenture be thought, that it were his owne ambicious minde and deuise, to depose the prince & take himself the crown. With which infami he wold not haue his honoure stayned for anye crowne.
(Thomas More, *The History of King Richard III*; 1514–1518; HC)

Quite interestingly, this construction is not limited to formal texts or translations from Latin, but can also be found in jest books or private letters.

(25) But when our lady cam to hym she asked hym what he had suffred for her sake/ which wordys made hym gretly abashyd bycause he had nothyng to say for hym selfe/
(*A Hundred Mery Talys*; 1526; HC)

Another section of subordinate clauses which was strengthened during the Early Modern period were non-finite constructions (infinitive, participle and gerund constructions). Although most of these constructions had already been available during late Middle English, their definite rise as a significant element of text structure only happens during the sixteenth and early seventeenth centuries. Non-finite constructions are a flexible means of syntactic compression, typical of the modern written standard. They usually have no tense marking and do not contain modal verbs. In many cases the subject is not expressed and there is no subordinating conjunction. In example (26) below the participle clauses *trembling, and almost fainting* could be rendered as "although she was trembling, and almost fainting", where the conjunction, the subject and the finite verb *was* have to be added.

(26) ... trembling, and almost fainting, she was oblig'd to suffer her self to be cover'd, and led away.
(Aphra Behn, *Oroonoko*; 1688; HC)

In a similar way, the infinitive clauses in example (27) below (*to offer ..., to carry me ..., to be engaged ..., to see ..., to have waited ...*) all lack overt subject, subordinator etc., which makes them an appropriate means of syntactic compression.

(27) Lady Long: was so kind to offer to carry me to ye Oppera to day with her and Lady Portland; but I was so unfortunate as to be engaged to go to Lady Denbighs to see ye famous Mrs Binges dance, or els I should have bin glad to have waited on Lady Long.
(Alice Hatton, *Letters*; 1700; HC)

Infinitive constructions could, for example, be used to replace clauses expressing purpose and result (*he went there to seek for his wife*) and relative clauses (*the first woman to attend school* "the first woman that attended school"). They could also be paraphrased by coordinated clauses (*he departed never to return* "he departed and never returned"). Latin influence is revealed in constructions following the pattern "object plus infinitive" (imitating the Latin accusative and infinitive construction, for example, *showes the Matine to be neere* (Shakespeare, *Hamlet*)). Participle constructions could be used to replace adverbial clauses, relative clauses and co-ordinate clauses (for an adverbial clause see example 26 above).

A special construction found even in Early Modern literate texts is the so-called "dangling" participle. Here the participle does not relate to the subject of the superordinate clause, as is required in contemporary Standard English. Hamlet's father says:

143

(28) ... sleeping in mine Orchard, A Serpent stung me
(William Shakespeare, *Hamlet*; First Folio Edition 1623)

Here it is, of course, the father who is asleep, not the serpent.

Traditionally, *ing*-clauses covering the position of noun phrases are called gerund constructions (for example, *Killing animals is nasty*). Gerund constructions are distinguished from *ing*-forms that are called verbal nouns. Verbal nouns form part of a noun phrase, for example, *The killing of animals should be forbidden*. (Note the definite article and the *of*-genitive, which contrasts with lack of definite article and direct object in the gerund.) While participle constructions started to spread already in late Middle English, the major period for the rise of gerund constructions is the second half of the Early Modern period. Quite interestingly, the spread of these constructions includes also several "mixed" constructions, which combine "nominal" elements of the noun phrase (for example, definite article, *of*-construction, premodifier) and "verbal" elements of clause structure (direct object, adverbial).

(29) And for the more effectuall preventing the Exportation of such Frames Bee itt further enacted by the Authority aforesaid That ...
(*Statutes* VII; 1695–6; HC)

(30) ... the roote of al the Cure is the wel purging of the body, whereby ...
(William Clowes, *Treatise for the Artificiall Cure of Struma*; 1602; HC)

The above constructions can be called "mixed" because in (29) we find a combination of definite article and premodifier on the on hand (*the more effectuall*), and direct object on the other (*the Exportation of such Frames*). In example (30) it is a definite article and the of-genitive (*the, of the body*) and an adverbial (*wel*). Such constructions become less frequent in the centuries following the Early Modern period.

5.2.4. Lexis and semantics

Like Middle English, Early Modern English is a period of significant growth of the vocabulary. However, while in Middle English the major donor language was French, it seems that now Latin had a more prominent role. If we want to understand the expansion of the lexicon in the Early Modern period, we need to look at the attitudes towards English that people adopted and how these views changed.

Since the fifteenth century, English had increasingly been used as the major medium of communication in society. Thus, when the Early Modern period started, it had developed a widening range of functions and genres. This spread across new domains, functions and registers required an elaboration of the language, especially in the field of lexis. Quite simply, in order to talk and write about things in all areas of life (including science, administration, education and the law) people needed a rich, suitable and accurate terminology. However, one of the prevailing attitudes during the sixteenth century was that English did not meet the requirements of a refined and "literary" language. According to many scholars, it lacked "copiousness", the varied and refined word stock offered by Latin, and therefore was not fit as a medium of communication when discussing topics normally covered in Latin. In fact, they thought, it was a "barbarous and rude" language. At the end of the Middle English period William Caxton (in his preface to his translation of the *Recuyell*) had already complained about the "simple and rude englisshe" and in the middle of the sixteenth century authors still saw English as "a base speche" (Barber 1997: 43). One way to deal with this problem and "improve" things was to introduce loan words.

The sixteenth century was a period of strong influence of Renaissance thought in England. The Renaissance advocated, among other things, the study of the classical languages and the ideals of Classical Antiquity. One of them was the model of "copiousness", mentioned above, the stylistic principle of lexical variation and lexical richness. So, in order to "improve" the English language, people chose new words from the classical languages, especially from Latin.

Typical examples of Latinate loan words are *abbreviate, acceleration, circumscription, emphasis, deficit, dogma, exit, formula, genius, gymnasium, inflection, metonymy, monopoly, orchestra, paradox, scholastic, sympathy, system, tenet, tolerate, tragic,* and so on.

If we trust the evidence from the *Oxford English Dictionary* (see Culpeper and Clapham 1996), Latin was the prominent donor language throughout the Early Modern Period, supplying more words than French. However, it is not always easy to decide whether a word entered the English language straight from Latin. Channels of borrowing could be quite "indirect". For example, many Latin terms reached English via French, Greek terms could come via Latin (see, for example, *dogma* and *paradox* in the above list) or French, and so on. Also, certain nouns might be the product of word-formation patterns (some of them going back to Middle English), not of borrowing (Nevalainen 2006: 52 discusses the case of *accommodate/accommodation* and *addict/addiction*).

As can be seen from the small selection of loan words above, the classical loans were mostly learned words or technical terms, which would be used in academic or "educated" contexts. Many classical loans did not survive or survived only as specialised terms.

Towards the end of the sixteenth century the negative, disparaging attitude towards the English language changed, to be replaced by a mixture of patriotism and pride, which saw English on a par with the classical languages, with similar resources and similar copiousness. However, the sixteenth century had also seen some heated debates about the advantages and limitations of loan words and excessive borrowings. First of all, there was the so-called "inkhorn controversy". The designation "inkhorn term" suggests that many loan words were not only artificial and too learned, but also mostly used for pompous effect and as a show of an elevated style. Many authors made fun of the unnecessary and excessive use of borrowings (among them Shakespeare and Ben Jonson). In 1553 Thomas Wilson warned in his *Arte of Rhetorique*:

> Among all other lessons this should first be learned, that wee neuer affect any straunge ynkehorne termes, but to speake as is commonly receiued: neither seeking to be ouer fine, nor yet liuing ouer-carelesse vsing our speeche as most men doe, and ordering our wittes as the fewest haue done. Some seeke so far for outlandish English, that they forget altogether their mothers language.

His famous fictitious "inkhorn letter", a supplicatory letter with an absurd and pompous accumulation of Latinate terms, was to serve as a deterrent, but even so a fair number of the Latinate terms included there have well survived until today.

Some of the opponents of an enrichment of the English vocabulary by classical words thought that elaboration could be achieved by native means, that is, by formations based on the Germanic word stock, following the established rules of English word-formation. Sir John Cheke (1514–1557), a classical scholar and Cambridge professor, published a translation of St Matthew's gospel in which he showed that, in order to express certain new concepts, native formations could be used. For example, he translated "centurion" as *hundreder*. This is a formation based on the native word *hundred*, with the affix *–er*, which is used to form agential nouns (like *singer, writer, driver*). Other translations include *toller* for "publican", *biwordes* for "parables" and *crossed* for "crucified". Edmund Spenser (?1552–1599), the famous poet, used words from late Middle English, especially those typical of Geoffrey Chaucer, for example, *eke* "also", *quoth* "said" and *ycleped* "called". In the preface to his *The shepheardes calendar* (1579) the writer with the initials E.K. says:

> he hath laboured to restore, as to theyr rightfull heritage such good and naturall English words, as haue ben long time out of vse.

However, the restoration of old words mainly served to give Spenser's works a special poetic archaic diction. Like John Cheke, he seems to have used loanwords from classical languages as well. There were other, less well-known people, who tried to reactivate English words of past ages or to form compounds consisting of native elements. But, basically, these purist and native trends were hardly successful. It is true that many learned formations and inkhorn terms were rather short-lived, but the influx of classical loanwords left its mark on the Early Modern period.

Apart from Latin, there was also extensive borrowing from other languages, most importantly from French, but also, although to a lesser extent, from Italian, Spanish and some more languages. Although French did no longer hold the important position it had had in Middle English, it was still used in the law courts and read in the form of literature. It was also used by French Protestant emigrants, who came to England late in the sixteenth century, and was common with English Royalists, who returned to England in the wake of the Restoration. Typical French borrowings included military terms, items connected with trade, social matters, art, literature and clothing (for example, *colonel, livre, bourgeois, ballet, champagne*). Whereas French loans underwent major changes while they were assimilated during the Middle English period, Early Modern English loans from French tend be adopted in a more or less unchanged form, especially towards the latter half of the seventeenth century (compare, for example, *liaison. faux pas, bureau*). The largely unaltered state of the loans suggests that they were adopted by members of the educated upper classes to serve as indicators of prestige and social weight.

Spanish and Italian loans mostly include national products and terms related to arts and society (examples from Italian are: *parmesan, gusto, umbrella, portico*; examples from Spanish are: *sherry, don, renegade*). From Spain came also some military and political terms (for example, *armada*) and many American-based designations (for example, *negro, banana, potato*). Other minor donor languages include Arabic, Chinese, Dutch, Persian, Turkish and Hindi. Not all loans, however, were direct borrowings.

Although Early Modern English appears to be much closer to contemporary English than, for example, Middle English, we still find many words that differ (sometimes fairly radically) in their lexical meaning and may thus be cause of confusion. For example, lexical meanings may have become more general or more specialised, they may have altered because of metaphoric extension, and their meaning may have become more positive or more negative (for the following sections see also Nevalainen 1999).

Examples of generalisation are the words *humour* and certain titles like *Master* and *Mistress*. In the Middle Ages *humour* had been the specialised term designating the four basic fluids of the human body (blood, phlegm, choler and melancholy), which were thought to determine a person's health and disposition. During the sixteenth century a more general sense was established, which refers to the general disposition of a person. The term later covered the more specific meaning relating to things which are funny or amusing. The terms *Master (Mr)* and *Mistress (Mrs)* had originally been reserved for the lower nobility and professional people. In the course of the period they were expanded to plain gentlemen and married and unmarried women of this rank. By the end of the period the terms had spread further down the social scale. As Nevalainen (1999: 438) points out, this "generalisation of titles in Early Modern Britain was motivated partly by increased social mobility, partly by reasons of courtesy and prestige."

Examples of specialisation of meaning are the terms *physic* and *science*. At first the term *physic* designated a medicine or cure and the general concept covering knowledge of the natural world. Here the word competed with the term *physics*, which during the eighteenth century acquired the general sense "natural science in general". In the eighteenth century, by contrast, *physick* was mainly "the science of healing". Since the fourteenth century, *science* had the general sense of "knowledge". During the Early Modern period it was also used in the sense of "skill", to denote mastery in any department of learning. From the seventeenth century onwards the word was increasingly used for theoretical knowledge (in contrast to more practical skills, which were denoted by the term *art*).

Metaphoric extension happens when the meaning of a term denoting one item is transferred to another item because the two items are perceived to have a similar shape or function. Thus, many plant names, which came up in Early Modern English, are based on similarity of shape, for example, *bear's foot, goosefoot, hare's palace, king's crown* (Nevalainen 1999: 444). A functional similarity seems to be involved in the meaning change of the word *parasite*, which originally referred to "one who eats at the table or at the expense of another" to "an organism living in or upon another" (Nevalainen 1999: 444).

Also, the meanings of certain words had more positive or negative associations than today. A good example is the term *boor* (see Nevalainen 1999: 441). The Middle English word simply denoted a person who lived in the country. During the sixteenth century the term came to be associated with a peasant lacking culture and elegance. This negative sense was generalised as the term was used to denote any male ill-bred and unmannered person. There were other lexemes which did not necessarily bear "negative" senses in Early Modern English but developed these negative connotations in the course of the period. For example, the adjective *cunning* had the meaning "able, skilful", *mediocre* meant "neither bad nor good, average" and *vulgar* was used to describe ordinary or customary things. By contrast, other lexemes had at first quite "negative" senses and developed more positive connotations during the Early Modern period, for example, *politician*, which had been used to refer to a plotter and intriguer, or *shrewd*, whose sense was "malicious, hurtful".

5.2.5. Regional and social distribution

In the chapter on Middle English dialects (4.2.5.) we saw that during the fifteenth century the dialectal provenance of texts was increasingly difficult to determine (except for texts stemming from the North). These tendencies towards standardisation continue during the next two centuries. In fact, Early Modern English can be called the period of the (orthographic) standardisation of the written language. At the end of the seventeenth century the written (or rather: printed) language appears fairly homogenous, with only few spelling features that do not conform to the contemporary standard (for example, spellings like *musick*).

However, there is no reason to assume that the spoken language showed the same standardising tendencies. On the contrary, there is ample evidence for the fact that the basic Middle English dialects were preserved in the spoken language (Görlach 1999a is a useful collection of evidence for and comments on regional and social variation). For example, the grammarian Alexander Gil gave in his (Latin) grammar of English (*Logonomia anglica*, 1619/21) a systematic treatment of the major dialect areas, distinguishing, apart from a general and a poetic dialect, a Southern, an Eastern, a Western and a Northern variety. The typical features he mentions (for example, the Southern voicing of initial fricatives, as in *vox* for *fox* and *zong* for *song*) point to the fact that these areas had preserved the distinctions between the major Middle English dialects (on southern voicing of fricatives in Middle English see Chapter 4.2.5.).

In the section on Early Modern English phonology we saw that dialect distinctions were also reflected in ongoing sound changes, most prominently in the so-called Great Vowel Shift, many steps of which were not carried out in northern dialects (see Chapter 5.2.1.). Also, the split of Middle English /u/ into /ʊ/ and /ʌ/ did not spread to most northern dialects (that is, here /ʊ/ was preserved in words like *but* and *cut*).

Quite often dialect speech is associated with lower prestige and textbooks on the Early Modern English period typically include citations from prominent works which comment unfavourably on the "rude" and "uncivil" language of regional dialects. For example, in the *The Arte of English Poesie* (1589), one of the most influential critical works of the Elizabethan period, the author (probably

George Puttenham), warns the young poet not to imitate the language of dialect speakers, in particular, people living more than sixty miles away from London. He recommends the language

> .. which is spoken in the kings Court, or in the good townes and Cities within the land. ... neither shall he take the termes of Northern-men, such as they vse in dayly talke, whether they be noble men or gentlemen, or of their best clarkes all is a matter: nor in effect any speach vsed beyond the riuer of Trent, ...: ye shall therfore take the vsuall speach of the Court, and that of London and the shires lying about London within lx. myles, and not much aboue.

It is clearly the high reputation of the Royal Court and the upper classes of the metropolis which led Puttenham to attach such prestige to the language of London and the neighbouring areas.

Along with this negative assessment of dialect speech, we find a growing tendency towards dialect levelling, that is, a process by which the distinctive features of regional dialects are evened out in areas where people stemming from different regions are in close contact. Dialect levelling is often the consequence of migration and urbanisation, typical processes which bring people from different districts in close proximity. Already in late Middle English there had been first waves of migration in the wake of the Black Death and the general appeal of the city of London, which had attracted many people especially from the Midlands. This process continued during the Early Modern period, again with people moving from rural areas to cities, especially London. London was unique in its position and the multiplicity of functions in England. It was the location of the Court and of Parliament, it had the major port and was the national centre of jurisdiction, business and trade, but also the heart of the emerging printing industry. People went to London in search of employment, in order to study (at the Inns of Court), to attend court sessions or sessions of Parliament and for all different reasons. It is estimated that during the Early Modern period the population of London grew tenfold. In this context London became the ideal setting for dialect levelling, a linguistic melting pot. Speakers stemming from differing regional backgrounds but living in close proximity tend to accommodate their (regional) speech to help others understand them or to avoid being associated with rural, probably stigmatised language varieties. All this contributed to the evolution of what Alexander Gil described as a general dialect (see above).

In contrast to regional variation, it is much more difficult to collect any hard and fast evidence of social dialects in Early Modern England. Most of the language users whose linguistic usage we can track down were literate and came from the well-to-do ranks of society. Linguistic evidence from the less well-educated and / or lower ranks is scarce. It can be found in the representation of lower-class characters in plays or other forms of dialogue. It can also be traced in descriptions of certain authors who comment on pronunciations or words which are stigmatised (for example, Puttenham's warning against "persons [who] doe abuse good speaches by strange accents or ill shapen soundes"). However, such representations and assessments are rare, they may overemphasise stereotypical features and are often highly subjective. Thus they do not always qualify as data for a systematic survey let alone a description of processes of language change. There are few writings (mostly letters) by less educated people (for example, tradesmen and servants), which may give first-hand evidence of linguistic usage in these ranks (Nevalainen and Raumolin-Brunberg 2003), but their number is small.

Social stratification and social change in Early Modern England are reflected in the use of titles (Nevalainen 1999: 438–439; 2006: 137–139). Originally, the titles *Lord* and *Lady* were only used for the nobility and top clergy (for example, dukes, barons, archbishops and bishops), *Sir* and *Dame* for the upper gentry (for example, baronets and knights) and *Mr* and *Mrs* for the lower gentry (esquire, gentleman). Yeomen and husbandmen (the top divisions of the non-gentry) had *Goodman* and *Goodwife*. In the course of the Early Modern Period, due to social mobility and changes in politeness conventions, the titles spread further down the social scale, and the address *Goodman* and *Goodwife* died out. Instead, *Master* and *Mistress* came to be used for yeomen and merchants. Also, all gentlewomen were addressed as *Lady*.

Social stratification can be reflected in the distribution of lexis. Latinate vocabulary is typical of the educated classes, whereas special languages, for example, thieves' cant, represent separate sections of society. (Thomas Harman, a country gentleman from Kent, gave a first description of this special language in 1567, *A Caueat or Warening for Common Cursetors, vulgarely called Vagabones*).

A chapter on the regional and social stratification of English should also cover the fact that English was spoken in other parts of the British Isles and spread to North America during the Early Modern period. In 1536 King Henry VIII definitely annexed Wales (Act of Union) and made English the official language there. The literary tradition of Welsh was, however, supported by Welsh translations of the Prayer Book and the Bible. The colonisation of Ireland was pursued during the sixteenth and seventeenth centuries (Plantation of Ulster in 1606, Cromwell's conquest), which laid the foundation for the emergence of Irish English. The political union with Scotland (Union of the Crowns in 1603) resulted in a further strengthening of English and an Anglicisation of Scots-English with a rapid spread of Anglo-English forms during the late sixteenth and the first half of the seventeenth century.

The Early Modern period is the time when English spread beyond the British Isles as well. Starting from 1607, permanent English settlements in North America evolved, which were followed by several new waves of immigration and settlement. The seventeenth century also witnessed the arrival of English in India (with the foundation of the East India Company in 1600).

5.3. Language use

5.3.1. Discourse and speech acts

In the field of discourse, Early Modern English may be called the period when some patterns of interaction emerged which are today associated with so-called polite forms of communication (in most Western societies). These developments can be traced in the changes of directive speech acts and in modifications in the system of pronominal address terms (*you* / *thou*).

In the chapters on discourse and speech acts in the Old English and Middle English periods (3.3.1; 4.3.1.) we saw that people in these eras tended to use requests that today would often be associated with impolite or rude behaviour (for example, explicit performative formulas, imperatives, modal constructions). The typical "indirect", polite manifestations common in contemporary English (*Could you give me a hand? Will you do me a favour?*) were not yet found. It seems that the Early Modern period brings a major change here.

A study of directive speech acts involving volition (that is, constructions including *wish, want, desire, had rather*, as in *I would like you to carry this for me*; see also Chapter 4.3.1.) showed that during the Early Modern period the frequency of requests with *wish* and *desire* increases considerably. Quite in contrast to the strict orders and commands we found in Middle English, the large majority of these items must be seen as rather polite manifestations (see examples 31–34 below).

(31) I have sent you a cake which **I desire you would be pleased to accept**.
(E. Oxinden, *Letters*; 1666; HC)

(32) *But* says he ***I would not wish you to approach***; *for I am sure you will be in love as soon as you behold her.*
(Aphra Behn, *Oroonoko*; 1688; HC)

(33) Also **I wold desire you to send mee word** of the letter that I wrote to my father and you ...
(R. Plumpton, *Letters*; 1536; HC)

(34) **I coold wish that you wold settell your self** to certin howers tasks euery day you rise: and those howld your self too with out any weariness.
(K. Paston, *Letters*; 1624; HC)

The writers in the above examples, rather than giving straightforward instructions (for example, by using an imperative sentence like *Accept the cake!* or *Send me word!*), express their desire that the addressee perform the act. The rather polite and cautious character of the requests is emphasised by the fact that they employ past tense forms and modal verbs (*would, could*). These suggest that the required act is not yet assumed to be real but rather remote and hypothetical (for example, in (34) the writer does not say that she wishes her son to settle down to regular working hours, but rather that she *could* wish this). All this suggests that we are dealing with fairly polite forms of directives. The speaker / writer does not assume any rights over the recipient but is careful not to infringe on his or her freedom of action.

It is quite instructive to contrast these requests with the manifestations that were found in Middle English (see, for example, (32) in Chapter 4.3.1., *we wol and charge you* "we order and charge you"). In Middle English, stating one's wish seems to have been a sufficient means of expressing a straight command. This typically occurred in an asymmetric communication situation (for example, a king addressing his subordinates). In Early Modern English this was obviously felt inadequate. The verbs which are used are much more tentative, implying that the addressee's cooperation is seen as more important for achieving the aims of a request.

Another typically polite request, involving an interrogative pattern with verbs like *can, could, will* or *would* (for example, *Will you do me a favour?*), also evolves during the Early Modern English period (see examples 35–37 below).

(35) Mr. Stanley, pray **can you recollect any Circumstance** how you came to remember that it was such and such Days that you saw him?
Yes, my Lord, I can.
What are they, tell them us?
I buried a Child that Morning, ...
(*Trial of Titus Oates*; 1685; HC)

(36) S. Walt.: **Wil't please you walke?**
T.I.: Sir I obey your time.
Exit.
(Thomas Middleton, *A Chaste Maid in Cheapside*; 1630; HC)

(37) **Will you do me the Favour** to conduct me to a Chamber?
(George Farquhar, *The Beaux Stratagem*; 1707; HC)

Here the indirect request is felt to be more polite because the speaker, at least on the surface, instead of issuing a straightforward command, simply asks a question and the hearer, if he or she should not follow the request, might simply answer a question (although, of course, in fact he rejects the request). The frequency of this construction still seems to be very low in Early Modern English and it was obviously extremely rare in the first decades of the sixteenth century. It is only towards the end of the period that the frequency approaches that of the constructions involving the volition of the speaker (see examples 31–34 above). In the beginning, some of the interrogative constructions still seem to have been ambiguous and were understood as simple questions (see example 35, where the interrogative is at first interpreted as a question and the addressor has to repeat the request in the form of an imperative). In later examples the directive meaning is revealed more clearly, for example, by words like *please* and *do me the favour*.

The Early Modern English examples which were found show an interesting pattern of distribution across genres. The large majority belong to two genres, trial records and plays. These two genres can be said to represent typical instances of formal and informal spoken interaction. The concentration of the interrogative pattern in these texts suggests that the construction started to spread in spoken discourse.

The general picture emerging in the development of directives is that the sixteenth and seventeenth centuries were obviously decisive for the emergence of two typical kinds of indirect requests, a development which reveals the general trend towards more polite forms of communication and a growing consideration of the position of the addressee in communication.

The same tendency is reflected in another development, the changes in the system of pronominal address terms, which eliminated the form of the second-person singular pronoun (*thou*). In the section on Middle English morphology (see Chapter 4.2.2.) we saw that the Middle English paradigm of the second-person pronouns still had the basic singular-plural distinction (*thou – ye*). In Old English the number distinction had also determined the possible uses of the personal pronouns as address terms. The singular pronoun was used for addressing a single person, whereas the plural form was employed when talking to more than one person. Apparently no connotations of social prestige or politeness were found in the use of the singular or plural forms of address. Starting from the late thirteenth century, the plural form *ye* was used as a polite form of address to one person. This was obviously modelled on French practice. Although the usage was far from consistent, the following basic pattern emerged in late Middle English and Early Modern

English: *thou* was used between equals and to address inferiors (in terms of rank and / or age); *ye* was employed in polite speech or to address a superior (again, in terms of rank and / or age). It was also used in the upper classes among equals. In addition, *thou* may also indicate intimacy whereas *ye* may communicate distance.

The important feature which distinguishes the Middle English and Early Modern English situation from contemporary systems of address employing a formal / distant and an informal / intimate option (for example, Modern German), is that the Middle and Early Modern English system was retractable. It was possible to switch from *ye* to *thou* and back with the same interlocutor, even within the same exchange (see example 38 below from Middle English).

(38) Al Denemark I wile you yeve to þat forward þu late me live.
"All Denmark will I give you in return for the agreement that you ('thou') let me live."
(*Havelok*; 1280; CMEVP)

There are quite a few studies on pronominal address terms in Chaucer's and in Shakespeare's works. Scholars point out that in Chaucer the fluctuations in use also reflect the interactional status of the interlocutors (which may be different from their social status and in fact become more important, for example, when a lower-ranking person knows a secret the higher-ranking person would like to find out etc.). In Shakespeare's works many deviations from the "regular" pattern have been observed. These deviations are obviously exploited in order to produce special effects. For example, *thou* is used instead of *you* to express scorn, disapproval, complicity, fondness and intimacy; *you* is employed instead of *thou* to show contempt, disapproval or formality.

In example (39) below, Falstaff addresses Pistol in his first turn with *thee*, which reflects his superior position as master. In his second turn he switches to *you* (which is employed in connection with the address term *Sir*). This usage is certainly ironic and expresses Falstaff's disapproval and criticism.

(39) *Fal.* I will not lend **thee** a penny.
    Pist. Why then the world's mine Oyster, which I, with sword will open.
    Fal. Not a penny: I haue beene content (Sir,) **you** should lay my countenance to pawne: I haue grated vpon my good friends for three Repreeues for **you**, and **your** Coach-fellow *Nim*; or else **you** had look'd through the grate, like a Geminy of Baboones...
(William Shakespeare, *The Merry Wives of Windsor*; First Folio Edition 1623; HC)

In the first act of *Richard III*, Richard consistently addresses Anne with *you*, whereas she usually retorts using *thou*. But when Richard's talk is associated with love and courting, he suddenly switches to *thou*. Clearly, in example (40) below, *thou* in Richard's turns expresses his attempts at establishing a more intimate relationship with Anne.

(40) Rich. These eyes could not endure y beauties wrack;
 You should not blemish it, if I stood by.
 As all the world is cheared by the Sunne,
 So I by that: It is my day, my life.
Anne. Blacke night ore-shade **thy** day, & death **thy** life.
Rich. Curse not **thy selfe**, faire Creature; **Thou** art both.
Anne. I would I were, to be reueng'd on **thee**.
Rich. It is a quarrell most vnnatural,
 To be reueng'd on him that loueth **thee**.
(William Shakespeare, *Richard III*; First Folio Edition 1623)

Conspicuous and more or less effective switches from *you* to *thou* are also found in texts which can be assumed to give a more faithful picture of everyday interaction in Early Modern England, for example trial records. In example (41) below, which is an excerpt from the trial records of Sir Walter Raleigh, the Attorney uses *thou* effectively in order to show his disapproval, scorn and contempt.

(41) Attorney. Nay, I will prove all: **Thou** art a Monster; **thou** hast an *English* Face, but a *Spanish* Heart. Now **you** must have Money: *Aremberg* was no sooner in *England* (I charge **thee** *Raleigh*) but **thou** incitedst *Cobham* to go unto him, and to deal with him for Money, to bestow on discontented Persons, to raise Rebellion on the Kingdom.
 (*The trial of Sir Walter Raleigh*; 1603; HC)

Given the negative connotations which *thou* seems to have had in many contexts, it does not come as a surprise that it was replaced by *you* during the Early Modern period. *Thou* is fairly rare towards the end of the seventeenth century, but it is difficult to decide when exactly the replacement took effect and became common. Jonathan Hope (1993) showed in his analysis of Durham court records stemming from the 1570s (which contain 377 relevant pronoun forms in 89 conversations) that *you* had already become the normal form of address, whereas *thou* was only used as a means of insult.

Among the reasons which are given for explaining this change, social mobility and the emergent politeness culture are the most frequent ones. The middle and upper ranks of English society, especially in the Tudor period, were less rigid and increasingly open to social aspirers (see Chapter 5.1.). Thus, it became increasingly difficult to tell in advance who belonged to which rank, especially if you were involved in a social interaction with unfamiliar people. Also, it seems that during the sixteenth and seventeenth centuries patterns of polite and genteel interaction were developing. Against this background it is plausible that, given the choice between *you* and *thou*, people would consistently opt for the more respectful *you*, just to avoid any difficult situation. In addition. it seems that with *thou* the prevalent message was not "we are intimate" but rather "I am superior".

5.3.2. Genres

As a matter of fact, the available text documents from the Early Modern English period are much more numerous and various than those which have come down to us from Middle English. This is mainly due to the further spread of literacy and the improvement of education on the one hand and to the introduction of the printing press, with a dramatic increase in the output of printed books, on the other. Thus, what has been said about texts and genres in the Middle English period (Chapter 4.3.2.) applies here to a greater extent. The number of texts and the variety of genres is so large that any short survey must necessarily be superficial and leave gaps. So, only the most important domains and the newly evolving genres will be dealt with in the following sections.

During the Early Modern era the religious domain still maintains a most important position. This is a result of the intricate link between religion and state. The sixteenth and seventeenth centuries were a time of religious dispute and – later – religious war. Religion formed the background of social and political controversy and the Reformation had a tremendous impact on England. Also, the most important books in terms of readership were the Bible, the *Book of Common Prayer* and Fox's *Book of Martyrs*, a collection of stories about saints and their spectacular deaths.

Many studies have confirmed that manuscripts and books containing religious documents show great circulation from the start. It seems that the sixteenth-century printers devoted a large part of their output to religious and devotional works. Apart from the traditional inventory of religious genres (ranging from prayer books to controversial treatises) we find two new items, catechisms and martyrologies. Catechisms form a novel genre, which is mainly associated with the Reformation and the time after. Catechisms present basic tenets and doctrines of the Christian faith in a concise way, mostly set in the form a dialogue between teacher and pupil. We also find a new form of religious biography, the martyrology, a collection of saints' stories. But these differ significantly from the traditional saints' legend found in the Middle Ages, since they no longer contain any miraculous incidents, wonderful healing and other supernatural elements.

These and other devotional writings covered an important position in society, but the most fundamental piece of religious writing was the vernacular translation of the Bible. The prominent status of the vernacular Bible was the consequence of one major corner stone of Protestant doctrine. According to the Protestant teaching, the Bible reflected God's law and every Christian was directly responsible to God. As a consequence, the Bible had to be made accessible to every Christian to ensure that he or she would become familiar with God's law. In other words, the vernacular Bible translation formed a pathway to salvation. Thus, it does not come as a surprise that the Early Modern English period is marked by a series of vernacular Bible translations. The first one, by William Tyndale (1530, 1534), was still incomplete but it was a ground-breaking enterprise since it was the first translation to be based on the original Hebrew and Greek texts, not on the Latin *Vulgate*. It also proved to be extremely influential because most of its text or phrases were adopted in later translations (especially the *King James Bible*). But also the immediate impact on contemporary readers must have been immense. Tyndale's New Testament was not only used as a source for learning about the Bible but also as the very means to learn to read. After several intermediate versions, for example *Coverdale's Bible* (1535), the first complete Bible in English, and the so-called *Matthew's Bible* (1537), it was only the more conservative project of the so-called *Great Bible* (1539) that gained official approval but never won great popularity.

A much more accepted Bible project was the *Geneva Bible* (1560), launched by Protestant exiles stationed in Geneva (on the so-called Marian exiles see Chapter 5.1.). It was a very much revised version of the *Great Bible*, shaped by Calvinist theology. It became famous and was feared for the marginal notes which gave political (and practical) comments on the text that could easily be applied in a contemporary situation (for example, the commentary on Daniel 6:22 and 11:36 said that a king's orders must be disobeyed if they are contrary to God's will, a serious challenge to the monarch). The *Geneva Bible* proved to be the most popular and powerful translation during the Elizabethan period (it was Shakespeare's Bible).

The *King James Bible* (1611), named after James I, who commissioned it after he had ascended the throne, is by far the most famous and most influential Bible translation in the history of the English language. It is a work very much restricted by specific regulations of committee work and by an entirely conservative spirit. As a consequence, the language and diction of the *King James Bible* very much preserved features which eventually go back to Tyndale's translation and included forms and constructions which were no longer part of the common language at the beginning of the seventeenth century. Typical conservative features are, for example, the retention of *thou*-forms throughout the text and the *eth*-affix for the third-person singular present tense of verbs. It is usually assumed that the *King James Bible* exerted considerable influence on the English language, especially in the field of lexis and idiom. After 1750 the *King James Bible* came to be seen as a great and adorable work of religious literature and a model of correct English. Also, people were continually exposed to the text right until the twentieth century, in church, at school and on several other occasions. So it seems quite plausible that the *King James Bible* influenced people's use of the language, although this has not been shown in any comprehensive way so far.

As was mentioned before, one major technological innovation that changed the inventory and distribution of genres during the Early Modern period was the introduction of the printing press. The new printing technology also introduced new publication types which may be called "higher-level" genres because they can include several genres. For example, pamphlets are a publication type that emerged during the Early Modern period. Pamphlets could serve as a platform for publishing a wide variety of genres. Letters could be published as pamphlets in order to reach a wider audience. In fact, many letters were especially designed for this publication format. But pamphlets could also include treatises, sermons, petitions and other genres. Since the texts contained in pamphlets were mostly fairly short, they could be produced quickly and were inexpensive, that is, could be bought by many people. Authors could react quickly to current events (and to other pamphlets). So, pamphlets marked many polemical controversies (often about religious issues) and rulers very much feared their immediate impact on wide sections of the population.

Another "higher-level" genre that emerged in the latter part of Early Modern English was the newspaper. Newspapers may be called a "higher-level" genre because they include and also gave rise to several sub-genres, for example, news reports, letters to the editor, announcements, lost and found, advertisements, and so on. The first English newspapers were published in 1620. These were mainly compilations of reports sent by correspondents who were stationed in important cities. The only organisational pattern found in these early newspapers was the headings of the individual reports which indicated the contribution of the correspondent. Internally, these reports had a chronological order and narrative structure. Only later do we find headlines and the introduction of the so-called "top down principle" (see Chapter 6.3.2.).

A further domain which saw major innovations was the area of scientific writing. The first vernacular scientific texts had been published in late Middle English, but Latin, the international language of scholarship, was still the prevailing medium for scientific writing. This situation only changed slowly, but in the course of the seventeenth century English emerged as the language of science. We find handbooks that contained the results of scientific thought, but also medical texts and recipe books that offered advice on maintaining health and on the preparation of medicine. Many handbooks from the Early Modern period were written in dialogue form. In most cases this was a fictional dialogue between a master or teacher and a student, and the information eventually directed at the reader was first passed on to the pupil. Today this kind of presentation may seem rather awkward and strange. Later a different mode of presentation became common, which was in the form of a report, stating personal observations and describing experiments, discussing results, also in relation to established positions of authorities. This new style was very much based on the foundation of the Royal Society and the principles advocated by its members.

Another section which shows a remarkable increase in the output of texts comprises genres associated with the private sphere. Personal letters had started in late Middle English, but due to the rise of literacy and the improvement of postal services in the latter half of Early Modern English, letter writing became much more popular. Other new genres of the private sphere which develop during the Early Modern period are personal diaries, autobiographies and personal accounts of journeys (travelogues).

A further new genre which evolved in Early Modern English times were the proceedings of state trials. Such court records are particularly interesting documents for historical analyses since they contain actual spoken interaction. Of course, we do not know in how far scribes were faithful in noting down details of the actual speech of the persons involved and in how far they edited the texts. Spoken interaction is, of course, also represented in drama. As we saw in Chapter 4.3.2., this genre developed out of the late medieval mystery plays and miracle plays. Since these plays were felt to go against the principles of the Reformation, their performance was suppressed and given up during the sixteenth century. At the same time, a new type of drama developed, with plays being performed in public theatres by professional actors. Major authors were Christopher Marlowe, William Shakespeare and Ben Jonson.

Summary

Early Modern English may be called the period of growing standardisation. Most of the remaining domains of language use (for example, scientific and academic prose) adopt English, and towards 1700 the spelling of printed works is nearly regularised. Early Modern English is also the period of the so-called printing revolution and growing literacy, and the era marked by the Renaissance and the Reformation.

Linguistic change is most noticeable in the fields of phonology and syntax. The Great Vowel Shift (a process which had already started in late Middle English and spreads out to the eighteenth century) restructures the system of long vowels, and many of the specific Modern English syntactic constructions (for example, *do*-support) emerged during Early Modern English. By contrast, in the field of morphology, Early Modern English only completed the sweeping changes which had happened in Middle English. The Early Modern English lexicon saw a significant new influx of loan words, above all from Latin, but also from French and Greek. The regional variation found in Middle English continues in the spoken language and the social stratification of Early Modern English can be traced, for example, in the use of titles, in the distribution of lexis and in letters stemming from less educated people.

In the Early Modern English period the output of texts and the variety of genres is further growing. Pamphlets and newspapers are among the innovative publications formats which emerge. But Early Modern English is also the period when many of the "polite" forms of communication which are common today developed (for example, the common address term *you* and the directives using interrogatives).

Further reading

Nevalainen (2006), Barber (1997) and Görlach (1991) are useful textbooks on Early Modern English. Nevalainen (2006) provides an excellent basic linguistic introduction, Barber (1997), in addition, emphasises socio-cultural aspects and Görlach (1991) offers a lot of linguistic detail and a valuable collection of text excerpts. Lass (1999) is better suited for the advanced reader. Rydén et al. (1998) is a collection of important research articles. Cusack (1998) is a useful reader with excerpts from Early Modern "everyday English". Jucker and Taavitsainen (2010) offers instructive articles covering, among other topics, important pragmatic aspects of discourse domains and authors of the Early Modern English period (for example, Shakespeare, religious discourse, courtroom discourse, news discourse etc.).

Questions and exercises

1. Early Modern English is often called the period of standardisation, in particular with regard to spelling. Which elements of modern standard languages are still missing in Early Modern English?

2. Using the presentation in Figure 1 in Chapter 5.2.1., reconstruct the development of the stressed vowel from late Middle English onwards in the following Present-Day English words: *sweet, heath, tale, fool, open, loud, light*.

3. Using the information given in Chapter 5.2.1., try to reconstruct the pronunciation of the text excerpt from Shakespeare's *Hamlet* below (III, i, First Folio Edition 1623). (If you need help, you might consider Chapter 3 of Barber 1997).

> To be, or not to be, that is the Question:
> Whether 'tis Nobler in the minde to suffer
> The Slings and Arrowes of outragious Fortune*,   *fate*
> Or to take Armes against a Sea of troubles,
> And by opposing end them: to dye*, to sleepe   *die*
> No more; and by a sleepe, to say we end
> The Heart-ake*, and the thousand Naturall shockes   *heart-ache*
> That Flesh is heyre* too*? 'Tis a consummation*   *heir - to - completion*
> Deuoutly* to be wish'd. To dye to sleepe,   *strongly*
> To sleepe, perchance to Dreame; I*, there's the rub*,   *"aye" - difficulty*
> For in that sleepe of death, what dreames may come,
> When we haue shuffel'd off* this mortall coile*,   *removed - confusion*
> Must giue vs pawse*. There's the respect*   *break - consideration*
> That makes Calamity* of so long life.   *misery*

4. Look at the affixes of the third-person singular present tense verb forms in texts A and B below. Does your finding confirm the distribution noted in Chapter 5.2.2.?
Determine the subjunctive forms in texts A and B and describe the syntactic contexts by which they occur.

A.
For the wit and minde of man, if it worke vpon matter, which is the contemplation of the creatures of God worketh according to the stuffe, and is limited thereby; but if it worke vpon it selfe, as the Spider worketh his webbe, then it is endlesse, and and brings forth indeed Copwebs of learning, admirable for the finesse of thread and worke, but of no substance or profite.
(Francis Bacon, *The Twoo Bookes of the Proficience and Advancement of Leaning*; 1605; HC)

B.
Mi. Ford.	... oh that my husband saw this Letter: it would giue eternall food to his	
Mis. Page.	iealousie. Why look where he comes; and my good man too: ... Let's consult together against	
Ford.	this greasie Knight: Come hither.	
Pist.	Well: I hope, it be not so.	with cut tail
	Hope is a curtall*-dog in some affaires:	aims at
Ford.	Sir *Iohn* affects* thy wife.	
Pist.	Why sir, my wife is not young.	courts
	He wooes* both high and low, both rich & poor, ...	

(William Shakespeare, *The Merry Wives of Windsor*; I, ii; First Folio Edition, 1623)

5. In *Hamlet*, (II,ii) Polonius asks Hamlet "What do you read my Lord?", and later, Hamlet, meeting Rosencrantz and Guildenstern, asks them "What make you at Elsonower?". Point out in how far these questions are ungrammatical and unidiomatic in contemporary English and what this reveals about Early Modern English syntax.

6. In the short letter below, Thomas Knyvett addresses his wife both with *you* (*y^r*, *you*) and *thou* (*thee, the, thy*). Try to determine the pragmatic meaning

163

communicated in these different addresses and what may have motivated them.

> My deere Harte
> the cause of my not writing to thee the last week was becaus I thought to haue been at home with the* before   *thee*
> my letter, and therfore I cannot chose but condemne y^{r*}   *your*
> to* rashe censure* of my forgettfullnes; which although   *too - disapproval*
> it proceeds from y^r infinite love, yet the assuered testimonies of my affection to you haue bene such as showld rather have layd the fault vpon something else, for I protest to god I love nothing but onely thee, and so rest assuered. […]
> and assoon* as ever all things be* finished betwixt vs I   *as soon - are*
> wilbe* with the, god willing, the next day, which wilbe,   *will be*
> I hope the next weeke. Till when and ever I rest
> Thy loving husband
> who loves the more
> then his owne life
> Tho: Knyvett.
> Houborn, Oct. 9.
> 1621.
> (*The Knyvett Letters*; 1621; HC)

7. The extract below is from a treatise on education. This text is presented in the form of a dialogue, a format that was quite popular in Early Modern English treatises and handbooks. Why would readers in Early Modern England prefer this interactive format to the expository prose we would expect in this genre today? What are the consequences for the linguistic form of the text if the dialogue format is used?

> *Spoud.*   That I may begin at the very first entrance of the Schoole: let me inquire this of you, how soon you would have your childe set unto the Schoole; for I thinke that worthy to be first knowne, if so be that you purpose to have your scholler* fitted for the Universitie, by fifteene   *pupil*
> yeeres of age.

Phil. I like your reason well, to enter there. But to the intent that I may more fully make knowne unto you, what I thinke, and have found in this behalfe, let mee heare first of you, as I wished in generall, at what age you use in your countrey, to set your children to begin to learne.

Spoud. For the time of their entrance with us, in our countrey schooles, it is commonly about seven or eight yeeres old: sixe is very soone*. If any beginne so early, they are rather sent to the schoole to keepe them from troubling the house at home, and from danger, and shrewd turnes, then for any great hope and desire their friends have that they should learne any thing in effect*. *early* *indeed*

Phil. I finde that therein first is a very great want generally;

(John Brinsley, *Ludus Literarius or the Grammar Schoole*; 1627; HC)

165

6. English after 1700 (Late Modern English)

The term "Late Modern English" does not belong to the traditional, "classic" designations for the periods in the history of the English language, like Old English, Middle English and Early Modern English. This seems to reflect an initial lack of interest on the part of historical linguistics. At first, historical linguists were not very much concerned about the linguistic developments after 1700, partly because they thought these were not attractive enough to merit their attention and the status quo of the language was "practically" like contemporary English. In fact, the changes during the eighteenth and nineteenth century are not as sweeping as those marking the Middle and Early Modern periods. Change seems to have been less categorical and much more statistical, in the sense that certain linguistic phenomena have become more or less frequent and common. It is only during the past two or three decades that interest in the developments of the English language after 1700 has been aroused, with significant numbers of studies being published. Along these lines, the general view emerged that the period roughly covers the years between 1700 and 1900 (or 1950) and that its name – in analogy to "Early" Modern English – should be "Late" Modern English.

6.1. Political and socio-cultural background

It is hard to find convenient extra-linguistic events which might serve as clear points of demarcation for the Late Modern period. In terms of kings and queens, the eighteenth and nineteenth centuries are known as the period of the Hanoverian dynasty and of Victorianism. Language history during this era is, however, less directly linked to the royal family but rather to general intellectual, socio-cultural, and political developments, such as rationalism, the Industrial Revolution, new technological developments, advances in education and, last but not least, colonial expansion. These will be discussed in the following sections.

The most influential intellectual trend towards the end of the seventeenth and the beginning of the eighteenth century, which set the scene for the Late Modern period, was rationalism, with its appeal to reason, observation and the rise of experimental sciences. The basic paradigm for conceiving the world was in terms of logical order. Whenever things failed to meet these requirements, they had to be regulated, and once a state of logical order was achieved, this state had to be fixed. Such a way of thinking shaped the attitudes towards the English language at the beginning of the eighteenth century. Since English was far from being fully standardised, people thought it had to be regularised, refined and fixed. Typical of such an approach is Jonathan Swift's *Proposal for Correcting, Improving, and Ascertaining the English Tongue* (1712), in which he sharply criticised any linguistic innovation, deplored the present state of the language, suggested to delete improper words and phrases in the language and then to "fix it for ever".

One way of "fixing" the language was, of course, by means of dictionaries and (prescriptive) grammars. The eighteenth century is, thus, often seen as the "age of correctness", which witnesses the beginning of the normative tradition of dictionaries and grammars, for example, Samuel Johnson's *Dictionary of the English Language* (1755) and Robert Lowth's *Short Introduction to English Grammar* (1762). The basic aim of the normative grammarians was to install rules for English which were governed by reason, analogy and the model of classical Latin, to criticise "improper" language use and to settle disputed points (on Late Modern dictionaries and grammars see Chapters 6.2.1., 6.2.4. and 6.2.5. below).

A further symptom of the spirit of this era was the call for an English language academy, following the examples of the *Accademia della Crusca* (1582) in Italy and *L'Académie Française* (1635) in France. Both institutions had succeeded in establishing an authoritative role in their respective countries, publishing important dictionaries. After earlier plans for an English academy in the Elizabethan era had been discarded, the idea gained new ground towards the end of the seventeenth and at the beginning of the eighteenth century. Despite the fact that the project had important supporters (for example, Jonathan Swift, Daniel Defoe and John Dryden), it never materialised and was more or less given up after the publication of Johnson's *Dictionary* in 1755.

Other developments which affected the English language in the eighteenth and nineteenth centuries relate to technological innovation and the Industrial Revolution. The shift from a still largely agrarian economy to an economy shaped by machine manufacture and large factories led to increasing urbanisation, especially during the late eighteenth and the nineteenth century. Large numbers of workers moved to the ever growing cities (particularly in the North). By 1900 nearly 80 per cent of the population lived in urban districts with populations of 10,000 or more (Rose 1985: 277). Urbanisation, of course, led to dialect levelling. People stemming from different dialect backgrounds, living in close proximity, tend to adapt their language habits, giving up the most salient features of their vernaculars. On the other hand, urbanisation also resulted in the formation of new dialects typical of the specific urban communities, which served as important models of identification and (local) pride.

The Industrial Revolution was also one factor which contributed to greater social mobility in the nineteenth century, creating a wealthy middle class. Many social climbers were fairly powerful and influential but, lacking the necessary education and being upwardly mobile, they were typically insecure about the "correct" language use. "Talking proper" came to be a mark of social respectability and education and those who failed to show it were unavoidably classed as poor, dishonourable and dull. This spirit of "talking proper" effectively combined with the spirit of "correctness" in language mentioned above, creating a vast demand for normative grammars and language guides.

Another consequence which the new technological developments had were advances in transport and communication. Travelling (and also travelling for pleasure) became much easier as new roads were built and a railway network developed in the nineteenth century. In 1840 the Penny Post was introduced, a uniform and cheap mailing system, which resulted in a multiplication of the numbers of private letters. In 1837 the electric telegraph was invented, the first of several inventions and innovations which increased the possibilities of written communication.

In the sphere of education and literacy the Late Modern period witnessed significant advances, although mainly towards the end of the era. In the eighteenth century the numbers of schools were increasing, but standards of teaching in provincial schools must still have been low, with teachers being neither well qualified nor well paid. Basically, a proper education was still a privilege of a minority, accessible to those who lived in urban areas or whose parents were rich enough to pay. In the nineteenth century the situation gradually improved and a (still grossly inadequate) system of state funding was introduced in the first half of the century. It was only in 1870, with the Elementary Education Act, that primary compulsory education was introduced. Still, we may well assume that literacy, especially reading skills, had spread throughout the period.

A major political development which has affected the English-speaking world right until the twentieth century and beyond was the colonial expansion of England. The first English settlements in the "New World" had already started during the Early Modern period (Jamestown 1607, the arrival of the "Pilgrim Fathers" in 1620). But it was the Late Modern Period that saw the unprecedented growth of English colonies and the foundation of the "Empire". There were further colonies in Canada, in India, in Australia and, in the nineteenth century, in South Africa and New Zealand and many more elsewhere. On the other hand, England also had to face the American Revolution (1775–1783) with the result of the independence of the United States.

The colonial expansion of England had far-reaching linguistic consequences. On the one hand it led to the world-wide spread of the language, with an increased opportunity of variation and several national standard varieties emerging in its wake (most importantly for the nineteenth century, American English). On the other hand, it resulted in an expansion of the vocabulary, first of all within the emerging varieties, but eventually also in the standard language.

6.2. Language structure

6.2.1. Spelling and pronunciation

By the end of the Early Modern period the spelling system was the most regularised section of the language, at least in printed works. Texts appear distinctly modern and there is no difference from contemporary English in the number of graphemes. However, some special features prevail, especially in texts stemming from the eighteenth century. The so-called "long s" <ſ> is still found. Modern readers unfamiliar with this allograph of <s> tend to confuse it with modern <f>. Thus <ſound> (*sound*) is easily misread as *found*. In some cases the final <e> was preserved (for example, *confesse, despaire*, also *comeing, haveing*). There was still variation in some endings, for example *–ick* instead of *–ic* (*musick, politick*), *-or* instead of *–our* (*savior, humor*) and *–l* instead of *–ll* (*cal, hal*), but here the modern forms spread in the course of the eighteenth century. The apostrophe was used to mark omission of letters, for example, to realise a "phonetic" spelling in past tense forms of verbs (*chang'd, rebuk't*) or just for abbreviations of specific words (*tho'* for *though, thro'* for *through*).

Some of the variation still possible in the eighteenth century was used by Noah Webster in order to establish some specifically American spelling features, for example, in *The American Spelling Book* (1783) and later in *An American Dictionary of the English Language* (1828). These features included spellings like <er> in *center*, <or> in *humor* and <se> in *defense*.

Another feature that makes English texts from the (early) eighteenth century look different from modern texts is capitalisation. In the first decades of the eighteenth century there was a custom to use capital letters, for example, for marking nouns or other important parts of a sentence, probably in order to make sentence structure more transparent. The number of initial capital letters increased considerably until about 1750, affecting other parts of speech as well, but was then suddenly dropped. By the end of the eighteenth century the custom was completely abolished.

When we say that spelling was more or less regularised in the eighteenth century, this statement must be restricted to printed matter. Especially in private correspondence we find a lot of variation. Even respected authors and critics (for example, Samuel Johnson, Laurence Sterne and Robert Lowth) seemed to follow different conventions when writing personal letters. Osselton (1984/1998: 34) assumes a dual spelling standard: a public one, which was found in printed works, and a private one, which people used when writing letters. Thus, with one and the same author we may find standard forms and more idiosyncratic forms, for example *easier* vs. *easyer*, *unworthiness* vs. *unworthyness* and *opportunities* vs. *opportunitys*. A good example, mentioned by Tieken-Boon van Ostade (2009: 44), is the memoirs of Laurence Sterne, which exist in a handwritten and a published version (1767 and 1775). The manuscript includes spellings which probably reflect Sterne's personal style and which may go back to the author's youth (for example *supplyed*, *orderd*, *Arch Bishop*, *Designe*). These "anomalies" were, of course, all expunged in the printed version. This "double format" of public and private spelling persisted throughout the eighteenth century and also in the nineteenth century we find divergences in the orthography between letters and diaries on the one hand and printed matter on the other.

Although spelling was the most standardised part of the English language by the nineteenth century, it was still in need of reform because of its irregularity, in the sense that there was no conventional link between orthography and pronunciation. Most people saw that there was need for a spelling reform but both the eighteenth and the nineteenth centuries were quite reluctant about introducing reforms. In part, this lack of reform reflected the prevailing attitude that language, especially written language, should be "fixed" and not adapted to speech, which obviously changed through the centuries. Although the late nineteenth century saw a notable innovation in the transcription of sounds with the development of the International Phonetic Alphabet, this alphabet had never been intended as a replacement of the conventional spelling. Despite new suggestions towards the end of the nineteenth century (for example, amendments suggested by the British Spelling Reform Association), the general attitude remained critical and reserved, and no general reform could be launched.

This persistent conservatism in matters of orthography may also be said to reflect a rising attitude which saw proper spelling as a mark of respectability and good education. Despite the idiosyncratic spellings mentioned above, educated writers were increasingly expected to follow the conventions laid down in respected works like Johnson's *Dictionary of the English Language* (on this see Chapter 6.2.4. below). The following decades saw the publication of a growing number of spelling books, as correct spelling came to be seen as a major mark of social distinction, similar in importance to "talking proper" in speech.

In the field of pronunciation we must distinguish between systematic / categorical changes in the sound system and processes by which certain pronunciations (for example, h-dropping) became stigmatised and socially undesirable. The latter will be dealt with in the chapter on regional and social distribution (see 6.2.5. below).

The available evidence for tracing the pronunciation of English in the eighteenth and nineteenth centuries is much richer than that of all the previous periods. There are large pronouncing dictionaries, for example, John Walker's *Critical Pronouncing Dictionary* (1791), sections in grammar books and spellers, and proposals made by spelling reformers. All of these may be biased since they often only reflect the subjective perspective of one individual. In addition, there are naïve spellings, spelling mistakes, rhyme and wordplay, which may be used to infer the pronunciation of individual words. Lastly, there are representations of speech in drama and novels. Here, again, we cannot be sure whether these are authentic, because they may only reflect the writer's subjective perception or use of stereotype. In the nineteenth century we find more objective descriptions of certain pronunciations by phoneticians and the first phonetic transcriptions, which of course deserve more trust.

In the sphere of long vowels, it is safe to assume that the merger of /e:/ (in words spelt like *meat* and *beat*) and /i:/ (in words spelt like *meet* and *beet*) was completed for most speakers by the end of the seventeenth century (on this stage of the Great Vowel Shift see Chapter 5.2.1. above). In the course of the eighteenth century we find evidence for the last stage of the shift. This is the diphthongisation of the vowels /e:/ (as in *face* and *name*) and /o:/ (as in *home* and *boat*), resulting in the modern pronunciation /ei/ and /əʊ/. Most evidence suggests that the long vowels stayed monophthongs until the end of the century and the new emerging diphthongs were not very prestigious at the outset. It seems that they were only accepted in high-status speech by the middle of the nineteenth century.

In the eighteenth century we find more evidence for the phonemic split between /ʊ/ and /ʌ/ (as in *look* and *luck*), which can be traced to the seventeenth century (see Chapter 5.2.1. above). Most of the evidence here is "negative", however, in that commentators see pronunciations of *but* as [bʊt] and *cut* as [kʊt] as provincial and typically Northern. The eighteenth century saw another vowel change which, if not followed, would similarly result in a "Northernism" later. This was the lengthening of the vowels in words like *bath*, *laugh* and *grass*. But it seems that the lengthening was not universally accepted in the nineteenth century and sometimes seen as a vulgarism.

In the area of consonants, the most noteworthy change during the Late Modern period is the loss of postvocalic /r/. Evidence suggests that the r-less forms took a long time before they were accepted in "respectable" speech and were stigmatised until the second half of the nineteenth century. As a consequence of the loss of postvocalic /r/, the short vowels preceding it (as in *bird, burn, Bernese*) merged as /ɜ:/ and a number of diphthongs with schwa as a second element emerged (as in *peer, bear, fare, pair*).

Other changes in pronunciation, like h-dropping and the so-called g-dropping, which were very much discussed and commented on in this period, reflect the changing social value of "correct" pronunciation in English society and the rise of "talking proper" in the nineteenth century. These issues will be dealt with in the chapter on the regional and social distribution in the Late Modern period (6.2.5.).

6.2.2. Morphology and word-formation

inflectional morphology

In the field of morphology we find few changes, in particular few categorical changes, during the Late Modern period. The categorical changes had mostly started in Early Modern English and were fully completed during the eighteenth and (sometimes) the nineteenth century. In some cases certain forms became stigmatised, that is, they were no longer part of Standard English or the kind of language use considered appropriate for communicating among the "respectable" classes.

Two changes had affected the inflectional endings of verbs in the present tense during the Early Modern period. The second-person singular *–st* ending was lost due to the demise of the personal pronoun *thou* and its related forms. And in the third-person singular the competition between the (more formal) *–th* ending and the (more informal) *–s* ending was settled in favour of the incoming standard form *–s*. Thus, starting from the eighteenth century, we find *thou* and its related forms only in biblical language, certain religious and literary registers and in regional dialects. In a similar way, the *–th* ending is restricted to the biblical and legal register. However, high-frequency forms like *doth, hath* and *saith* are still found in the eighteenth and even in the nineteenth century.

The Early Modern period had also seen a reduction in the inventory of morphological forms of irregular verbs. This process continued in the Late Modern period. In particular, the final *–n* in the second participle is lost (*spoke* for *spoken* and *got* for *gotten*). Also, preterite forms are used for the participle (for example, *write, wrote, wrote*) and, vice versa, participle forms for the preterite (for example, *fling, flung, flung*). As a result, we find great variability in the past tense forms of many verbs. This situation was even intensified by new weak variants of strong verbs and the occasional introduction of archaic forms (derived from Shakespeare or the *King James Bible*). For example, Görlach (2001: 103) notes *wrote, wrate,* and *writ* as variants for the past tense and *wrote, writ* and *written* as variants of the past participle of *write*. With *shrink* we find *shrank, shrunk* and *shrinked* in the past tense and *shrank, shrunk* and *shrinked* in the past participle. In addition, the spelling of regular weak verbs in the eighteenth century was often different from contemporary English in that it tended to represent the voiced or voiceless quality of the dental suffix (for example, *dropt* for *dropped, stuft* for *stuffed* and *lov'd* for *loved*).

With nouns and pronouns there was much less variation. The s-genitive in nouns with a final *–s* was not marked in the eighteenth century and it was only in the nineteenth century that forms like *boss's* became the rule. Similarly, the conventions for marking the genitive plural (*kings', wives'*) were not established until the end of the eighteenth century. The so-called irregular plurals (*mice, teeth* etc.) were the same as in contemporary English, but there was some uncertainty about the plural forms of Latin and Greek loanwords, which were often formed according to the plural forms of the donor language (for example, *theses, species, opera*).

In the personal pronouns the situation of the late seventeenth century was firmly consolidated: *thou* and related forms were extremely restricted (see above), the distinction between *ye* and *you* was given up and only retained in biblical writings. The new genitive form *its* was fully accepted, but the alternatives *thereof* and *of it* were still frequently found.

One issue which raised (and still today raises) considerable concern is the "correct" choice of the case forms of personal pronouns in certain constructions, for example: *It is I* vs. *It is me*; *between you and I* vs. *between you and me*. The selection of the correct, that is in most cases, the more formal option, turned out to be of superior importance since it was considered to reflect the education and social acceptability of a speaker, a symptom of the rise of "talking proper", which marked especially the nineteenth century (see Chapter 6.2.5.).

word-formation

There are hardly any comprehensive investigations of Late Modern English word-formation, and some researchers say that there are not many innovative formations which may be called specific for the eighteenth or the nineteenth centuries. But this may be due to the lack of adequate documentation or the simple fact that the Late Modern era is still found to be too "close" and "familiar" with regard to contemporary English. Manfred Görlach, in his textbooks on eighteenth- and nineteenth-century English (2001: 169–177; 1999b: 118–125) lists some interesting new developments, some of which will be mentioned below.

In the field of derivational suffixes, the noun ending *–ess*, which expresses gender, became increasingly popular. But many new formations do not seem to have survived or were created just for the moment (for example, *citizeness, editress*, in the nineteenth century *seductress, visitress*). Suffixes indicating diminutives (*–ette* and *–let*) became popular in the nineteenth century (*balconette, novelette*; *booklet, starlet*). The nineteenth century saw also an increase in formations ending in *–ism*, which were often added to a personal name (for example, *Victorianism, Darwinism, Pre-Raphaelism*), with the respective *–ist* denoting a follower (*Darwinist*) and *–ite* for an adjective (*Darwinite, Pre-Raphaelite*). It seems plausible to assume that such formations reflect a situation typical of the nineteenth century, where the supporters of different ideologies and divisions in society were competing with each other. The ending *–ise* (for example, *idealise, revolutionise, legalise*) is typically associated with a new international technical vocabulary. While it does not seem to have been very productive in the eighteenth century, the nineteenth century, with its progress in science and technology, saw a significant growth of these formations. They are also often associated with other, mostly technical, formations which were based on Latin and Greek elements, and which are traditionally called neo-classical formations. These new coinages will be dealt with in the chapter on lexis (see 6.2.4.). As regards prefixes, there seems to have been a noticeably increase in prefix-formations in the nineteenth century, most of them associated with technological progress (for example, *ante-orbital, demoralise, interactive, pre-Christian* etc.).

In the field of compounding, Noun + Noun and Adjective + Noun formations comprised the most frequent new items (for example. *witch-doctor, steam engine*; *red-fish*). With regard to other word-formation processes, a substantial increase in backformations can be noted in the nineteenth and twentieth centuries (for example, *stagemanage, housekeep, typewrite* and *handshake*).

6.2.3. Syntax

In Late Modern English the situation in the field of syntax is quite similar to that in phonology and morphology. Categorical changes which had been introduced during the Early Modern period were fully established, with incoming standard constructions becoming more frequent and (in most cases) entirely regulated.

Among the more noticeable developments is the rise of the progressive construction. Before 1700, that is, during the Early Modern period, this construction had been optional (compare, for example, Polonius's question in Shakespeare's *Hamlet* "What do you read, my Lord?" not "What are you reading, my Lord?"). The basic structural meaning of the *ing*-form was a focus on the on-going action. Later, during the eighteenth century, but particularly during the nineteenth century, this construction saw a remarkable increase, both in terms of the numbers of tokens found in texts and in terms of the predicates with which the form could occur. While the progressive became an obligatory category during the eighteenth century, it still lacked passive forms. Passive meaning was expressed through the active forms (*the book is printing*, meaning the *book is being printed*) or through the simple passive form. The first passive progressive forms are found in the late eighteenth century, spreading in the wake of the dramatic rise of progressive forms during the nineteenth century. Quite interestingly, prescriptive grammarians severely criticised the new progressive forms, especially those involving longer verb phrases with future and perfect tenses (for example, *they will have been being silly*). In the course of the nineteenth century the number and types of predicates with which the progressive could co-occur expanded, too. For example, it could be used with stative verbs, with verbs denoting momentary events and acts (*explode, nod*) and with adjectival complements (*He is being silly.*). Recent studies confirm that the spread of the progressive continued right through the twentieth century.

The passive progressive expanded the options of the passive voice in Late Modern English. Quite generally, one can say that the frequency of passive constructions increased during the Late Modern period. In particular they are found more often in eighteenth-century texts than in contemporary ones. Also, certain phrasal verbs developed passive constructions (for example, *They were met with.*). Görlach (2001: 117), however, notes that some constructions were fairly inelegant (for example, *She was gone up to by him.*). In addition, a further passive form, the construction with *get*, developed in the second half of the eighteenth century.

Another development in the verb phrase, which had already started in the Early Modern period, was the demise of *be* as an auxiliary in the present and past perfect. Originally, the auxiliary of verbs denoting motion and change (for example, *go, come, grow, become*) had been *be* (*he is come, she was become* etc.). During the Early Modern period the auxiliary *have* had started to spread in these verbs, resulting in variation between *be* and *have*. By the nineteenth century, this change was more or less complete, leaving *have* and *had* as the only options for perfect tenses of the active voice. One of the results of this development was a clearer distinction between active and passive constructions. On the other hand the possibility of distinguishing between action (*he has gone*) and result (*he is gone*) in the present perfect was lost.

One of the major syntactic innovations during the Early Modern period had been the introduction of the so-called *do*-support. By 1700 most negative and interrogative clauses had *do*-support. However, there were some exceptions, which vanished only during the late eighteenth or the nineteenth century. Certain short and frequent verbs (for example, *know, think, write, speak, doubt*) were still found without *do* in negated sentences (*I know not, he wrote not* etc.). Later, such constructions were restricted to biblical and poetic texts. In addition, so-called empty *do* could still be found in declarative sentences during the eighteenth century, mostly in poetry (where *do* served as a metrical filler) or in legal texts, which traditionally were written in very conservative and formulaic style. Also, it seems that lack of *do*-support or empty *do* in declarative sentences was an indicator of low social status and lack of education. Writers like Jane Austen, Thackeray and Dickens employ this feature to depict "lower", uneducated characters in their novels.

Another area where the regularisation of tendencies that had emerged in Early Modern English could be found is relative clauses. Here, the first tendency was the use of *who* with animate antecedents on the one hand and of *which* with inanimate antecedents on the other. *Which* with animate antecedents is only found in non-standard speech by the end of the eighteenth century. The second tendency involved the restriction of *that* to restrictive (or defining) relative clauses. This pattern also emerged during the eighteenth century. As a third tendency, zero-relatives came to be limited to object position. Such "contact clauses" were particularly associated with informal style and were often criticised by conservative authors, especially when the relative pronoun was in subject position.

A last change linking back to Early Modern English and developing further in Late Modern English was a shift in the complementation system of verbs. This shift has not been mentioned in the syntax chapter on Early Modern English and it was less categorical than the other developments mentioned so far. Shift in the complementation system means that in the course of the centuries verbs tended to be followed less often by finite clauses (above all *that* clauses) and more often by non-finite clauses (at first infinitives and later gerunds). During the nineteenth century in particular, we witness a shift from infinitives to gerunds. Verbs like *remember* were no longer complemented by an infinitive (*He remembered to have forgotten his purse.*) but by a gerund (*He remembered forgetting his purse.*). In a similar way, verbs like *avoid, forbear, decline, deny, refuse* were rather followed by gerunds, not by infinitives. Other verbs showing the same tendencies were *forget, recall, try, enjoy, hate* and *like*.

6.2.4. Lexis and semantics

After Middle English and Early Modern English, as periods of a major expansion of the vocabulary, Late Modern English seems to have been more modest in terms of lexical growth. Studies based on the *Chronological English Dictionary* (in which the entries of the *Shorter Oxford English Dictionary* (SOED) are arranged in chronological order) suggest a slower increase in the number of new words, especially for the eighteenth century, but a noticeable rise towards the middle of the nineteenth century. Some researchers have raised the question whether this finding may just reflect the compilation methods of the *Oxford English Dictionary* (OED), on which the SOED is based. Here the eighteenth century was less extensively represented than the previous centuries of the Early Modern period and the nineteenth century. But even so, most researchers still believe that the low rate of lexical innovation in the eighteenth century reflects the spirit of the time, characterised by a typical reluctance to accept new words or any innovations and changes in the language (see Chapter 6.1.).

Quite similar to the Early Modern era, however, most new formations found in Late Modern English are based on Latin and Greek (apart from French) and they belong for the most part to a learned, scientific background, reflecting technological progress and scholarship. Particularly noteworthy is here the evolution of a neo-Latin and neo-Greek terminology, which can already be found in the eighteenth century, but saw its peak in the nineteenth century. Typical neo-classical formations are so-called neo-classical compounds, for example, *biology, telegraph, democrat, chronometer* (for a detailed list see Görlach 2001: 166–167 and Görlach 1999b: 112–113; see also Chapter 6.2.2.). These formations are also called quasi-compounds because, like compounds, they can be split up into separate elements (for example, *bio-* and *-logy*, *tele-* and *-graph*) which can be re-combined to form other neo-classical formations (*biosphere, theology, television, monograph*) but cannot be seen as independent free forms, as in regular compounds. Typical first elements are *anthropo-, bio-, chrono-, eco-, demo-*, typical second elements *–crat, –cracy, –gamy, –meter, -nomy*. Such terms had already existed from the Renaissance onwards, but increased dramatically with the technological progress in the eighteenth and nineteenth centuries. The majority of terms in the Late Modern period are technical terms and might be more or less transparent for a language user with some knowledge of classical languages. Görlach (1999b: 114) points out that such coinages must have been international in the sense that similar formations with similar meanings were found in other European languages. This made international communication in science and technology much easier, at least in the written medium. On the other hand, many of the nineteenth-century neologisms are hardly ever found in an everyday context (compare such words as *autoerotism, monomorphous, polyptych* and *thermophile*).

We also find some lexemes which seem to have been borrowed straight from Latin or Greek (like *excursus, omnibus, bacillus, pylon*), but these are obviously also restricted to learned or specialised contexts.

Apart from Latin and Greek, French is the major third donor language in Late Modern English. Both in the eighteenth and nineteenth centuries, French was the most prominent foreign language, enjoying a high prestige, associated with refined and luxurious life and polite communication. Many of the borrowed words can be assigned to the fields of dress and fashion, furniture, cooking, art and literature. Typical examples are *ballet, negligee, brunette, cuisine.*

There were also borrowings from other European languages on the Continent. German provided terms associated with mineralogy and mining (for example, *cobalt, sinter, nickel*) and designations for particular products and concepts (*pumpernickel, waltz*). Dutch supplied nautical terms (*schooner, caboose*), and Italian, among others, musical and architectural terms (*cantata, soprano, loggia*), whereas Spanish contributed only a few isolated items (for example, *fandango, flotilla*). – Due to British colonialism and the spread of English across the globe, we also find many loans from languages outside Europe, sometimes also via American English.

In all these borrowings it is often difficult to recognise a coherent pattern, for example, in terms of semantic fields, and the generalisations made above must be seen rather as tendencies. Especially in the nineteenth century there are few consistent patterns of borrowing and in most cases we are dealing with an accumulation of individual "word-cases" and "word-histories" (Görlach 1999b: 117).

However, there are two generalisations which can be made about loanwords in the Late Modern period. First, loanwords borrowed during the Late Modern period (whether they were of French, Latin, Italian or other provenance) were no longer fully integrated into the language but retained much of their foreign character (see, for example, *brunette, cuisine* and *machine*, stemming from French, and *nucleus, excursus, bacillus* borrowed from Latin, or *cantata* and *soprano* from Italian). In the case of French one can assume that the approximately "original" pronunciation might be shown off as a sign of genteel education, whereas in the case Latin, speakers might fear that more adapted forms could be taken as mistakes.

Secondly, apart from neo-classical formations, the number of borrowings decreased in the course of the nineteenth century. This is one of the major changes in the history of the English language: Whereas the previous centuries saw the influx of large numbers of foreign words, making the English vocabulary extremely multifaceted, complex and flexible, the trend shifted towards exportation at the end of the nineteenth century. Now English gradually became one of the major languages which contributed words to other languages, a development which reached a first peak in the middle of the twentieth century.

One major new development in the Late Modern period that affected the documentation of the vocabulary was the emergence of English lexicography. The first monolingual dictionaries stemmed from the seventeenth century (for example, Robert Cawdrey's *Table Alphabeticall* from 1604 or Thomas Blount's *Glossographia* from 1656), but they mostly contained hard words, that is, words which were inaccessible to people lacking (classical) learning and education (for example, women and businessmen). Thus they were far from covering the complete vocabulary of the English language. At the beginning of the eighteenth century dictionaries slowly expanded their scope and moved beyond mere lists of hard words (for example, John Kersey's *New English Dictionary* from 1702 and Nathan Bailey's *Universal Etymological English Dictionary* from 1721). However, the major lexicographic work of the eighteenth century, which set new standards for dictionary making, was *A Dictionary of the English Language* by Samuel Johnson, published in 1755. Johnson's *Dictionary* covered much more of the English vocabulary than any other work before him. He also offered a stabilised orthography, which had a standardising effect on the spelling of the large majority of English words. Johnson included thousands of quotations which were supposed to illustrate the use of the words. Since Johnson mainly focussed on the "best writers", it does not come as a surprise that most quotations are from Shakespeare, Milton and Dryden. Johnson very much improved the definitions of the senses of the words, but was sometimes criticised for being too Latinate (compare, for example, the often cited definition of *cough* as "a convulsion of the lungs, vellicated by some sharp serosity"). Criticism was also expressed about the choice of some words and the etymologies he offered. But despite these flaws, Johnson's *Dictionary* stands out as the major lexicographical achievement of the century.

The most conspicuous gap left in Johnson's description of words was pronunciation. Some hint was given occasionally, for example, in connection with the entry on *cough* mentioned above, where Johnson adds: "It is pronounced coff." But generally no information was included. This gap was closed with the publication of John Walker's *Critical Pronouncing Dictionary* in 1791. Both Walker's and Johnson's works remained highly influential during the first half of the nineteenth century. No new innovative lexicographic initiatives can be found during this period, and by the middle of the century there was no comprehensive and reliable dictionary available apart from the not quite up-to-date editions of Johnson's and Walker's works.

On the other side of the Atlantic, in the United States, Noah Webster published his *American Dictionary of the English Language* (1828). With this work he documented and established the American conventions of English, both in terms of spelling and in terms of lexis, and these conventions were increasingly seen as a specific mark of national identification and pride.

In England, the second half of the nineteenth century saw the emergence of the greatest lexicographical project (so far) in the history of English, which finally led to the publication of the *Oxford English Dictionary* (first called *A New English Dictionary on Historical Principles*). The initiative started from a growing awareness of the lack of an adequate lexicographic reference work and in 1857 a committee was founded by the Philological Society, which finally set out the basic requirements for a new dictionary project. It should include every word recorded after 1150, trace their history in terms of variant forms, spellings, uses and, of course, meanings, and provide a large number of quotations covering all the recorded writings in English. In order to collect the required quotations, a huge reading program was launched, with hundreds of helpers gathering some six million slips. The first instalment, which contained part of the letter A, was published in 1884. The final work was not complete until 1928, when the first full edition of the *Oxford English Dictionary* was published. It contained more than 15,000 pages and more than 240,000 head words. In 1989 the second edition followed. The *Oxford English Dictionary* became the major lexicographic institution for the English language during the twentieth century. At the beginning of the new millennium it was rounded off with the online-edition (with more than 600,000 headwords and 3 million quotations) and the OED3 project.

Given the fact that Late Modern English is so much closer to contemporary English than Middle English or Old English, one might assume that semantic change is not as pervasive and relevant as in previous areas. This is certainly corroborated by the general impression that reading a novel by Jane Austen or Charles Dickens does not seem to create great difficulties with regard to the meaning of individual words. However, we find quite a few lexemes in the eighteenth and nineteenth centuries whose contemporary, "common" senses were not yet as widespread as they are today. For example, *match* ("a small stick for lighting fires") became prominent only in the 1830s; *traffic* had the primary meaning "exchange of goods, trade" through the larger part of the nineteenth century, and the contemporary sense "road traffic" emerged only from the 1830s on. Other examples are *sport* ("recreation, amusement" as opposed to "games and exercises", which emerged only in the 1860s), *star* ("a person distinguished in art, industry or science" from the 1830s) and *train* ("railway carriages", from the 1830s).

Other reasons for different lexical meanings can be found in social history, for example, in prudery. Thus common designations for women's undergarment were systematically avoided, leading to respective senses of words like *inexpressibles, indescribables, inexplicables* or *unmentionables*. In a similar way, terms designating drinks or vehicles may cause difficulties for modern readers: *bishop* ("a sweet alcoholic drink"), *porter* ("a kind of beer"), *purl* ("hot beer with gin"); *dog-cart* ("a cart with a box for dogs"), *chaise-cart* ("a light cart"), *cabriolet* ("a light two-wheeled chaise drawn by one horse"). These and other examples nicely illustrate that semantic changes are quite often triggered by changes in attitudes and habits and by new technological developments.

6.2.5. Regional and social distribution

During the Late Modern English period regional spoken dialects were pervasive in everyday communication, following basically the same pattern of distribution as in Early Modern English. However, towards the end of the period the extensive migration in the wake of the Industrial Revolution caused a large-scale levelling of dialects and an emergence of new urban varieties of speech. At the same time, we find a growing awareness of the social value of language. With the codification of the written standard and the formation of a spoken norm in the course of the nineteenth century, members of the middle class emphasised the importance of correct grammar and respectable pronunciation, associating non-standard forms with lack of education and even corruptness. So the nineteenth century becomes the period of "talking proper" and the social evaluation of speech.

For the eighteenth century we can assume that regional dialects could be heard on most occasions in everyday communication, sometimes even among members of the upper classes. There are reports about respected politicians who kept their local accents even in the nineteenth century (for example, Walpole and Gladstone). Early dialectologists (for example, Alexander Ellis and Joseph Wright) mention that local dialect was common in the towns in the nineteenth century, especially in the North, an account which is corroborated by the reports of the school inspectors.

At the same time, we witness an immense loss of dialect during the nineteenth century, which even affected the countryside and smaller towns. The large number of people who were employed in the ever-growing factories stemmed mostly from rural areas. Once they were living in close proximity, many dialect features were levelled and lost. In some cases new metropolitan varieties emerged (for example, in the large industrial cities of the North).

The weakening of the traditional rural dialects was also due to the spread of the written standard and the evolution of a spoken norm. Already in the eighteenth century, the prescriptive tradition of the grammars and dictionaries had stigmatised non-standard varieties and advocated, apart from the use of "correct" grammar and lexis, the written (standard) form of a word as a model for pronunciation. "Good" pronunciation was linked to the educated and "polite" speech of Londoners, "good" grammar and lexis could be found in the various handbooks and dictionaries (for example, Robert Lowth's *Short Introduction to English Grammar* (1762) and Samuel Johnson's *Dictionary of the English Language* (1755)). From 1791, when John Walker's *Critical Pronouncing Dictionary* appeared, people could also refer to an institution which provided a norm for the pronunciation of every single word.

The close association of "proper" language with education and class is mainly a development of the late eighteenth and the nineteenth century. It can in part be traced to the effects of the Industrial Revolution and the new money-based economy, which would allow people from the lower classes or the lower middle class to rise quickly in the social hierarchy. Such upwardly mobile risers are usually linguistically insecure and keen to imitate the prestigious norm of the middle class. On the other hand, the members of the middle class will defend their "standard" by stigmatising all forms of non-standard speech, attaching all kinds of flaws to the speakers / writers using them. Such disapproval included lack of education, lack of social acceptability and even weakness of character. The social pressure to conform to the norms of "talking proper" were so great, that in the course of the nineteenth century the spoken standard came to be defined as *Received Pronunciation* (*RP*), that is, the speech of best-educated persons showing no traces whatsoever of local dialect. It is likely that one of the most important institutions promoting and establishing the norms of *RP* were the public schools and the close-knit social networks associated with them. It was here that upwardly mobile children were sent by their well-to-do parents in order to be immersed in the norms of correct grammar and respectable pronunciation. On the other hand, non-standard forms were not only shared by the lower classes but also by the highest class (see below). Obviously, members of the top sections of society did not feel the need to adjust their speech to any other class, let alone the middle classes.

The most notorious pronunciation features associated with non-standard speech are the so-called h-dropping and g-dropping. H-dropping, that is, the pronunciation of words like *horse* as [ɔːs] and *holy* as [əʊlɪ], seems to have been a common feature of English pronunciation since Middle English, but it only attracted negative comments in the second half of the eighteenth century and was highly stigmatised in the nineteenth century (as it is today). Access to the rules and the several exceptions presupposed teaching and education. As a symptom of the linguistic insecurity we also find many hypercorrections, that is, insertion of /h/ where it is not appropriate (for example, *horange* and *hastronomy*). G-dropping, the pronunciation of *–ing* as [ɪn] (*laughin*, *ridin*) was also recorded earlier in the history of English, and only later seen as incorrect and vulgar. Quite interestingly, this pronunciation was found both in the lower classes and the highest class. The underlying motivation for criticising both h-dropping and g-dropping was obviously the assumed superiority of the written word over speech and the basic orientation towards writing as a guide to pronunciation (*air* vs. *hair*, *look in* vs. *looking*) (Mugglestone (2007 [1995]).

In the field of grammar (morphology and syntax) the eighteenth-century prescriptivists had offered a long list of undesirable constructions, which were banished by many of them, and a corresponding list of "correct" construction, which they advocated, for example, the distribution of *shall* and *will* in future time reference (*I shall*, *you will* etc., not the other way round), the choice of the subject (not the oblique) forms of the pronoun in predicative constructions (*it is I*, not, *it is me*) and after prepositions (*between you and I*), and the use *whom*, not *who* in oblique cases, so-called preposition stranding (*the person I was talking about*) as well as the shifting of past tense and past participle forms of strong verbs (*I seen him.*). The use of *ain't* (*We ain't there.*) and the use of *don't* as a singular form (*he don't come*) were similarly condemned, although both forms were found in the lower and in the highest classes. All these forms were also exploited by eighteenth- and nineteenth-century novelists for characterising non-standard speakers (like servants or nannies). This prescriptive grammar tradition had started in the eighteenth century but was continued in the nineteenth century in the form of numerous handbooks and usage guides, some of which are still popular today (for example, Fowler's *The King's English*).

Quite recently, researchers have questioned the traditional image of the eighteenth-century prescriptivists as staunch supporters of a Latinate, logic-based view of language who imposed arbitrary rules on English, suggesting a modified view. Could it be that these men only introduced as norm what they knew was already common best practice? Using corpus-based methods, new investigations try to gauge the impact of the rules prescriptive grammars set up, by testing them in large Late Modern English corpora. The initial results give a rather mixed picture. It seems that at least some of the rules (for example, the prohibition of double negatives) were already being followed by most Late Modern English language users. Thus, Joan Beal suggests that some prescriptive grammars "would be better described as occupying different points on a prescriptive-descriptive continuum" (Beal 2004: 90).

To round off the rather complex relationship between standard language on the one hand and non-standard language or dialect on the other, it is quite interesting to see that especially the nineteenth century entertained a quite positive, nostalgic view of rural dialects. According to this view, rural dialects were ancient representatives of a lost "golden age", preserving old "true" words and phrases, "gems" which should be collected and saved for future generations. This desire to save the dialects that were in danger of being lost is also reflected in the foundation of the English Dialect Society in 1873, whose explicit aim was the preservation of rural forms of speech and dialect lexis.

This romantic view on dialects is not in contrast to but rather in accordance with the prevalent depreciation of non-standard speech. Non-standard dialect was seen as the product of industrialisation and urbanisation, the corrupted means of communication between members of lower-class urbanised communities, infinitely distant from the pure manifestations of the "true" language of a past age. The archetype of an "evil" urbanised dialect was Cockney, the lower-class speech of London, typically associated with poverty and crime, but also stereotypically employed in novels to depict vulgar and lower-class characters.

6.3. Language use

6.3.1. Discourse and speech acts

From a socio-historical perspective, Late Modern English may be seen as a period of upward social mobility. In the wake of rapidly expanding commerce and the Industrial Revolution, social climbers and members of the middle classes became increasingly rich. The new wealth created a new class consciousness and a growing assumption that members of the "genteel" classes should show an appropriate conduct, in particular with regard to language. The key term was "politeness". Polite behaviour, in the sense of refinement in speech and manners, became a constitutive feature of one's social status. The norms of elegant and sophisticated language use formed the border line dividing "genteel" and lower classes. This "ideology of politeness" shaped discourse and the manifestations of speech acts during the Late Modern period to a considerable extent. The present section will deal with two speech acts that are particularly sensitive to interpersonal relations and politeness, compliments and thanks, and with another way of showing respect or marking social position, modes of address.

In a recent study Irma Taavitsainen and Andreas H. Jucker (2010) have looked at compliments and thanks in eighteenth-century English. As sources they used educational handbooks, newspapers and novels. Both speech acts show realisations quite distinct from modern complimenting and thanking, and they also reflect the ideology of politeness typical of their time. Taavitsainen and Jucker found what they called "ceremonious compliments", long and elaborate formulations of praise following the rules of elegant diction and courtesy. These compliments are "ceremonious" because they often mark certain conventional stages in a conversation or social interaction, like greeting and introduction, thus constituting a ritual of genteel society. Handbooks presented model conversations like the following exchange.

(1) A: Sir, I esteem it a singular Happiness, to have met with such good Company, seeing I have by this Means obtained the Favour of being acquainted with you.
B: Sir, if the same Chance which brought us together in this place, did likewise render me capable of making my Friendship as useful to you as your Goodness is pleased to esteem it acceptable, I should think myself doubly happy; but till Opportunity presents itself, I shall pray you to accept of the good Will.
(*A New Academy of Compliments*; [1669] 1784; cited in Taavitsainen and Jucker 2010: 168)

These extremely elaborate and notoriously exaggerated formulations (for example, *esteem it a singular Happiness, to have met with such good Company* or *render me capable of making my Friendship as useful to you as your Goodness is pleased to esteem it acceptable*) must appear stilted, inappropriate and even hilarious to a contemporary speaker, but they seem to have exactly met the requirements of conduct prevalent during the eighteenth century. The same applies to compliments on looks and other characteristics found in the data (for example, *You are the Glory of your Sex, and bear the Palm of Beauty from them all* or *The Music of the Spheres is not so ravishing as your Voice*; cited in Taavitsainen and Jucker 2010: 169). Such compliments had less the character of expressing personal feelings but rather were conventional moves in the polite interaction required by genteel society. This "ritual" character of the compliments is also revealed in the ways they are referred to in reports and descriptions. See the excerpt below from a novel presented by Taavitsainen and Jucker:

(2) He saluted me with politeness; and having replied to the usual compliments of introduction, He motioned to Theodore to quit the chamber.
(Matthew Lewis, *The Monk*; 1796; cited in Taavitsainen and Jucker 2010: 172)

The notion of *the usual compliments of introduction* indicates that compliments were seen as part of conventionalised polite conversational moves (in the above example the compliment is part of a greeting exchange). It is fair to assume that compliments have become more private and personal in the course of the centuries, losing their ritual and purely conventional features in favour of the expression of less excessive and more individual attitudes and feelings.

Similar developments can be observed for thanks. Expressions of gratitude and indebtedness in the eighteenth century are formulated in a highly elaborate and refined way, which strikes us often today as stilted if not exaggerated (see example 3 below)

(3) Sir, should I not render you thanks for your many favours, I should die in deep impatience or Sir, your goodness hath forced me to a silence that I am not able to render you sufficient thanks for so great a favour.
(*The New Academy of Compliments*; [1669] 1781; cited in Taavitsainen and Jucker 2010: 174–175)

Here again, eighteenth-century politeness conventions seem to have required such ritual acts of thanking. The conventionalised, ritual character of thanking can also be seen in designations like "address of thanks", which "seems to have been a formalised part of a ceremonial compliment, a speech act required at certain occasions" (Taavitsainen and Jucker 2010: 177), as in *the Speaker of the House of Commons presented their Address of thanks to his Grace* (177). Such ceremonial functions of thanking are today mostly restricted to special occasions (for example, when accepting an award). In contemporary English, thanking has acquired new discourse marking functions, for example, terminating an interaction. Such functions are hardly ever found in the eighteenth century.

Modes of address are another way of expressing politeness and showing respect. Quite interestingly, developments in this field during the eighteenth century show, on the one hand, a decrease in distinctions, that is, a spread of more common terms of address. By 1700 *thou* had been given up in favour of universal *you* (see Chapter 5.3.1. above). In the course of the eighteenth century the title *Mr* and *Mrs* became more and more common and the designation *Madam* lost its exclusive touch. On the other hand, handbooks on conduct emphasised the necessity of addressing

187

people with their distinguishing titles. For example, when writing letters, a prince received *his Highness*, an ambassador *his Excellency*, an Archbishop *the most Reverend Father in God* and so on (Taavitsainen and Jucker 2010: 165–166).

Modes of address were also used in Victorian England in order to sustain class distinctions (see Phillipps 1984, who used mostly novels, etiquette books and letters as data). Members of the aristocracy received *my lord, my lady, your grace* etc., whereas servants were addressed with the bare surname. The kind of distance and aloofness maintained in social relations is reflected in the custom of married couples to refer to each other with *Mr* or *Mrs*. Also, a young woman was not allowed to call a young man by his Christian name, and the same applied to men with regard to married women. Usually, Christian names, also among men, were restricted to intimate family communication, except for the lower classes. Thus, it is quite remarkable that, while the linguistic structure of the English language in nineteenth-century England is so close to contemporary English, language use seems to have been remarkably different.

6.3.2. Genres

The Late Modern English period continued a general trend which had affected genres already in the Early Modern era. Genres become more diversified and new genres develop in the wake of the new technology of printing. This chapter will deal with the further development of newspapers and the associated subgenres (including advertisements) and one new (or almost new) genre that is characteristic of the professional diversification of communication, the experimental report, which, among other things, leads up to the modern medical research article.

The first newspapers in England emerge during the seventeenth century, but, as was pointed out in Chapter 5.3.2., these early editions were mostly compilations of individual reports, which followed a basically chronological and narrative pattern. The internal organisation and structure of newspapers changed along with their further development and spread.

The eighteenth century saw a fast growth of newspapers, apart from a great variety of journals (for example, the *Gentleman's Magazine*). Daily newspapers became common in larger cities, and provincial papers were published in towns. The first daily newspaper of London was published in 1703 (*The Daily Courant*), later in the century, more dailies and some evening papers were added. All these London papers, of course, had a wide circulation not only in the capital, but also throughout the country. But the countryside had its own papers, too. In 1725 there were twenty-two provincial newspapers, a number which had risen until fifty in 1780. It is estimated that from 1760 more than nine million newspapers were sold in Britain each year. The provincial papers, of course, very much relied on the London press, borrowing extracts from the metropolitan papers.

It goes without saying that the growth of the press very much enhanced public discourse. People who had not had access to political information or news from society before could now participate to a much larger extent, following their country's military victories or defeats, political scandals and controversies. Politics and social debate were no longer restricted to (the male part of) the upper classes. During the nineteenth century the numbers and distribution of newspapers rose further. This growth was favoured above all by two legislative acts, the repeal of the stamp duty for newspapers in 1855 and the abolition of the tax on paper in 1861.

Among the more noticeable developments in newspapers during the Late Modern period is the further diversification of sub-genres and the emergence of specific (linguistic) profiles for these (see Fries 2012). For example, in the news section, we find home news and foreign news, but also shipping news and crime reports. The letters-to-the-editor sections start in the first half of the eighteenth century. Death notices or obituaries begin as short announcements of deaths and towards the end of the eighteenth century expand to form longer assessments of the life and achievements of the deceased. A separate sports section only appears in the course of the nineteenth century.

In some sub-genres the major development was first of all quantitative expansion. Crime reports (on thefts, robberies, murders etc.) were fairly short at the beginning of the eighteenth century, giving just the necessary information and hardly exceeding one sentence. Later in the century, more appealing details and some commentaries are included, leading to those kinds of stories which were to form a major component of the popular press. A similar expansion can be found in the change of obituaries from short death notices to long presentations (mentioned above). Other developments involved more qualitative changes, the most important one being the evolution of the specific structure of news reports.

The common structure of news reports to which we are used today (headlines, leads, main events) is the product of a rather late development. The common paragraphs in early eighteenth-century news reports were rather long, corresponding in many cases to the report of one correspondent and including many different items. The only headlines found were mostly "datelines", which contain the date of the report together with the respective place. In the course of the eighteenth and nineteenth centuries news reports become longer but also acquire a more transparent structure (Ungerer 2002). The narrative approach is abandoned in favour of reports describing events from different perspectives or structuring the report by the insertion of headlines. But headlines and leads only become widespread in the second half of the nineteenth century. The so-called top-down structure, where the most important items are presented first, with the minor elements left to the end, is a development which belongs to the beginning of the twentieth century.

Occasional advertisements could already be found in the earliest versions of newspapers in the seventeenth century, but they become more popular only after 1700. The first newspaper which systematically devoted large sections to advertisements (but also included news sections) was the *Daily Advertiser*, whose first edition was published in 1730. In the course of the eighteenth century advertisements became a sub-genre closely associated with newspapers. However, these texts are conspicuously different from today's advertisements. They are unusually long, purely descriptive and typographically quite similar to the other texts found on the page. The articles offered in these early advertisements reflect the wants of the fairly well-to-do readership of the eighteenth century, who would buy fashionable and expensive items (for example, tobacco, tea, precious textiles etc.). Another typical feature of such texts is the unrestrained praise heaped on these articles due to their unique quality, with many superlative and strongly positive adjectives, accompanied by numerous learned words (Görlach 2002). In the course of the nineteenth century advertisements become shorter and more eye-catching, due to their more distinctive typography and the increasing number of illustrations added to them. But against the background of contemporary advertising, these texts still appear fairly elaborate, formal and wordy.

Experimental reports form a genre that, similar to news reports, goes back the seventeenth century but developed its specific character only in the Late Modern English period, finally leading to the modern research article. In the late seventeenth century, the Royal Society of London, with the publication of the *Philosophical Transactions*, had imposed new stylistic guidelines for the formulation of texts. Authors of experimental reports were to place the focus on the representation of observable facts and concrete events. Quite interestingly, many of these early reports had the form of a letter. This meant that they started with an explicit address (to the editors) and that the descriptions were presented mainly from the perspective of the writer (with many first-person pronouns and many actions typically predicated of the author). In the course of the eighteenth century, predominantly narrative accounts gave way to more abstract discussions. Towards the end of the century, experimental reports developed slowly into what may be called the modern scientific article. Now the focus is more on general theories and laws of nature, with a detailed justification of methods. Specific observations and descriptions of experiments only serve as a bridge leading to a general conclusion. The pattern is no longer "experiment plus result", but rather "hypothesis plus experiment". Thus, the experiment on which the text reports, has changed from a "noteworthy" affair which deserves a description in itself to a means of promoting scientific progress and insights into the laws of nature (Bazerman 1988, Atkinson 1992).

Summary

Late Modern English has been called the "age of correctness", when prescriptive grammars and dictionaries set out to improve and fix the language. On the other hand, it was the period when technological innovations, advances in transport and communication and political developments (for example, the Industrial Revolution and colonisation) had far-reaching consequences on the development of the language.

In the fields of phonology, morphology and syntax, many of the categorical changes that had started in Early Modern English were fully established and (in many cases) entirely regulated. The Late Modern English lexicon saw a substantial number of borrowings and new formations (mainly based on Latin, Greek and French), but the end of the period witnessed a shift to a major donor language, contributing large quantities of words to other languages.

The most important new development in the regional and social distribution of the language was the explicit social evaluation of speech and the idea of "talking proper", which resulted in the emergence of a spoken standard during the nineteenth century. In the field of discourse, the period was dominated by the "ideology of politeness", which shaped the ceremonious and ritual character of most speech acts especially in the eighteenth century. Like in Early Modern English, the variety of genres and the output of texts were growing further in the wake of the development of the printing technology.

Further reading

Görlach (2001) and Görlach (1999b) are instructive textbooks, containing detailed information about the development of the language and offering, in addition, a valuable collection of text excerpts. Tieken-Boon van Ostade (2009) is an accessible introduction, whereas Romaine (1999) is a more advanced collection of articles. Mugglestone (2007 [1995]) gives a detailed account of the rise of the ideology of talking proper. Bergs and Brinton (2012, sections 56–67) give instructive information about language use, genres and discourse in the Late Modern English period.

The website of the *Oxford English Dictionary Online* is www.oed.com.

Questions and exercises

1. Late Modern English is often seen as the period that is very close to contemporary English, but this view may be misleading. Reviewing the sections on Late Modern English phonology, morphology and syntax (6.2.1–6.2.3.), work out the major differences which still obtained in the first half of the eighteenth century.

2. The excerpt below is from an eighteenth-century letter (Lady Wentworth to her son, 18th September 1705; cited from Görlach 2001: 297). Look at the orthography and trace the non-standard spellings. Are the non-standard spellings coherent? What may have been the reasons for the idiosyncratic orthography?

   My dearist dear and best of children, I am much rejoysed at your fyne present, I wish you may often have such and better, tell you ar as ritch as the Duke of Molberry whoe is billding thy fynest hous at Woodstock that ever was seen; thear is trescore rooms of a flower, noe stairs, only a little pair that goes to the uper rooms, which ar only for sarvents, and staitly wood ... and fyne gardens that are fower myles about. It is beleeved furneture and al cannot cost les than three hundred thoussand pd, the house will cost above a hundred thousand pd. Why should you not be as fortunate as he?

3. Below is an excerpt from an early eighteenth-century advertisement (from Görlach 2001: 298). Compare the spelling with that of the letter in exercise 2 above. What is the probable motivation for the capital letters found in the advertisements? In how far does this advertisement meet the description of early advertising given in Chapter 6.3.2.?

   The true Cephalick, or Head Snuff, twice or trice using, which does infinitely more real good, than 50 times using any other sort; for by its peculiar Operation and Effects, it Cures the most Stubborn and Dangerous Distempers of the Head; such as Apoplexies, Epilepsies, Lethargies, Vertigoes, Megrims, Pains in the Head, Humours in the Eyes ... 2 Papers at most times making a perfect Cure; it being what is daily prescrib'd and approv'd by the most Eminent Physicians ...

4. The following excerpt from a "Fashion report" was published in 1851 (cited in Görlach 1999b: 257). Trace the French loan words and adaptations from French found in the text. Can you find them listed in the *OED*? What specific function(s) do these items seem to serve and what does this suggest about the position of French in nineteenth-century England (see also Chapter 6.2.4.)?

Boulogne, Dieppe, and Trouville, have the privilege of attracting the greater number of Parisiennes, ... Morning *negligés* are composed of peignoirs with their vestes, or pelerines *châles* of jean, quilting, valencia of toile cashemire, in shades, grey, dust-coloured, and pale brown; the greater part are trimmed with broad braids, and lined with pink or blue taffetas. A second sleeve is worn under the pagode of the redingotes of the same material, with a small turn-up cuff trimmed with braid; the same trimming in two or three rows forms a ruche around the throat ...

5. The following text is an excerpt from a foreign news section of the *London Daily Advertiser* published in 1751. What is the basic structure of this short text and how does it differ from foreign news sections in contemporary newspapers?

Paris, Oct. 8.
    The King, who has been at Crecy for some Days, returns this Day to Versailles; during his Majesty's Stay at the former Place, seventeen poor Maidens were married, Portions being given them by the Marchioness de Pompadour. The King intends to distribute a Sum at Versailles, Choisy, and Fontainbleau for the same good Purposes.
The Duchess de Ruppelmonde, Court Lady to the Queen, made her Profession Yesterday in the Carmelite Nunnery in St. Francis-street. Her Majesty intending this Lady the Honour of her Presence, and of delivering her the Veil, came hither, accompanied by Mesdames de France: At the Barrier she was received by a Detachment of each of the Regiments of French and Swiss Guards, and the Corporation of the City, with the Duke de Gesvres at their Head, who paid her a Compliment. At her Entrance within the City, she was saluted by the Guildhall and Invalids Guns, and several private Discharges. It was about Three when her Majesty reached the Convent, where she staid till Five; and in her Return went to view the Invalids; from whence, after a most respectful Reception, she set out for Versailles, and was saluted as at her coming.
(ZEN; corpus file 1751lda00184).

6. Although the text excerpt below stems from an article published in the *Philosophical Transactions* already in 1667 (and thus would belong to

the Early Modern period), it nicely illustrates the beginnings of the genre of the experimental report, which shaped this genre very much through the eighteenth century (see Chapter 6.3.2. above). Show how the letter format affects the form of this text and how the descriptions given are presented mainly from the perspective of the writer. The text is taken from the *Early Modern English Medical Texts* Corpus (Taavitsainen and Pahta 2010).

SIR,

I Hinted to you in my last something about the Original of the Experiments made in Italy, by injecting Acid Liquors into Blood: To explain which, I shall now tell you, That about this time three years I mentioned at Gresham Colledge to the Royal Society, an odd Experiment I had formerly made (not by Chance, but Design) upon Blood yet warm, as it came from the Animal, viz. ...

This Experiment I devis'd, among other things, to shew the Amicableness of Volatil Spirits to the Blood. And I remember, 'twas so much taken notice of, that some very inquisitive Members of the Society came presently to me, and desired me to acquaint them more particularly with it; which I readily did, though afterwards I made some further Observations about the same Experiments, that I had no occasion to relate. ...

If it be thought fit, that any mention be made of what I related so long since, I think I can send you some other Circumstances belonging to it: For I remember, I tried it with other Liquors (as Spirit of Wine, Oyl of Tartar, Oyl of Turpentine) and I think also I can send you some Remarks upon the Colour of the upper part of the Blood. And I shall on this occasion add, in reference to Anatomical matters in general, that after I saw how favourably the usefulness of Experimental Philosophy was receiv'd, I was invted to inlarge it in another Edition; and for that, I provded divrs Anatomical as well as other Experiments, and designed many more, so that I hav by me divers things that would not, perhaps, be unwelcome to Anatomists, &c.

(*Philosophical Transactions*; 1667; EMEMT)

7. Perspectives on present-day English

The emphasis of this book has been on the more distant parts of the history of the English language, with the traditional periods of Old, Middle, Early Modern and Late Modern English. It does not attempt to cover all the recent developments of the (later) twentieth century and the beginning of the new millennium. Nevertheless, and still in accordance with the broad, long-term orientation of the book, the last chapter will include a short account of some perspectives on present-day English and its possible future developments.

Among the many (sometimes highly speculative) lines of thought forecasting the future of English I will select two aspects which link back to language-external developments of the Early and Late Modern periods. These are, firstly, the information revolution based on the new media and computer technology, which can be seen as a further stage in the innovations initiated by the printing press in the late fifteenth century, and, secondly, the position of English as a world language, which (among other factors) is a result of the colonial expansion which began in the Early Modern era.

The advent of telephone, radio and television during the twentieth century has certainly left a mark on language use in most modern languages. Some researchers talk about a new, secondary orality (Ong 1982: 11), characterised by (partly new) oral forms of communication, which, however, depend to a large extent on writing and print. But the (so far) most pervasive influence on language use has emerged from the advent of computer technology and computer-mediated communication, resulting in many new forms of communication and ways of spreading information, most importantly, the introduction of email, the World Wide Web and, more recently, the development of "participatory", "user controlled" forms such as blogging.

Talking about long-term developments in language use triggered by the internet seems to be a fairly speculative undertaking since computer technology is very much an evolving field, with new inventions / applications and their impact on digital discourse hardly being predictable. On the other hand, English has been one of the languages most involved in computer-mediated communication, at least in the initial stages. While English can still be called one major language of the web today, the internet becomes increasingly multilingual, the importance of English remaining at best stable if not decreasing. For example, Crystal (2006) reports on a significant decrease in the proportion of internet hosts in English (less than 70 per cent in 2003) and the proportion of internet users in English-speaking countries (35.8 per cent in 2004). But even so, it is fair to say that English is still one of the major internet-languages, probably used by hundreds of millions of native and non-native speakers.

A well-known impact of electronic communication on the structure of English (and other languages) is found at the typographic and orthographic level. Digital communication is characterised by an unusually high number of abbreviations and acronyms, some of them newly invented. There are also new cues such as emoticons, new interjections, an extensive use of punctuation marks and a rather loose, often idiosyncratic and phonetic handling of spelling. Such features are, as was mentioned above, well-known and probably familiar to any internet user. But what about other levels of linguistic description?

With regard to other aspects of language, researchers are much more tentative with their statements. In fact, many of the issues should actually be formulated in the form of questions. For example, can we assume a specific variety of "netspeak" (Crystal 2001), which is seen as a general linguistic use typical of the internet, or are such generalisations premature and can linguistic variation in digital discourse be better captured in terms of differing genres? Are we witnessing the evolution of new genres specific to digital discourse or is it rather a slow transformation of traditional forms into new ones? What about the strange "intermediate" position of the internet language between speech and writing, with its basic manifestation as written language, but with many informal and dialogic features of oral discourse? Can computer-mediated communication be seen as an independent force in language change or does it merely reflect (and spread) changes which have originated elsewhere? A last question concerns the status of a text in digital communication. In its electronic form a text seems to have become much more changeable and indeterminate than in its fixed printed form. In particular, many electronic texts found on the internet do not show the well-known linear structure encountered in most printed books. Rather, they are increasingly "interrupted" by links to other texts or text modules, also called hypertexts. This basic constitution as hypertext, a structured arrangement of textual elements linked together, may have far-reaching repercussions on the basic structure and coherence of texts and the cohesive means which are used to mark such structures. But so far, any hard and fast statements about future long-term developments do not seem possible.

The second perspective on present-day English included in this chapter involves the future of English as a world language. The position of English as a world language reaches back to the colonial expansion of the British Empire, beginning in the Early Modern period, and its further expansion to Australia, New Zealand, (South) Africa, South Asia and other places around the globe. As a result of this expansion, many countries that are former British colonies have English either as a national language or as the language of administration and / or education. But beyond this spread in former colonies, English has become a world language, a *lingua franca* used in a large number of domains.

Crystal (2006: 424) lists some recent estimates of speakers of World English, divided up into first, second and foreign language users. Estimates on first-language speakers range between 350 and 450 million and estimates on second-language users range between 235 and 400 million. Foreign-language users, who are often difficult to distinguish from second-language users, cover an even larger range, between 600 and 1,000 million. Here, of course, a lot depends on the assumed competence in English the person included in the category should have. Crystal suggests a "medium level of conversational competence in handling domestic subject matter" (2006: 425), reaching a grand total of around 1,500 million speakers of World English in all three categories.

The status of English as a world language, with these impressive numbers of users, does not only go back to colonial history and, one may add, the emergence of the United States as a superpower in the course of the twentieth century. Crystal (1997 [2003]) lists other factors which undoubtedly have also contributed to this position (for example, the press, advertising, broadcasting, motion pictures, popular music, education, communication). It is quite instructive to recall in how many domains English is established as the major medium of communication. It is the *lingua franca* for scientists, for most international news agencies, it is the language for air and sea traffic control, for safety instructions and tourism and, last but not least, one of the major languages of the internet.

Some people think that a language becomes a world language because it is "simple" and "easy to learn". In the case of English they may point to the reduced inflectional morphology or the straightforward word order. But linguists agree that such language-internal factors (for example, the relative complexity of the syntactic, morphological and orthographic rules) are mostly irrelevant. It is for language-external factors that a language becomes a world language.

The status of English in various countries of the world is often described in terms of three concentric circles, with an inner circle, an outer circle and an expanding circle (see, for example, Kachru 1985). The inner circle comprises countries in which English functions as the native language of the majority of the population and is used as the primary means of communication (for example, the United Kingdom, the United States, Ireland, Canada, Australia and New Zealand). In the outer circle we find countries where English is not a native language but covers a privileged position as one of the official languages and is an important means of communication in several domains (for example, in the administration, in educational institutions or in the literary domain). Crystal (2006: 423) reports that English has "some kind of special administrative status" in over seventy countries (e.g. Ghana, Nigeria, Zimbabwe, India, Singapore). Many of them are, of course, former colonial territories. The expanding circle comprises countries which have no colonial background and where English does not have any official status. However, in these countries the language is given a privileged position as a second language and is often recognised as an important *lingua franca*. Crystal says that there are more than 100 countries in Europe, Asia, North Africa and Latin America which fall under this category (for example, Japan, Israel, Greece, Poland, Germany).

This enumeration of countries where English plays an important role is of course impressive, but this wide circulation may also pose a threat to the future of English as a world language. The numbers of language users presented above reveals that the proportion of speakers using English as a second language by far exceeds the number of native speakers. It is estimated that the ratio is around 3 to 1 (Crystal 2006: 425). What happens to a language which is spoken by a large majority of non-native speakers in a global setting? What consequences does this have for the linguistic structure? Will the language continue to be used and seen as "one language" or will it split up into several "sub-languages" drifting apart in the course of time?

The problem is that it seems fairly difficult to tell what exactly will happen. There does not seem to be any precedent known in history developing on a similar scale. Neither do we know how the relevant language-external factors function in a global setting. Linguists express a range of different views about the future status of the English language in the world (see Crystal 2006). They include continued spread as a global *lingua franca*, a weakened global position including competition with other languages (for example, Chinese and Spanish), and a disintegration into several "Englishes" accompanied by increasing multiglossia. But it seems extremely difficult to anticipate exactly what will happen.

Crystal (2006) points out that the future development of English will probably be determined by two opposing forces which reflect two basic communicative needs, the need to make oneself understood to a largest possible audience and the need to show that you belong to a specific group and express your identity. The former force will drive towards mutual intelligibility by means of an international standard variety of English, the latter force will drive towards a differentiation of various "Englishes" which represent their speakers' identity by being unlike each other. On the one hand one could argue that the wide range of uses of English in different domains across the world requires a large common core ensuring that the message comes across to everybody speaking English. On the other hand we witness that particular regions stress their autonomy and that individual "Englishes" maintain a national identity, with regional varieties acquiring prestige (sometimes even on an international scale). Nobody can predict whether the force towards mutual intelligibility or the drive for identity and differentiation will prevail. Perhaps the result might also be a compromise between the opposing forces. For example, in Singapore some kind of international Standard English is indispensable for maintaining the various economic and political relationships across the world and also as a means of communication between Singaporeans of different linguistic backgrounds. Singlish, the special variety of Singaporean English, is on the other hand important for maintaining their own identity. Why not imagine a situation where both varieties co-exist, each serving its respective function?

Crystal (2006) points out that the possibility of fragmentation seems quite real, even if it starts only with mixed varieties that serve as prestigious markers of identification:

In fifty years time, we could find ourselves with an English language which contains within itself large areas of contact-influenced vocabulary, borrowed from such languages as Malay or Chinese, being actively used in Singapore, Malaysia and emigrant communities elsewhere. First-language speakers from those areas would instinctively select this vocabulary as their first choice in conversation. Everyone else would recognise their words as legitimate options – passively, at least, with occasional forays into active use. (Crystal 2006: 434)

A scenario which would go further beyond a mixed vocabulary would envisage the emergence of several separate sublanguages, with English playing the same role as Vulgar Latin, which disintegrated into several unintelligible varieties today called Romance languages. But whether this will come true we will only know in more than fifty years.

Summary

In this short chapter we looked at two aspects which may contribute to the future shape of English and which link back to language-external developments of the Early and Late Modern periods: the information revolution based on the new media and computer technology, and the position of English as a world language.

While most prognostications about the future of the English language seem fairly speculative, one development that will strongly influence the position of English during the next decades is the fact that the number of non-native users exceeds the number of native speakers by far. Which exact consequences, however, this will have for the future of English is very much a matter of debate.

Further reading

Crystal (2001) gives an overview of the questions connected with the role of English as the major language in the internet. A more recent outline is given in Heyd (2012). For other languages see Danet and Herring (2007). – Crystal (1997 [2003]) and Crystal (2006) deal with the issues of English as a world language and possible future developments. A recent accessible introduction to World Englishes is Schneider (2011).

Questions and exercises

1. Based on your experience as internet user, identify some internet genres which can be seen as novel, web-specific developments and some which can be seen merely as transformations of more traditional genres.

2. Gather some English data from typical, web-specific sources (blogs, chats, posts etc.). Try to determine whether they contain more "oral" and less standard forms. Can you link this to the fact that the majority of internet users may be non-native speakers of English?

3. If you live in a country where English has no official status but enjoys a privileged position in many domains of life, spot the places where you encounter English words and phrases mixed with your native language (for example, in advertisements, in public transport, in educational institutions).

List of References

Electronic Sources

CMEPV: *Corpus of Middle English Prose and Verse*. The Humanities Text Initiative, University of Michigan http://quod.lib.umich.edu/c/cme/

DOEC: *Dictionary of Old English Corpus*; original release (1981) compiled by Angus Cameron, Ashley Crandell Amos, Sharon Butler, and Antonette diPaolo Healey (Toronto: DOE Project 1981); 2009 release compiled by Antonette diPaolo Healey, Joan Holland, Ian McDougall, and David McDougall. http://tapor.library.utoronto.ca/doecorpus/

EMEMT: *Early Modern English Medical Texts*. Taavitsainen Irma, Päivi Pahta, Turo Hiltunen, Martti Mäkinen, Ville Marttila, Maura Ratia, Carla Suhr, and Jukka Tyrkkö (eds.). CD-ROM. Amsterdam: John Benjamins. (see also see Taavitsainen and Pahta (2010); http://www.helsinki.fi/varieng/CoRD/corpora/CEEM/CEEMcorpora.html/

HC: *The Helsinki Corpus of English Texts* (1991). Department of Modern Languages, University of Helsinki. Compiled by Matti Rissanen (Project leader), Merja Kytö (Project secretary); Leena Kahlas-Tarkka, Matti Kilpiö (Old English); Saara Nevanlinna, Irma Taavitsainen (Middle English); Terttu Nevalainen, Helena Raumolin-Brunberg (Early Modern English). http://www.helsinki.fi/varieng/CoRD/corpora/HelsinkiCorpus/

LOB-Corpus: The LOB Corpus, original version (1970–1978), compiled by Geoffrey Leech, Lancaster University, Stig Johansson, University of Oslo (project leaders), and Knut Hofland, University of Bergen (head of computing). http://khnt.hit.uib.no/icame/manuals/lob/INDEX.HTM/

ZEN, Zurich English Newspaper Corpus Version 1.0. English Department of the University of Zurich. http://es-zen.unizh.ch.

References

Anttila, Raimo (1989): *Historical and Comparative Linguistics*. Amsterdam: John Benjamins.

Atkinson, Dwight (1992): "The evolution of medical research writing from 1735 to 1985: The case of the Edinburgh Medical Journal", *Applied Linguistics* 13(4), 337–374.

Barber, Charles (1997): *Early Modern English*, 2nd edition. Edinburgh: Edinburgh University Press.

Barnard, John & D.F. McKenzie (eds.) (2002): *The Cambridge History of the Book in Britain. Vol. IV, 1557–1695.* Cambridge: Cambridge University Press.

Baugh, Albert C. & Thomas Cable (2002): *A History of the English Language*, 5th ed. London: Routledge.

Bazerman, Charles (1988): *Shaping Written Knowledge: The Genre and Activity of the Experimental Article in Science.* Madison, WI: University of Wisconsin Press.

Beal, Joan C. (2004): *English in Modern Times 1700–1945.* London: Arnold.

Bennett, Jack A. & G.V. Smithers (1968): *Early Middle English Verse and Prose.* Oxford: Clarendon Press.

Bennett, Harry Stanley (1969): *English Books & Readers 1475 to 1557*, 2nd ed. Cambridge: Cambridge University Press.

Bergs, Alex & Laurel Brinton (eds.) (2012): *Historical Linguistics of English* (HSK 34.1). Berlin: de Gruyter.

Blair, Peter Hunter & Simon Keynes (2003): *An Introduction to Anglo-Saxon England.* Cambridge: Cambridge University Press.

Blake, Norman (ed.) (1992): *The Cambridge History of the English Language, Vol. II, 1066–1476.* Cambridge: Cambridge University Press.

Boitani, Piero & Jill Mann (eds.) (2003): *The Cambridge Chaucer Companion*, 2nd edition. Cambridge: Cambridge University Press.

Burrow, John A. & Thorlac Turville-Petre (2005): *A Book of Middle English*, 3rd ed. Oxford: Blackwell.

Campbell, Lyle (1998): *Historical Linguistics: An Introduction.* Edinburgh: Edinburgh University Press.

Cannon, John (ed.) (2002): *The Oxford Companion to British History*, rev. ed. Oxford: Oxford University Press.

Chaucer, Geoffrey (2008 [1987]): *The Riverside Chaucer*, 3rd ed. (with a new foreword by Christopher Cannon), ed. Larry D. Benson. Oxford: Oxford University Press.

Clackson, James (2007): *Indo-European Linguistics: An Introduction.* Cambridge: Cambridge University Press.

Clark Hall, John R. (1960): *A Concise Anglo-Saxon Dictionary*, 4th ed. Cambridge: Cambridge University Press.

Cressy, David (1980): *Literacy and the Social Order: Reading and Writing in Tudor and Stuart England.* Cambridge: Cambridge University Press.

Crystal, David (2001): *Language and the Internet.* Cambridge: Cambridge University Press.
Crystal, David (2003 [1997]): *English as a Global Language*, 2nd ed. Cambridge: Cambridge University Press.
Crystal, David (2006): "English worldwide", *A History of the English Language*, ed. Richard Hogg & David Denison. Cambridge: Cambridge University Press. 420–439.
Culpeper, Jonathan & Phoebe Clapham (1996): "The borrowing of Classical and Romance words into English: A study based on the electronic Oxford English Dictionary", *International Journal of Corpus Linguistics* 1.2, 199–218.
Cusack, Bridget (ed.) (1998): *Everyday English 1500–1700: A reader.* Edinburgh: Edinburgh University Press.
Danet, Brenda & Susan Herring (eds.) (2007): *The Multilingual Internet: Language, Culture, and Communication Online.* Oxford: Oxford University Press.
Davies, Norman (2000): *The Isles: A History.* Oxford: Oxford University Press.
Davis, Norman (1965): "The *Litera Troili* and English letters", *Review of English Studies New Series* 16, 233–244.
Edwards, Anthony S.G. (ed.) (1984): *Middle English Prose. A Critical Guide to Major Authors and Genres.* New Brunswick, N.J: Rutgers University Press.
Ellegård, Alvar (1953): *The Auxiliary "Do": The Establishment and Regulation of its Use in English.* Stockholm, Almqvist and Wiksell.
Fell, Christine E. (1984): *Women in Anglo-Saxon England.* Oxford: Blackwell.
Fischer, Andreas, Gunnel Tottie & Hans Martin Lehmann (eds.) (2002): *Text Types and Corpora: Studies in Honour of Udo Fries.* Tübingen: Gunter Narr.
Fisher, John H. (1996): *The Emergence of Standard English.* Lexington, Kentucky: The University Press of Kentucky.
Fisher, John H., Malcolm Richardson & Jane L. Fisher (eds.) (1984): *An Anthology of Chancery English.* Knoxville: University of Tennessee Press.
Fries, Udo (2012): "English and the media: Newspapers". In: Bergs & Brinton, 1063–1075.
Gneuss, Helmut (1955): *Lehnbildungen und Lehnbedeutungen im Altenglischen.* Berlin: E. Schmidt.
Godden, Malcolm & Michael Lapidge (eds.) (1991): *The Cambridge Companion to Old English Literature.* Cambridge: Cambridge University Press.
Gordon, Robert Kay (1954): *Anglo-Saxon Poetry.* London: J.M. Dent.
Görlach, Manfred (1991): *Introduction to Early Modern English.* Cambridge: Cambridge University Press.
Görlach, Manfred (1999a): "Regional and Social Variation". In: Lass, 459–538.

Görlach, Manfred (1999b): *English in Nineteenth-Century England: An Introduction*. Cambridge: Cambridge University Press.
Görlach, Manfred (2001): *Eighteenth-Century English*. Heidelberg: C. Winter.
Görlach, Manfred (2002): "A linguistic history of advertising", *Sounds, Words, Texts and Change. Selected Papers from 11 ICEHL. Santiago de Compostela, 7–11 September 2000*, ed. Teresa Fanego, Belén Méndez-Naya & Elena Seone. Amsterdam: John Benjamins. 83–104
Greenfield, Stanley B. & Daniel G. Calder (1986): *A New Critical History of Old English Literature*. New York and London: New York University Press.
Heyd, Theresa (2012): "English and the Media: Internet". In: Bergs & Brinton, 1105–1118.
Hock, Hans Henrich (1991): *Principles of Historical Linguistics*, 2nd rev. and updated edition. Berlin: Mouton de Gruyter.
Hogg, Richard M. (1992): *The Cambridge History of the English Language, Vol. I, The Beginnings to 1066*. Cambridge: Cambridge University Press.
Hogg, Richard M. (2002): *An Introduction to Old English*. Edinburgh: Edinburgh University Press.
Hope, Jonathan (1993): "Second Person Singular Pronouns in Records of Early Modern 'Spoken' English", *Neuphilologische Mitteilungen* 94, 83–100.
Horobin, Simon (2013): *Chaucer's Language*, 2nd edition. Basingstoke: Palgrave Macmillan.
Horobin, Simon & Jeremy Smith (2002): *An Introduction to Middle English*. Oxford and New York: Oxford University Press.
Jucker, Andreas H. (2000): "Slanders, slurs and insults on the road to Canterbury: Forms of verbal aggression in Chaucer's *Canterbury Tales*", *Placing Middle English in Context*, ed. Irma Taavitsainen, Terttu Nevalainen, Päivi Pahta & Matti Rissanen. Berlin and New York: Mouton de Gruyter. 369–389.
Jucker, Andreas H & Irma Taavitsainen (eds.) (2010): *Historical Pragmatics*. (Handbook of Pragmatics 8). Berlin: Mouton de Gruyter.
Kachru, Braj B. (1985): "Standards, codification and sociolinguistic realism: The English language in the outer circle", *English in the World*, eds. Randolph Quirk & H.G. Widdowson. Cambridge: Cambridge University Press. 11–31.
Kastovsky, Dieter (1992): "Semantics and Vocabulary". In: Hogg, 290–408.
Kohnen, Thomas (2000): "Explicit performatives in Old English: A corpus-based study of directives", *Journal of Historical Pragmatics* 1 (2), 301–321.
Kohnen, Thomas (2002): "Towards a history of English directives". In: Fischer et al., 165–175.

Kohnen, Thomas (2004): "Methodological problems in corpus-based historical pragmatics. The case of English directives", *Advances in Corpus Linguistics. Papers from the 23rd International Conference on English Language Research on Computerized Corpora (ICAME 23) Göteborg 22–26 May 2002*, eds. Karin Aijmer & Bengt Altenberg. Amsterdam: Rodopi. 237–247.

Kortmann, Bernd (1997): "Typology and language change", *Anglistentag 1996. Dresden*, ed. Uwe Böker & Hans Sauer. Trier: Wissenschaftlicher Verlag. 109–124.

Lass, Roger (1994): *Old English: A Historical Linguistic Companion*. Cambridge: Cambridge University Press.

Lass, Roger (1997): *Historical Linguistics and Language Change*. Cambridge: Cambridge University Press.

Lass, Roger (ed.) (1999): *The Cambridge History of the English Language, Vol. III, 1476–1776*. Cambridge: Cambridge University Press.

Lehmann, Winfred P. (1992): *Historical Linguistics: An Introduction*, 3rd ed. Abingdon: Routledge.

Marsden, Richard (2004): *The Cambridge Old English Reader*. Cambridge: Cambridge University Press.

McIntosh, Angus, M.L. Samuels & Michael Benskin (1986): *A Linguistic Atlas of Late Medieval English*, 4 vols. Aberdeen: Aberdeen University Press.

Mitchell, Bruce (1995): *An Invitation to Old English and Anglo-Saxon England*. Oxford: Blackwell.

Mitchell, Bruce & Fred C. Robinson (2012): *A Guide to Old English*, 8th edition. Malden and Oxford: Wiley-Blackwell.

Mossé, Fernand (1968 [1952]): *A Handbook of Middle English*, 5th impr. Baltimore: Johns Hopkins.

Mugglestone, Lynda (2007 [1995]): *'Talking Proper': The Rise of Accent as Social Symbol*. Oxford: Oxford University Press.

Nevalainen, Terttu (1999): "Early Modern English Lexis and Semantics". In: Lass, 332–458.

Nevalainen, Terttu (2006): *An Introduction to Early Modern English*. Edinburgh: Edinburgh University Press.

Nevalainen, Terttu & Helena Raumolin-Brunberg (2003): *Historical Sociolinguistics: Language Change in Tudor and Stuart England*. Harlow: Pearson Education.

Ong, Walter (1982): *Orality and Literacy: The Technologizing of the Word*. London and New York: Methuen.

Orme, Nicholas (1973): *English Schools in the Middle Ages*. London: Methuen.
Osselton, N.E. (1998 [1984]): "Informal spelling systems in Early Modern English: 1500–1800". Reprinted in: Rydén (1998), 33–45.
Phillipps, Kenneth C. (1984): *Language and Class in Victorian England*. Oxford: Blackwell.
Powell, Susan (ed.) (1981): *The Advent and Nativity Sermons from a Fifteenth-Century Revision of John Mirk's Festial*. (Middle English Texts, 13) Heidelberg: Carl Winter.
Pulsiano, Phillip & Elaine Treharne (eds.) (2001): *A Companion to Anglo-Saxon Literature*. Oxford and Malden: Blackwell.
Richardson, Malcolm (1980): "Henry V, the English Chancery and Chancery English", *Speculum*, Vol. 55, No. 4, 726–750.
Romaine, Suzanne (ed.) (1999): *The Cambridge History of the English Language, Vol. IV, 1776–1997*. Cambridge: Cambridge University Press.
Rose, Michael E. (1985): "Society: The emergence of urban Britain", *The Cambridge Historical Encyclopedia of Great Britain and Ireland*, ed. Christopher Haigh. Cambridge: Cambridge University Press. 276–281.
Rydén, Mats, Ingrid Tieken-Boon van Ostade & Merja Kytö (eds.) (1998): *A Reader in Early Modern English*. Frankfurt a.M. et al.: Peter Lang.
Samuels, Michael L. (1963): "Some applications of Middle English dialectology", *English Studies* 44, 81–94.
Sauer, Walter (1998): *Die Aussprache des Chaucer-Englischen: Ein Übungsbuch auf der Grundlage des Prologs der Canterbury Tales*. (Sprachwissenschaftliche Studienbücher). Heidelberg: Universitätsverlag Winter.
Schendl, Herbert (2001): *Historical Linguistics*. (Oxford Introductions to Language Study). Oxford: Oxford University Press.
Schneider, Edgar W. (2011): *English Around the World: An Introduction*. Cambridge: Cambridge University Press.
Taavitsainen, Irma & Andreas H. Jucker (2010): "Expressive speech acts and politeness in eighteenth-century English", *Eighteenth-Century English: Ideology and Change*, ed. Raymond Hickey. Cambridge: Cambridge University Press. 159–181.
Taavitsainen, Irma & Päivi Pahta (eds.) (2010): *Early Modern English Medical Texts. Corpus Description and Studies*. Amsterdam and Philadelphia: John Benjamins.
Tieken-Boon van Ostade, Ingrid (2009): *An Introduction to Late Modern English*. Edinburgh: Edinburgh University Press.

Ungerer, Friedrich (2002): "When news stories are no longer just stories: the emergence of the topdown structure in news reports in English newspapers". In: Fischer et al., 105–122.

Weimann, Klaus (1990): *Einführung ins Altenglische*. Heidelberg: Quelle & Meyer.

Wilcockson, Colin (ed.) (2008): *The Canterbury Tales: A Selection*. Oxford: Blackwell.

Textbooks in English Language and Linguistics (TELL)

Edited by Magnus Huber and Joybrato Mukherjee

Band 1   Ulrike Gut: Introduction to English Phonetics and Phonology. 2009.
Band 2   Jürgen Esser: Introduction to English Text-linguistics. 2009.
Band 3   Rolf Kreyer: Introduction to English Syntax. 2010.
Band 4   Alexander Bergs: Synchronic English Linguistics. 2012.
Band 5   Alexander Tokar: Introduction to English Morphology. 2012.
Band 6   Thomas Kohnen: Introduction to the History of English. 2014.

www.peterlang.com

www.ingramcontent.com/pod-product-compliance
Ingram Content Group UK Ltd.
Pitfield, Milton Keynes, MK11 3LW, UK
UKHW021300180426
11947UKWH00015B/943